Nonviolence, Peace, and Justice

Nonviolence, Peace, and Justice

A PHILOSOPHICAL INTRODUCTION

Kit R. Christensen

broadview press

BROADVIEW GUIDES to PHILOSOPHY

Library and Archives Canada Cataloguing in Publication

Christensen, Kit Richard
  Nonviolence, peace, and justice : a philosophical introduction / Kit R. Christensen.

Includes bibliographical references.
ISBN 978-1-55111-996-0

  1. War (Philosophy). 2. Violence—Moral and ethical aspects. 3. Peace—Philosophy. 4. Social justice—Philosophy. I. Title.

B105.W3C57 2009   172'.42   C2009-905953-3

Edited by Joel Buenting and Alex Sager

Broadview Press is an independent, international publishing house, incorporated in 1985. Broadview believes in shared ownership, both with its employees and with the general public; since the year 2000 Broadview shares have traded publicly on the Toronto Venture Exchange under the symbol BDP.

We welcome comments and suggestions regarding any aspect of our publications—please feel free to contact us at the addresses below or at broadview@broadviewpress.com.

North America
PO Box 1243, Peterborough, Ontario, Canada K9J 7H5
2215 Kenmore Ave., Buffalo, New York, USA 14207
Tel: (705) 743-8990; Fax: (705) 743-8353
email: customerservice@broadviewpress.com

UK, Europe, Central Asia, Middle East, Africa, India, and Southeast Asia
Eurospan Group, 3 Henrietta St., London WC2E 8LU, United Kingdom
Tel: 44 (0) 1767 604972; Fax: 44 (0) 1767 601640
Email: eurospan@turpin-distribution.com

Australia and New Zealand
NewSouth Books
c/o TL Distribution, 15-23 Helles Ave., Moorebank, NSW, Australia 2170
Tel: (02) 8778 9999; Fax: (02) 8778 9944
email: orders@tldistribution.com.au

www.broadviewpress.com

Typesetting by Aldo Fierro

This book is printed on paper containing 100% post-consumer fibre.
PRINTED IN CANADA

FSC
Mixed Sources
Product group from well-managed forests, controlled sources and recycled wood or fibre

Cert no. SW-COC-003438
www.fsc.org
© 1996 Forest Stewardship Council

Contents

Introduction   1

Chapter 1: Ethical Evaluation   7
   Section 1: Relevant Situations   7
   Section 2: Moral Responsibility and Moral Standing   12
   Section 3: Relativism and Universalism   16
   Section 4: Guiding Moral Principles   19
   Section 5: Morality and Law   27
   Further Reading   29

Chapter 2: Violence, Nonviolence, and Conflict   31
   Section 1: The Nature of Violence   31
   Section 2: The Nature of Nonviolence as a Strategy of Conflict
           Resolution   38
   Further Reading   45

Chapter 3: The Relevance of Human Nature   47
   Section 1: The Concept of Human Nature   47
   Section 2: Humans as Good but Corruptible   48
   Section 3: Humans as Evil but Controllable   54
   Section 4: Humans as Inherently neither Good nor Evil, but
           Educable   58
   Section 5: Biology and Environment   66
   Further Reading   69

Chapter 4: Life, Death, and Moral Goals: Religious and Secular
           Perspectives   71
   Section 1: Belief Systems and Violence   71
   Section 2: Some Religious Views   72
   Section 3: Religious Fundamentalism   87

Section 4: Tolstoy, Gandhi, and King   91
Section 5: Some Secular Views   96
Further Reading   107

Chapter 5: War and Peace   111
Section 1: War and Realism   111
Section 2: Just War Theory   115
Section 3: Pacifism   124
Section 4: Negative and Positive Peace   130
Further Reading   132

Chapter 6: The Shaping of Public Opinion   135
Section 1: Ideology, Propaganda, and Truth   135
Section 2: Entertainment and Violence   142
Section 3: Revenge, Retribution, and Reconciliation   152
Further Reading   159

Chapter 7: Concluding Hopes, Fears, and Dilemmas   163
Section 1: Our Global Community   163
Section 2: Dilemmas in the Struggle for Social Justice   173
Further Reading   181

Introduction

Books on peacemaking and on the rejection of organized violence as a means of resolving social conflict seem to be appearing at a greater rate in the last decade or so, and I take this to be a good sign. Although in the US some of this increased interest is still a response to the September 11, 2001 terrorist attacks in New York and Washington, DC, it also indicates a growing social concern about the militaristic approaches to national and international affairs that for too long have been given privileged status in public discourse. Peace studies curricula offered at academic institutions, and a variety of peace and conflict resolution institutes, also have attracted more attention in recent times as they have focused both on theoretical issues and on practical strategies of conflict mediation and reduction of social tensions in many regions of the world. The theories and practices of peacemaking have been appropriately interdisciplinary and eclectic, but in this book I have confined myself to a philosophical overview of concepts and questions that I think should be addressed if we are to make sense out of the connections between nonviolence, peace, and social justice as well as the problems of violence generally, war in particular, and injustice.

As a professional philosopher myself, I see philosophical inquiry basically as the critical analysis of our beliefs and how we go about justifying those beliefs. Since we have beliefs about almost everything within the range of our conscious experience, and since we are often compelled to justify those beliefs to ourselves or to others, there is hardly any limit to what we can investigate philosophically as long as we have the curiosity to do so. But since we also all have beliefs that significantly influence how we actually live our lives, and how we treat fellow humans as well as other living beings, it really does matter what those beliefs are and especially whether or not they are rationally defensible. We do have choices in what we believe, and insofar as our beliefs determine our conduct, deciding if they are based on good or bad reasons is certainly of practical value. In the present context then, if somebody claims that killing

1

in self-defense is morally permissible, or that capital punishment is wrong, or that modern war is all about financial profiteering, it is not just the pleasures of idle speculation that lead many philosophers to ask questions about what is meant by these claims and whether a reasonable person should be persuaded by arguments for them. Beliefs about different kinds of killing are often re-flected in law and policy decisions affecting large numbers of people, and so there is quite a bit at stake in our choosing as individual citizens to accept or contest official justifications of such judgments. Peace and justice activists can be understandably impatient with what they might see as too much theory and not enough practice in this regard, because many people in many countries are being victimized right now by violence and injustice, and careful philo-sophical analysis of the issues may seem like a time-consuming luxury. But education and progressive activism should be mutually reinforcing, and being adequately educated here requires going beyond a merely impressionistic view of what is good and what is bad about the current state of our world, as well as some facility in assessing our belief options with respect to the facts of specific situations and relevant moral values.

Having said that, I will actually proceed in this book in a way contrary to the philosopher's usual tendency to go into more depth on a narrower subject, and instead emphasize breadth in the range of topics to be covered in order to provide, again, an explicitly philosophical introduction to the value judgments and other assumptions underlying an agenda of peacemaking and social justice. As part of this broader focus I will put into historical context most of the issues discussed, since in one form or another they have been sources of debate for centuries if not millennia. I will also try to clarify the cultural contexts within which many of these questions have been addressed in the past, showing how that understanding can be useful in making sense of our multicultural and globally interconnected present. That is, identifying differences and similari-ties in historical circumstances and cultural norms puts us in a better position to see why some people in the contemporary world respond to conflict the way they do, for example, by seeking revenge for perceived wrongs done, by being willing to die for what they believe is a righteous cause, or by interpreting their social environment in terms of "Us *versus* Them."

Although normally in philosophical study we should try to operate with as few presuppositions as possible, in addition to the belief that reason is the best means of handling disagreement there will be throughout this text at least one other guiding assumption: In interpersonal, inter-group, and international relations the burden of proof should always be on those who advocate violence in order to achieve somebody's ends or resolve conflict. This may not seem like a controversial assertion on its face, but in fact it has been more often the case in many societies that the burden of proof was presumed to fall on those who recommended nonviolence, especially in situations of collective strife between clans, ethnic groups, governments, or other political organizations. For there to be any realistic chance in the human future for widespread, sustainable peace, however, one thing that has to change is this bad habit of treating violence as a normal means of "getting our way" when nonviolence and civility are inconvenient or falsely associated with weakness. Of course, I will also be looking into why this bad habit has not yet been given up in human affairs, along with inquiry into the possibilities for substantial change in the direction of nonviolent, mutually respectful interaction between all persons and peoples.

Since most of the issues addressed in what follows center around the values of nonviolence, peace, and justice together with the disvalues of violence, war, and injustice, I provide in Chapter 1 a pretty standard summary of the different aspects of ethical evaluation and decision-making as most ethics professors would treat them. I include: (1) A description of the kinds of situations where ethical evaluation becomes relevant in the first place; (2) the nature of moral responsibility in such situations as well as whose interests have to be taken into account; (3) an explanation of the preliminary choice between ethical (or moral) relativism and universalism which we all have to make in deciding what is ethically/morally right or wrong, good or bad; (4) some of the more historically influential moral principles (at least for philosophers) that can be applied to the determination of ethical obligation in specific situations; and, (5) clarification of the relationship between law and morality.

In Chapter 2, I address first the nature of violence itself, since we can't plausibly say that it is ever wrong or right until we understand what it is and what it is not. I also identify the differences between physical violence, psychological violence, and institutional (or structural) violence. Second, I discuss the nature of nonviolence primarily (but not only) as a strategy of conflict resolution, as well as particular tactics and policies that have been used successfully by nonviolent social activists over the years.

In Chapter 3, I discuss possible answers to what really is an age-old question: Is human nature itself a major obstacle to people living nonviolent, peaceful, and socially just lives? How we decide this issue of course will influence what we believe is achievable regarding widespread social change and moral progress along these lines. Without arguing for or against any one of them, I summarize some relevant views on human nature from a representative sample of famous philosophers in the distant and recent past, organized in terms of their agreement that (1) Humans are basically good but corruptible, or, (2) humans are basically evil but controllable, or, (3) humans are basically neither good nor evil, but educable. I conclude with a brief discussion of how human nature looks from the current standpoint of the biological sciences, and why that matters.

What people think about the acceptability of violence is often based on the value and meaning they attach to life and death, which in turn informs their view of the proper goals in life, and what sort of relationships (if any) they think should obtain between humans and some supernatural or divine power, between fellow humans, and between humans and the rest of the natural world. In Chapter 4, I offer an overview of a number of religious and secular belief systems, focusing on what their adherents typically would say about these topics as they relate specifically to the morality of violence. In addition, I include an account of religious fundamentalism (as separable from any one set of traditional religious doctrines), and a summary of the religiously grounded nonviolentism of Leo Tolstoy, Mohandas Gandhi, and Martin Luther King, Jr.

In Chapter 5, I deal more directly with the ethical problems of war and peace, in the first place by describing basically what war is apart from all euphemism and romanticizing distortion, as well as identifying different kinds of war. In light of recent history some may be surprised that I don't provide a separate analysis of "war against terrorism" here, but terrorism is more accurately understood as one type of "unconventional" strategy employed both by governments and by non-governmental groups (and sometimes by isolated individuals) whether or not there is an actual war going on. Thus, it can be evaluated like any other violent tactic used for political ends such as torturing prisoners, bombing civilian targets, or the systematic raping of females associated with an identified "enemy" group. I also look at three general positions on the morality of war: (1) Realism; (2) Just War Theory; and (3) Pacifism. Arguments for and against all three are explicated, though I try to clarify why I am more in agreement with the pacifist ethical approach than with the other two. In addition, I explain differences between negative and positive peace as two distinct though related goals in peacemaking, and the connection of the latter especially with social justice.

As communications technology has advanced dramatically in the last two centuries, more people can be reached more quickly by those who want to influence public opinion for or against warmaking, for example, or by those who just want to sell products by preying on people's fears and their fascination with violence. I point out in Chapter 6 some of the problems peacemakers face in contemporary societies where most of the population is regularly bombarded (so to speak) with violent imagery, and with as much disinformation as

4

actual information about who or what is to be feared "out there"; all of which can have the effect of encouraging more violence or at least the passive acceptance of it as an unchangeable part of life like the weather. These problems include the power of propaganda and ideological conditioning, violence in entertainment, the attractions of vengeance, and the need for reconciliation in situations where people want to move forward with their lives after they have experienced violent conflict and suffering.

Chapter 7 brings the book to a close on a less than completely optimistic note, as I describe factors to consider in assessing the chances for radically reducing violence (especially instances of war) and injustice around the world in the foreseeable future. Always emphasizing the relationship between local conditions and our global connectedness, for better or worse, I first identify some of the major challenges yet to be overcome in interpersonal, inter-group, and international arenas of moral choice. I then conclude by focusing on two continuing dilemmas in people's struggles for social justice in many different countries: (1) The problem of means and ends, that is, whether only nonviolent means can bring about truly peaceful ends; (2) how do people who have suffered massive abuses and oppression in the past, or who are still being similarly victimized, keep up their hopes and their efforts at nonviolent liberation and social transformation, without finally giving up in despair or giving in to the temptation to "fight fire with fire"?

It is my intention in this text to offer information, ideas, and arguments that can provide a starting point for readers who want to explore the range of what already has been accomplished in thought and action by some of those who have cared about peace, and see what still needs to be done in confronting the problems of violence, war, and injustice. In this kind of introduction to the diverse field of Peace Studies, readers will only get a first taste in many instances of complex issues that really deserve more in-depth investigation elsewhere. For the sake of both brevity and breadth of coverage, I have also excluded case studies and extensive analyses of specific historical events as illustrations of theories or concepts. This might make some of the material covered seem a little abstract or overly generalized. But I am hopeful that the book will serve not as a source of dissatisfaction but of stimulation to pursue some of these life and death questions further, and as a provocation to study the world around us with a more critical eye.

CHAPTER 1

Ethical Evaluation

SECTION 1: RELEVANT SITUATIONS

In the course of our day-to-day lives, we regularly make judgments about the appropriateness or inappropriateness of somebody's actions, and come to decisions regarding what we should do in particular circumstances. Most people also tend to care about the predispositions, intentions, and personality characteristics discernible in others and themselves, largely because there is a common sense understanding that such character traits translate into conduct that can have good or bad personal, interpersonal, or more widely social effects. In the history of moral philosophy around the world these areas of human concern have given rise to extensive discussion of justifiable criteria of right and wrong actions, on the one hand, and of good and bad (or virtuous and vicious) moral character on the other hand. As obviously interconnected as conduct and character are in our daily affairs, however, in this chapter I will focus more on what is involved in the ethical evaluation of actions and policies of individuals and groups (including governments, militias, and business corporations). I take this approach here because most of the time, when we think morally about occurrences of violence in the world and possible nonviolent alternatives, we are thinking about what someone is *doing* to someone else, and whether or not they should be doing it. So, by explaining a fairly typical philosophical approach to ethical analysis of conduct generally, I can go on to show how it provides a thoughtful, consistent, and rationally defensible foundation for understanding why violence is wrong more often than not, and why nonviolence especially in resolving conflict is morally preferable.

In moral reflection on human action, we can see in the first place that not all behaviors are appropriately susceptible to evaluation. That is, we all regularly engage in actions that for all practical purposes are morally neutral, for example, because they are involuntary (reflex behaviors such as flinching at sudden loud noises), or because in a particular setting they may not have any relevant impact on anyone or anything that matters (say, a specific act of looking through a telescope). Still, a fair amount of our conscious activity during any given day is subject to ethical appraisal, as becomes clear when we "stand back" from what we are doing for a moment and think about why we are doing it. What is it about any life situation, besides the fact that the people involved are engaged in conscious voluntary action, that prompts us to bring to bear moral standards of some kind in making sense out of it? Many philosophers would answer this question by pointing to four features of such a situation that make it a relevant one for moral scrutiny.

First, in plausibly deciding whether someone's action is morally justified or unjustified, that actor must in fact have a choice about what he or she is (or what they are) doing. Whether we are trying to decide the right course of conduct for ourselves in a situation, or evaluating the actions of others, the belief that someone ought to do something or not only really makes sense if that actor can choose to do so. This means that the actor realistically is *capable* of doing what might be morally expected, and that he/she/they *could do otherwise*, that is, there are alternative courses of action available. This is more or less what many philosophers have been getting at over the years in using the formula "ought implies can," and this is also one very traditional way (though certainly not the only way) of making the concept of moral responsibility practically meaningful. So, for example, if someone tries to convince you that, alone among all humans, you are the one responsible for ending all poverty in the world, from a rational point of view you don't have to take too seriously such a claim. Unless you were many times over a billionaire, even if you wanted to eliminate world poverty you couldn't, at least as a single individual. On the other hand, if someone claims that you personally have an obligation to "contribute somehow" to ending global poverty, this makes more sense, and is realistic insofar as you actually are capable of making such a contribution. The question for you then becomes, not whether you have a viable choice in the matter, but which choice, morally, is the right one.

Not surprisingly, one very common strategy people use for avoiding ethical responsibility for their actions, or for defending conduct or policies that otherwise probably wouldn't be defensible, is to convince themselves or others that, in a particular case, they "have no choice" but to do what they do. The human capacities for self-deception, dissembling, and "rationalization" (as distinct from rational justification) are extensive and often well-developed in the domain of moral decision-making, and themselves have been the subject of moral critique down through the ages to the extent that people have recognized that we are not fated to succumb always to their influence. And yet, in many situations it is not clear what viable choices the actors really do have, and so adequate ethical evaluation does also require knowing enough about the relevant facts of the case to make that determination.

A related issue here has to do with actors' responsibility for their own knowledge or ignorance of the options open to them in a particular situation. If a person really believes that he or she has no choice but to follow a certain course of conduct despite the possible harm to others, but could easily acquire information indicating that there are in fact viable alternatives available involving less harm to others, does that person somehow act immorally by remaining ignorant of possibly better choices of which he or she *should* have been aware? To what extent do we have an ethical obligation to be knowledgeable enough about our world so that we can be, in some meaningful sense, competent moral actors? What if people we trust systematically deceive us about relevant facts, or what if, as a result of our upbringing, we are conditioned to believe that we have no choice in some matters when in reality we do? When can we say justifiably that people's ignorance about moral alternatives is "not their own fault," and when can we hold them responsible for that ignorance? In more recent times in western philosophy these problems have been associated with what has been called the "ethics of belief," and as will be seen later, when I discuss, for example, citizens' credulity in response to governmental rationales for military violence, they too must be addressed if we are to formulate successful strategies for moving toward a more nonviolent, truly peaceful world.

A second feature of situations susceptible to ethical evaluation is that our decisions regarding relevant conduct are based on our value preferences. Again, whether we are reflecting on our own choices of what to do in a situation or on the choices made by others, understanding both what is happening and what should happen is guided by what we consider desirable or undesirable, laudable or condemnable, good or bad, valuable or not. Obviously actors' values inform and provide motivation for what they choose to do in any particular case, so from a philosophical standpoint it becomes a matter of first identifying what distinctively moral values are involved, and then determining which course of conduct in that case is most consistent with, or best actualizes, those values.

As you might imagine, in the global history of moral philosophy there has been plenty of disagreement about what the most important values and disvalues are, as well as about the most rationally compelling ethical standards based upon them. But there seems to have been at least some commonality too in the history of human value preferences, which is also reflected in the more systematic reflections of thinkers in a very wide variety of cultural and historical settings. For example, other things being equal, sane, rational individuals have always seemed to prefer happiness to unhappiness, pleasure to pain, and health to sickness. People everywhere also have normally viewed being treated with respect, or the experience of safety, as good things, while personal degradation by others and living in constant terror are seen as bad things. There has always been great diversity of opinion regarding how some of these fundamental values and disvalues are related to each other, how they might be rank ordered when trying to resolve moral dilemmas, even how they are to be defined in specific social contexts, and of course who deserves which and to what extent. But I think the anthropological evidence shows that there is a cross-cultural and trans-historical consistency in the identification of this admittedly rather small set of "goods" and "evils" that we can take as basic to the human condition. And really, this shouldn't be surprising to us when we remember our biological commonality as members of the same species with the same basic mental and emotional faculties, in spite of the differences in life experience for all human individuals that contribute to the differences in value judgments in most other respects.

The third factor that allows us to characterize a decision-making situation as an "ethical" one is the relevance of determining the actors' obligations in those circumstances (i.e., what they would be morally obliged, or have a moral "duty," to do or refrain from doing). As implied above, and as assumed by all ethical theories and lived moral codes focusing on conscious action, the value judgments identified as "moral" in the first place always come down to some question about how people "ought" to conduct themselves, beyond simply a factual account of how they actually, or will likely, act in the situation. Although there has been some philosophical debate about this over the years, at a practical level there is normally a clear distinction between claims about what someone *in fact* does, and claims about what he or she *ought* to, or *should* do, and it is this latter kind of claim that is the central concern in ethical analysis. Thus, if I read about the military bombing of a city, or a street mugging, from my recognition of the fact that these violent actions occurred, I cannot immediately conclude that the actors' behavior in those cases was either consistent or inconsistent with how they were morally obliged to behave. Further reasoning is required to take that step, and in thereby deciding what duties were fulfilled or violated, again, I am deciding whether conduct in that situation was morally right or wrong. Also, a moral judgment about what someone is obliged to do by its very nature universalizes to some degree, determining from a more impartial standpoint what any actor in the same or similar circumstances of choice ought or ought not to do. This is why philosophers often treat as distinct (though not necessarily incompatible) moral judgments and judgments regarding what someone "ought" to do if he or she simply wants to achieve some selfish end. The latter are sometimes called "prudential" judgments and are in effect intended as recipes for the successful pursuit of self-interest, oriented explicitly by a kind of partiality rather than by an impartiality beyond this or that party's exclusive interests.

A fourth element considered crucial in many philosophical traditions for rationally defensible ethical evaluation is some kind of overarching principle or rule, appealed to for guidance in the determination of our more situation-specific obligations. There are many such trans-situational principles that have been formulated and applied in a variety of cultural and historical contexts, and a good deal of debate always has centered around which principles should take precedence in which situations. Some of these general moral principles will be discussed in Section 4, but here the main ideas to keep in mind are that, in the first place, we have some rational choice about the principles we think are most appropriately applied in deciding particular actors' obligations; and second, once we make this choice we are bound by the standards of rational integrity and consistency to accept the implications that will in fact follow for those and similar cases. So, for example, in trying to decide if capital punishment is morally justified in the case of a convicted murderer, I might ask what the principle of justice would imply in this situation, regarding both what that person deserves, and whether the state is overstepping its rightful responsibilities in killing someone convicted of such a crime. On the other hand, I could instead decide this issue by appealing to some version of the principle of utility, which generally recommends that actions and policies (including penal law) be judged by their tendency to maximize benefit and minimize harm for everyone significantly affected by them. Or, I can choose the principle that people should always follow the will of Heaven, applying it in this case by determining if such an instance of government-directed killing of a human being is required by, or consistent with, or goes against this divine will. Of course, these examples of historically influential moral principles, along with the many others possible, do not have to be seen as mutually exclusive, or as rank ordered in any fixed and final way (though their various advocates have sometimes treated them as if they were). Still, even pluralistic combinations of moral principles need to be logically consistent and nonarbitrary, so that persuasive, relevant, and insightful accounts of what is morally justified in specific situations can result.

SECTION 2: MORAL RESPONSIBILITY AND MORAL STANDING

As we try to evaluate conduct and policies ethically by identifying the choices, values, obligations, and principles involved for particular actors in particular circumstances, we also have to understand just what it is about any "actor" that makes plausible the attribution of moral responsibility. That is, we don't expect a human fetus, or a tree, or a shark, or bacteria to act in accordance with moral duties, and we don't judge their activity as immoral when they fail to do so, even though that fetus might cause the death of the pregnant woman carrying it, the tree might damage someone's house by falling on it, and sometimes sharks and bacteria attack people. We do, however, expect a functional human adult to fulfill his or her obligations, at least in terms of refraining from avoidable harm to innocent others. This difference in expectation can be traced, once again, to the concept of choice, where those who we appropriately consider to be morally accountable for their actions have available to them alternative courses of conduct in this or that situation, which they can rationally understand and from which they can choose in light of self-consciously identified ethical considerations. In other words, we typically think of a "moral actor," or "moral agent," as someone or something capable of understanding the content of specific moral obligations, understanding his, her, or its own status as one upon whom such ethical demands can be made, and recognizing the responsibility for voluntary choice in the matter at hand.

Answering the question "Who is morally responsible?" becomes more complicated, however, not only when we start investigating the cognitive capabilities that might imply some sort of "moral sense" in non-human species of living beings, but also when we try to decide whether human collective entities such as towns, governments, or business corporations can ever be judged as fulfilling or violating *their* moral obligations. As will be further explained in Section 5, such obligations, if they exist, are not logically identical simply with whatever legal constraints guide action by these collectivities, even though legal duties and rights, and moral duties and rights, are closely connected. In any case, people often do praise or blame as "agents" whole societies (e.g., France, America, China) as well as the distinct governments of those societies; they talk about the desirable or undesirable competition, for example, between this city and that city for attracting some arms manufacturing enterprise; and, they refer to the responsibility to be a "good corporate citizen" on the part of this or that big business. Is all this just a confused, or overly simplistic, way of referring to the moral responsibilities of individual humans who are members of these organized groups? Or, is there some meaningful sense in which such organizations can be said to be actors "themselves," intentionally pursuing their perceived interests and attempting to follow agendas for which we can justifiably hold them accountable? Resolving this issue is necessary if we are to evaluate with any thoroughness the war and peace policies of a national government, the trials of persons charged with war crimes, the lending practices of the World Bank and the International Monetary Fund that have increased the suffering in many already impoverished communities, or the environmental damage caused by companies in search of fossil fuels.

In addition to determining who is morally responsible for how they treat others, we also have to determine which "others" moral agents are obliged to take into account if their conduct is to be ethically defensible in particular situations. This is sometimes referred to as the problem of "moral standing," that is, who (or what) deserves "moral consideration" when what we do will likely affect her, him, it, or them in some way. Different moral principles will emphasize different kinds of consideration regarding relevant others, whether it is their moral rights that are at stake, or the degree of benefit and detriment that might accrue to them, or their likely preferences, or their inherent worth. But the issue here is what kinds of beings have any of these ethically significant attributes in the first place, so that we must take them into account if our actions are to be rationally justified.

Throughout history this concern with who counts morally has been dealt with quite differently in a variety of cultural contexts, and even today there is much more diversity of belief on this matter than we might initially assume. For example, on the one hand, in both the European and the Chinese intellectual traditions going back at least a few thousand years, the most commonly held view has been an anthropocentric one, that is, that among "earthly" beings only human interests count morally. The moral value of nonhuman living beings in these traditions typically has been indirect and instrumental at best, insofar as how they were treated affected some humans' interests. But this anthropocentrism (also called "humanism," though distinguishable from the somewhat narrower social and political theory affirming the historical progress and moral self-improvement of humankind) itself has generated many variations, including the options of an unqualified individualism (all and only individual human beings have moral status), a qualified individualism (only human individuals who meet some further criterion such as self-consciousness, have moral status), or some version of communitarianism (specific human communities themselves deserve moral status, while the individuals populating them may or may not). In addition, within this general range going from what has been called an extreme social atomism to an extreme social organicism, people have

13

argued that we only have moral obligations to existing fellow humans, or that we also owe consideration to future, not-yet-existing generations of humans, or that we also have duties to our ancestors and other no-longer-physically-existing humans. And, one way or another all these anthropocentric accounts of moral standing have been linked historically to particular religious and/or secular philosophical doctrines (for example, the Jewish and Christian use of the creation stories in the book of Genesis, as well as the seventeenth-century natural rights theory of John Locke in European culture, and Confucianism in China).

On the other hand, in the second half of the twentieth century more western intellectuals started voicing the concern that the usual anthropocentric approaches to ethical decision-making were too exclusive and thus inadequate. Instead, some argued, many nonhuman living beings deserved moral consideration in their own right and not simply because they may have extrinsic value with respect to human interests. Among moral philosophers this perspective became known as "extensionism," because it affirmed the extending of moral standing beyond *homo sapiens* to other classes of individuals who were sufficiently like humans in some relevant way. Some extensionist theories took a "first phase" approach, either extending varying degrees of moral status to all sentient animals (i.e., those capable of experiencing pleasure and pain, in some meaningful sense of those terms), or in a more restricted manner emphasizing the moral standing of all human and nonhuman animals possessing self-consciousness and thus definable as "persons." Other extensionists have put forth "second phase" theories, arguing for some significant degree of moral consideration owed to all or most non-sentient as well as sentient living things, whether they are plant or animal.

The belief that we have direct obligations to nonhuman as well as human individuals, while still viewed by many in contemporary western societies as deviant and not to be taken seriously, is in fact not unique to recent western thought. The spiritual traditions of Hinduism, Buddhism, and Jainism, originating in India and still widely followed today, also emphasize in different ways the intrinsic rather than merely extrinsic moral status of most living beings. At the most general level this is because all three have in common the doctrine of karma and rebirth, which asserts that all actions of some kind of individual "self" have consequences that will be experienced by that being, either in this mortal life or another. This requires being reborn, and dying, again and again in a wide variety of possible life forms, until one is able to transcend all ego related concerns and "this-worldly" attachments that keep one tied to mortal existence, eventually liberating the "self" forever from this "wheel of rebirth." Thus, every living thing we encounter might be viewed as involved in its own spiritual journey, and also deserves consideration to some extent on that basis.

There is a third general approach to this question of moral standing that has both ancient and contemporary variants, in recent times often called "ecocentrism." In ecocentric moral evaluation the focus is not only on humans (individually and collectively) and individual nonhumans. What is emphasized here is the interrelated totality of all living things, so that the well-being of the whole planetary biosphere itself, its numerous local ecosystems, the species inhabiting those ecosystems, and the individual members of those species, all should be taken into account in relevant decision-making. In other words, a collective entity such as an ecosystem or a biological species also has moral status in its own right, as do the individuals populating it, because it too can benefit or be harmed by what morally responsible parties do in relation to it. Further, it is often argued that the health and integrity of these living systems and the species constituting them is of greater moral concern than the life or death of particular organisms, so that our moral obligations to these "biotic communities" (to which we moral agents belong as well, naturally) presuppose a social organicism expanded beyond intra-species relations among humans, to include inter-species relations at a very fundamental level.

As the interest in environmental ethics has grown in recent decades within the academic world, hand in hand with developments in the biological science of ecology, ecocentrism has become a more common option as a conceptual framework for ethical evaluation generally. In the moral assessment of war, for example, questions about environmental damage and violence against local ecosystems are more regularly raised than they once were, and not only out of concern for the human interests negatively affected. Once again, however, this way of thinking about who or what counts morally is not new in human cultural history, but in fact also forms the basis of the moral codes traditionally followed by many indigenous peoples in North and South America. For example, it has been typical in Native American thought to reject the usual western assumption that humans comprise a special species set apart from the rest of "Nature," who can only be in direct moral relation with other humans. It is widely believed as well in western hemisphere native cultures that there are different kinds of intersecting biological communities, human and nonhuman, local and global, which are morally valuable in themselves as living systems, even apart from the fact that every single living thing is also dependent on them for its own well-being.

SECTION 3: RELATIVISM AND UNIVERSALISM

Before we engage seriously in the enterprise of morally evaluating our own or other moral agents' choices of action in relevant situations, there is another preliminary decision we have to make. Regarding questions about the rightness or wrongness of personal conduct or social policies, should we assume that one answer is as good as another or that some answers are discernibly better than others? Put in very basic terms, this is what the debate between ethical (or "moral") relativism and ethical (or "moral") universalism is about, and until we decide how to proceed here we won't know what counts as a good or bad reason for any of our normative beliefs. In general then, the relativist position is that what really *is* right or wrong, good or bad, *is* what any particular individual or group believes it to be, so that the moral justification of actions or practices is simply a function of what people actually think is justified (i.e., just because they think so). In contrast, the universalist (or "objectivist") position asserts that what really is right or wrong, good or bad, is not simply equivalent to whatever anybody thinks it is, but that whatever the moral truth might be in specific relevant situations, it is so for every moral agent in sufficiently similar circumstances of choice, independently of what she, he, or they may think about the matter.

As usually characterized, ethical relativism comes in more moderate and more extreme versions, the former focusing on moral justification as being relative to particular societies or cultural groups, each with its own presumably distinct *ethos*. That is, this moderate relativism asserts that conduct is morally right or wrong depending entirely on what any particular society/culture generally believes to be the case. For example, if in one society slavery is a morally approved practice, it really is morally right just because of that cultural approbation, while if slavery is generally seen as immoral in another society, it also really is morally wrong, just because of that cultural disapprobation. And, in this view there is no way to rationally decide which of the opposing beliefs about slavery is more *ethically* defensible. The more extreme version of ethical relativism, on the other hand, takes this unresolvable moral diversity down to the level of the individual person, so that what is morally right or wrong becomes what any such individual thinks it is, regardless of his or her cultural affiliation. This approach is expressed in everyday life by common utterances such as "Morality is just a matter of opinion anyway," "What's moral for me may not be moral for other people," or "Who am I to judge anybody else?" and it is a viewpoint with which most of us are familiar. One implication here then, is that if someone believes it is always right to punish children violently, it is always right because he or she thinks so, and if that person's next door neighbor believes it is always wrong to punish children violently, it is always wrong just because that other person thinks so. Again, we have no adequate moral basis for determining which of the opposing beliefs is more justified.

These versions of ethical relativism have often been supported by appealing to the facts of cultural or individual diversity of beliefs, on the one hand, or, on the other hand, by appealing to the moral principle of tolerance, interpreted as a nonjudgmental respect for beliefs and practices different than one's own. In the estimation of most philosophers these days, however, the problems with any of these versions are of both a logical and a practical nature. In the first place, the relativist position allows for the logical contradiction that the assertions "X is morally justified" and "X is not morally justified" can both be true at the same time. Further, the relativist argument based on the demands of tolerance cannot rule out the implication that those morally advocating intolerance of all cultural or individual diversity are equally justified in their beliefs and whatever bigoted actions follow from them. Secondly, if what we are interested in is how we ourselves or anybody else *morally ought* to act in a particular situation, then we don't receive any adequate guidance simply by identifying what somebody's feelings, attitudes, or opinions are regarding the issue. Such information might be useful in considering the range of possible options from which to choose, but what we need are good reasons for why one belief rather than another should be transformed into conduct which, after all, will most likely have some kind of beneficial or harmful effect on someone. Specifically concerning the ethical evaluation of interpersonal, inter-group, or international violence, the fact that some moral agent thinks that certain violent acts are okay is just not a good enough reason, by itself, for us to accept uncritically that party's opinion as justified or convincing, given what is practically at stake. If critical analysis and rational persuasiveness are to be at all useful or relevant in deciding how people should treat others in this world, then we not only need to work with the distinction between "good" and "bad" reasons for our ethical conclusions, but also to maintain a coherent distinction between "mistaken" and "correct" moral beliefs from the outset, even if we aren't sure which beliefs are which in particular cases.

The universalist approach to the search for "correct" as opposed to "incorrect" moral beliefs has always been the predominant one in most if not all philosophical traditions, but it also has appeared in many different versions. These differences can be located on a continuum, from more absolutist accounts at one end that assert the objective existence of a fixed and invariable, eternally true "moral law" (usually divinely ordained) applicable in the same way to all people everywhere and at all times, to more context-dependent interpretations of "moral truth" on the other end emphasizing the possibility of rational agreement among reflective, well-informed, sufficiently impartial parties, based on at least some commonality of values, and focused on determinate ethical decision-making situations. Along this continuum the concept of universality itself is used variously, from more inclusive to more exclusive versions of moral responsibility, as is the concept of objectivity, from references to that which is eternally so independent of all cognition, to reliance on what is called in the sciences "intersubjective verification" as the way to ground nonarbitrary rational judgments about justified and unjustified ethical choices.

There have been a number of problems with ethical universalism/objectivism identified over the years, and for the most part the relativist position which emerged at least within the western intellectual tradition was a critical response especially to the more absolutist, ahistorical accounts of moral truth aimed at all humankind. One common criticism, often offered by social scientists rather than philosophers, has been that any universalizing normative ethical theory must have an empirically discoverable universal foundation, and given the fact of widespread cultural, historical, and individual differences among humans in their value beliefs, there just is no such foundation. Another problem with universalist ethical evaluation has been its tendencies toward ethnocentrism which, as a chauvinistic devaluation of cultural "otherness" as only deficiently human, is to be opposed presumably on moral grounds (but again, it doesn't seem as though the moral relativist can consistently criticize the unabashed champion of ethnocentrism as somehow "wrong" either). A third kind of criticism has rejected the whole enterprise of developing normative theories, or standards of ethical evaluation, arguing instead that moral opinions are translatable either into factual self-reports about what one feels or thinks in response to a situation, or into simple attitudes which may or may not align with those of someone else, but about which we cannot rationally argue.

In response to these criticisms many moral philosophers point out in the first place that the evidence for a species-wide foundation of at least some kinds of ethical determination seems to be increasing, and that the empirical argument for irreconcilable moral incommensurability between persons and/or peoples is not so well-founded. This is most obvious if we recognize the historical and cultural ubiquity of some human value judgments: that health is better than sickness, that pleasure is intrinsically more desirable than pain, that personal respect is preferable to personal degradation, or that living in conditions of safety and security is better than living in constant fear and insecurity. Secondly, the dangers of ethnocentric bias in our ethical evaluations and theory construction are more often recognized and taken into account than they once were, though admittedly they will continue to exist into the foreseeable future as something about which we should always be concerned. Although ethnocentrism can affect our moral judgments, it does not necessarily or unavoidably do so in ways that rule out any cross-cultural common ground achievable among rational inquirers.

Finally, to say that our conclusions regarding what actions or policies are ethically justified or unjustified in real life situations are merely reducible to unarguable self-reports or attitudes is to reject as irrelevant and pointless, again, all critical analysis and rational discussion aimed at actually deciding on principled grounds which line of conduct among the available alternatives is most likely the best one to follow. To take this position is to give up the effort to discern good and bad reasons for people's beliefs, to identify mistaken moral judgments, and to discover which conclusions about moral right and wrong are more or less persuasive. The most obvious and problematic practical consequence of this is that in disagreements about what ought to be done, the opinions that prevail will tend to be those of the parties with the most power to assert their will over others, in other words, "Might makes right." This seems to be an inescapable implication for ethical relativism generally, and thus one of the main reasons why most moral philosophers currently will instead opt for some version of ethical universalism.

SECTION 4: GUIDING MORAL PRINCIPLES

As I indicated in Section 1, moral philosophers have often pointed to overarching principles or rules as the source of our more situation-specific ethical obligations, and a good deal of philosophical debate over the centuries has centered around which principles should take precedence when decisions about conduct need to be made. I will not attempt to resolve the controversies in that domain here (countless books already have been written on the subject), but I would like to offer a brief summary of some of the more historically influential moral principles that have been applied to questions about interpersonal and inter-group violence and nonviolence, along with some of their compatibilities and incompatibilities.

1. Given the links often made between nonviolence, peace, and justice these days by progressive social activists worldwide, the principle of justice itself is naturally the first one that comes to mind for many people when they reflect ethically on relevant actions or policies. The idea of justice has a

very long history in human affairs, and it has been defined quite diversely in different places and times. But there does seem to be a common thread running through at least most of its various characterizations, and that is, that we should treat others as they *deserve* to be treated. Now, this very general notion of justice as having to do with what someone deserves (in other words, the concept of "just deserts") does not by itself get us too far in the determination of our moral obligations in specific situations, since people can agree that this is what justice demands of them and at the same time significantly disagree about both what anyone actually does deserve in any particular case, and again, what beings have moral standing within the scope of justice in the first place. Still, this abstract formulation of action in accordance with what relevant parties deserve together with its conceptual opposite, action contrary to what they would deserve (i.e., "injustice") provide useful parameters within which concerns about the moral rightness or wrongness of violence can be meaningfully worked out, once other circumstantial factors are also taken into account. For example, one might argue that during a time of war enemy combatants deserve to be treated violently until they surrender, but that non-combatants "on the other side" deserve not to be targeted for violence, and if they are, they are being treated unjustly and the perpetrators thereby are doing what is morally wrong.

Justice has been conventionally subdivided into four main types, or four arenas of application, beyond the everyday considerations of "fairness" that usually inform our understanding of how we and relevant others deserve to be treated. One such type has to do with the role of punishment in organized social life, and is commonly referred to as the principle of "just retribution." This is the ethical idea that those who have wrongfully harmed others deserve to be harmed in return, and that the amount of harm they deserve should be proportionate to the amount of harm they inflicted on those others. In the context of law enforcement this rule of retributive justice is often given the formulation "crime must be punished, and the punishment must fit the crime." A second "species" of justice shifts the focus from the wrongdoer to the victims of wrongdoing and what they deserve, and thus constitutes a principle of "just compensation." As usually understood, compensatory justice recommends that those who have been wrongfully harmed deserve compensation for that harm, and that the amount of compensation again be proportionate to the degree of harm suffered. If people are wrongfully killed, or if they were persecuted or abused generations ago and have since died, obviously there is no way to directly compensate them, and in contemporary society this has given rise to some difficult questions regarding possible compensation owed to families and later descendents of victims as a way of finally "making things right," as well as who exactly is responsible for providing that compensation.

A third kind of justice has to do with the access to limited resources in social environments where it is assumed that the needs and wants of everybody concerned are at least roughly similar. This is the principle of "just distribution," and it requires that things of value (goods, services, life opportunities, and so on) be distributed in a fair and equitable manner. So, if people deserve a certain level of preference satisfaction under determinate conditions, and they are thwarted in the achievement of that goal by other moral agents, or those others cause and/or maintain an avoidable maldistribution of the relevant things of value, then the principle of distributive justice is violated and the violators are guilty of injustice. A lot of the contemporary ethical discussion concerning "globalization," world hunger, medical care, educational opportunity, the weapons market, and human rights, as well as the continuing debate regarding the pros and cons of capitalism and various socialist alternatives, is often framed in terms of distributive justice and injustice, so this third arena of "just deserts" tends to be broader and even more multifaceted than the prior two. And as you might guess, much of the disagreement in this domain again comes down to the intertwined problems of who really deserves what in which cases, and who has the corresponding duty to act accordingly.

The fourth type of justice covers contractual agreements and exchanges, and is thus often identified as the principle of "just commutation." In other words, commutative justice requires that exchanges (say, between buyers and sellers) are fair, with reasonably equivalent benefits accruing to both parties. In contractual relationships (which often involve exchanges too, of course) all participants owe each other compliance with the terms of the agreement, with noncompliance normally constituting unjust treatment of the other parties until the contract itself is nullified or renegotiated. As usually construed, however, there are two morally necessary prerequisites for fairness in this arena. In the first place, all exchanges and agreements must be voluntary in the sense that all parties are able to exercise autonomous choice in entering into such relationships. Secondly, each participant must be adequately informed regarding the conditions and implications of what she, he or they would be making commitments to, without which presumably rational choice cannot be truly exercised. What this means is that if people enter into binding transactions because they are coerced, desperate, or incompetent, and don't really have a viable choice in the matter, or, because they are kept ignorant by others' active or passive deception about relevant information on the basis of which they could autonomously decide if it was in their best interests to participate, then those exchanges or contractual arrangements are essentially unfair and thus also unjust for those people.

2. Another common approach to grounding our obligations is to appeal to the moral rights thought to be possessed by some identified population, so that we would be required to act in ways that respect everyone's rights, and conduct violating someone's rights is thereby morally wrong. In most ethical discussions, to have a moral right to something means that one can *justifiably* demand a certain kind of treatment from others. So, for example, if I possess a right to life I can legitimately demand of others that, at the very least, they not kill me, and they also then have a corresponding moral duty to refrain from doing so. Further, rights are usually categorized as either "negative" or "positive," so our negative rights (if we have them) indicate what other morally responsible parties should *not do to us*, while our positive rights (if we have them) indicate what those others should *do or provide for us*. The former are also often referred to as "rights of noninterference" or "liberty rights," and moral agents can fulfill their correlative duties to the right-possessor simply by doing nothing or leaving that party alone (e.g., the rights to property, privacy, free speech, and again, life). The latter specify some kind of aid from others (and thus are sometimes called "welfare rights," such as the right to food, housing, medical care, or education), which would require positive action on the part of others in order to fulfill their duties.

As was the case with the principle of justice however, beyond these general definitions of moral rights the main difficulty and source of debate in ethical evaluation is deciding who has which rights in which life situations, and under what conditions one party's rights might override another's. For example, even though there is fairly widespread agreement these days that there exist basic "human rights" globally, and the 1948 United Nations document, titled the "Universal Declaration of Human Rights" (still officially in effect), actually lists many such rights, there continues to be much disagreement around the world regarding how equally applicable they are in circumstances of conflict and material scarcity, how morally and legally accountable violators of these rights should be, and how many negative and especially positive rights people justifiably can claim. On the other hand, it is often assumed within these areas of controversy that justice and injustice themselves can be understood in terms of conduct consistent with or in violation of human rights (as well as the rights of any other beings with moral standing), although obviously the attribution of rights is not the only way to make sense out of "what is deserved."

3. In the history of moral reflection on violence and nonviolence many thinkers in many different traditions have appealed to the concept of a morally ordered

universe within which we all exist, as the ultimate source of our duties. Though often quite compatible with various justice-based or rights-based approaches to ethical evaluation, this belief that there is a moral law inherent in the very nature of things which is binding on all moral agents can be distinguished as a third guiding principle of right conduct. It also has had long-standing and wide-ranging influence mainly because of its association with many religious and other spiritually oriented doctrines. In the western monotheistic religions (that is, the Abrahamic religions of Judaism, Christianity, and Islam) when this principle is appealed to it sometimes has been formulated as "natural law," or "the law of nature," emphasizing the idea that there is a proper way for us to act and live our lives in this world in accordance with our God-given human nature and thereby consistent with God's expectations. Actions are wrong then because they are somehow unnatural and contrary to the natural moral order of the world established for us by the Creator. So, one might argue that, given our common humanity and its inherent rather than merely "earned" value, all intentional killing of other humans is always immoral even if occasionally excusable, because it is a deviation from our true nature and thus a violation of natural law. Of course, this position on homicide clearly does not represent the majority opinion in the history of these three religions; but, especially in recent times, it has been given voice by more and more religiously affiliated nonviolentists.

In the predominant religious and philosophical traditions originating in India the belief in a morally ordered universe is given form primarily in the central doctrine of *karma*, referring to the moral law of causality whereby all thoughts, words, and deeds have consequences which will be experienced by the moral agent himself or herself, either in this material life or another. This law of karma together with the presumed goal of spiritual liberation (*moksha*) from reincarnation is the basis for ethical duty (*dharma*) especially in Hinduism, Buddhism, and Jainism, and since ancient times has been used both to justify (more often in Hinduism) and to condemn (more consistently and thoroughly in Jainism) particular acts of violence. Similarly, in ancient Chinese philosophy (distinct from later Buddhist influence) the basically "this-worldly" principles of living in accordance with "the Way" (*Dao*) of nature in Daoism, and following "the Mandate of Heaven" (*Tien ming*) in Confucianism were variously employed in ethical evaluation without either version of "natural law" ever generating unanimity regarding violence and nonviolence. Finally, in the religious cosmologies and related ethical systems of many indigenous peoples in the Americas and Africa there always has been a strong emphasis on the interrelatedness and mutual dependency of all living things, constituting a created natural order which must be respected and not disrupted by moral agents if they are to live well. In this general conceptual framework, moral right and wrong often have been characterized in terms of that which helps maintain balance and functionality in all relationships making up this "web of life," as opposed to that which creates imbalance and dysfunction, and all acts of violence are evaluated accordingly.

4. The principle of utility is a fourth option as a foundation for our moral obligations, and another one that continues to be very influential in most modern ethical debates while having more ancient roots. Simply put, this principle demands that we act so as to maximize benefit and minimize harm for everyone affected to any significant degree. That is, an action or policy is morally justified if it appears to lead to more good consequences and fewer bad consequences for all parties whose interests are at stake, compared to the alternative choices; it is unjustified, on the other hand, if it appears it will lead to less good and more bad/evil for all concerned, compared to alternatives. In the last few centuries there have been a number of different utilitarian ethical theories advanced by philosophers, but for present purposes I will just distinguish generally between what is now called classical utilitarianism and preference utilitarianism. In the former approach, most famously elaborated by Jeremy Bentham in the late eighteenth century and John Stuart Mill in the mid-nineteenth century, conduct is to be judged right or wrong depending on the total quantities of happiness and unhappiness it is likely to bring about for everyone affected. Here, happiness and unhappiness themselves are conceived of hedonistically, in terms of the presence or absence of pleasure and pain. The latter approach has been developed in more recent times to overcome the perceived problems of treating utility only as a happiness-maximizing and unhappiness-minimizing imperative, and emphasizes the likely preferences of each individual party concerned in any particular decision-making situation. So in this interpretation of the principle of utility we are obligated to act in accordance with the preferences (whatever they are) of all relevant individuals as much as possible, and to avoid acting in ways contrary to those preferences as much as possible, given the available choices.

As is the case with our everyday considerations of fairness in our social interactions, there is something very commonsensical about taking into account the consequences of our actions, and their effects not only on us but also on others. And, it is certainly not unusual or inappropriate for people to think about what will lead to more benefit and less harm for everybody affected, when they morally assess violent and nonviolent alternatives in cases of interpersonal and inter-group conflict. On the other hand, utilitarianism also has been criticized as an unreliable basis for moral evaluation, because it lends itself too easily to the rationale that "the end justifies the means." Others have challenged the principle of utility on the grounds that it is overly dependent on accurate factual information, unfortunately not always available in real life conditions, on the basis of which (inevitably fallible) predictions concerning good and bad outcomes for everybody must be made. Further, various advocates of the other principles already mentioned have argued that if utility is employed as the primary criterion of right and wrong it would allow for possible cases where, in the name of "the greater good for the greater number," treating some persons unjustly, overriding their natural or civil rights, etc., would be morally correct. Since such a conclusion could never be rationally justified according to these critics, at best utility should be seen as a secondary or derivative rule, but never as the foundational principle guiding ethical judgment.

5. In modern western moral philosophy, another theory sometimes clearly distinguished from and sometimes treated as a further development of the above options, is contractarianism. In the history of political theory it has aimed mainly at providing a rational and voluntaristic foundation for a legitimate state, but as an ethical theory the contractarian approach characterizes the criteria of right and wrong conduct simply in terms of moral rules that prudent, well-informed persons most likely would agree to. In other words, based on the factual assumptions of the ability for rational self-determination (and in many versions the exclusive motivation of rational egoism) in the case of each involved party, and the purely atomistic and ultimately artificial rather than organic nature of all social relations, actions and policies are justified if reasonable, self-interested individuals would find them mutually agreeable, and they are unjustified if such individuals would most likely agree that they be rejected. Viewing moral evaluation as a function of this sort of "social contract" has been recommended because it is a more well-developed account of both the Golden Rule and the principle of commutative justice, and because it is most consistent with our natural motivational tendencies anyway. However, critics have argued that taken by itself contractarianism is an inadequate ethical theory, in the first place because it has difficulty accounting for the possible differences between people's perceived self-interests and their actual self-interests without arbitrariness, ethnocentrism, or ideological bias. Secondly, the presumed rational egoism and subsequent artificiality of all social relations upon which this normative theory usually is based, are highly contestable as species-wide generalizations, even though still quite popular among apologists of western capitalist economic practices over the last few centuries.

6. One more basic moral value that sometimes has been formulated by philosophers as a distinct moral principle is the concept of care, which as a

guide to conduct would require us to actively take responsibility for the welfare of others with whom we are in relation, protecting them from harm while maintaining the viability of the relationship itself, and acknowledging everyone's needs as inclusively as possible. As a theoretical response to the observed experience especially of women in modern patriarchal society, the "ethics of care" has developed within the larger framework of feminist analysis in explicit contrast to the typical modernist appeals to formal justice and negative rights. To a greater extent than the other "guiding principles" identified here, however, care also has been at least as often treated as a morally valuable character trait (a "virtue"), rather than primarily as a rule governing actions. In any case, because of the emphasis on concretely contextualized relationships among flesh and blood, vulnerable beings, and on inculcating a personal responsibility to aid and protect others in need where we can, the care ethic has been explored by a number of thinkers for its promise in providing a more honestly realistic, less abstract approach to the infliction of suffering and the need for nonviolent conflict resolution.

As I indicated earlier, a good deal of philosophical debate historically has centered around the question of which moral principle should be the primary guide for moral agents in the determination of their obligations. Frequently it has been assumed that one principle must be chosen above, or even to the exclusion of the others, so that in effect a priority list of decision-making criteria can be established, "universalized," and adhered to consistently to make our ethical judgments rationally defensible. This tendency is still exhibited in western academic philosophy, for example, in the disagreements between utilitarians and various nonconsequentialist proponents of the theoretical primacy of justice, or rights, or natural law. In contrast to this focus on which principle universally trumps the others, however, we could choose to take a more pluralistic approach which trades on the fact that all of these principles in their own way offer understanding of important moral values at stake in a very wide range of ethical situations. Since obviously we can conceptualize justice, rights, natural law, utility, the social contract, and care in ways that make them all basically compatible without reducing them to mere equivalents of each other, an ethical pluralism can emphasize a much more contextualized and flexible orientation to moral evaluation which nonetheless remains within the bounds of logical consistency and also avoids the pitfalls of relativism. And, although I will not be arguing for one particular normative ethical theory in the rest of this book, my accounts of different "peace and justice" issues as well as the possibilities for nonviolent conflict resolution will be in the spirit of this kind of pluralism most often.

SECTION 5: MORALITY AND LAW

Some kind of moral code is discoverable in every society throughout human history, contributing essentially to whatever identifying *ethos* exists for this or that people, but not all societies have been governed by laws. Even though both moral norms and legal codes specify right and wrong behavior for people in the context of community life, law is usually seen as the product of more explicit, public decision-making by some recognized political authority which also possesses the power of legally specified enforcement. As a typical institutional feature of politically organized societies, especially in recent centuries, a set of laws is used to govern a certain group of people and/or geographical region, and we can learn what conduct is allowed and prohibited as well as what the penalties are for noncompliance within that jurisdiction, simply by consulting what that particular legal code says on the subject. So, deciding what our legal duties and rights are in a situation becomes largely an empirical matter, leading some people to leap immediately to the conclusion that what is morally justified or not is also reducible to existing law, with no need to look further. But if this is true then, first, all moral disagreement with any actual laws becomes meaningless, and second, we end up back in the position of a kind of moderate ethical relativism referred to earlier, whereby what is morally right or wrong is what the laws in any political community dictate. Since it is highly implausible that all legislation becomes morally sound and beyond criticism once it has been enacted, or that the same conduct is at the same time justified and unjustified morally solely because it is allowed or mandated in one legal jurisdiction and prohibited in another, we should instead always keep clearly in mind the distinction between morality and the law for both logical and practical reasons. After all, the fact that an action is legally required does not necessarily mean that it ought to be required, and it does not follow that we have a moral right to something just because we have a legal right to the same.

On the other hand, since moral beliefs and legislation both "regulate" how we treat each other in society, there is a crucial connection between them as well. For example, most people think it is morally wrong to intentionally kill an innocent person against his or her will, and in fact many legal codes historically have also treated such killings as punishable offenses in one way or another. At the very least, there is a significant overlapping in the content of many moral and legal rights and duties, and more often than not legal rules are created in response to and defended in terms of ethical considerations already influential in group life. Similarly, when laws are changed or repealed it is often as a result of someone challenging their ethical defensibility, as in the case of former racial segregation laws in the southern United States. Of course, in any ethical argumentation used publicly in favor of or against particular laws, it is often worthwhile to determine how much sincerity, mere rhetoric, or cynicism is behind it all. But even less honorable uses of moral discourse provide further evidence of how widespread the belief is in the first place that legislation should be somehow ethically grounded.

In the following chapters, the discussions of violence and nonviolence, war and peace, and their relevance to questions of justice and injustice, will require clarity regarding both the distinctions and interconnections between morality and law because of the recurrent emphasis on ethical evaluation of legislative efforts at social control as well as other government policies in various places around the world. For example, in many nation states judicial systems have been created basically as institutional means of resolving conflict between different parties, both domestically and in foreign relations, and in principle they aim at achieving some kind of legal justice. For this to happen it is also necessary to legally determine what is owed to all citizens, non-citizens, and "persons" whose interests are at stake (which again, in a state like the US would include business corporations as possessors of civil rights), in terms of possible benefits and punishments. But as will be shown, sometimes there is good reason to conclude that what has been declared legally just is not at all morally just, and that accordingly "the law must change." This in turn raises ethical questions about how far our obligations go in obeying existing laws, and what legitimate strategies (possibly including civil disobedience) are available to us for changing either those laws themselves or at least the legal decisions allegedly based upon them.

As social conventions associated with a certain binding force for everyone within an identifiable community, legal "do's and don'ts" operate at many different levels in human affairs. There are municipal ordinances, state or provincial statutes, national laws, and even a somewhat more ambiguous body of international law. In all of these legal domains, however, evaluating the justifiability of laws is inseparable from deciding whether the specific kinds of coercion they imply also are justified, assuming that, other things being equal, making people do things against their will is contrary to their personal preferences. Because the means of law enforcement and their outcomes can be more or less harmful to persons subject to them, and can involve greater or lesser degrees of violence, the study of nonviolence must also address a number of issues surrounding the uses of governmental coercion. Although many people these days tend to think of human violence as mostly illegal or extralegal, it is more likely in fact that more violence worldwide continues to be carried out directly by government agents or sponsored by them, and in other ways, allowed by some legal authority. Obviously, executing criminals is one example of violent law enforcement, and war is organized, intentional, group violence usually engaged in by governmental personnel, but imprisonment, debilitating monetary penalties, and economic embargoes that cause increased poverty, disease, and death among whole peoples, also are strategies of legally supported coercion that are intended to make actual human beings suffer.

These different means of enforcing laws and achieving other political goals have been defended variously in the name of public safety, "law and order," national security, retributive justice, economic prosperity, or human rights, and the very idea of an organized society without punitive legal coercion is simply unthinkable for many. Whether the latter results only from a lack of imagination and historical knowledge, or instead reflects the recognition of a social necessity in larger human populations, in any case the evaluation of a particular coercive strategy must focus on its nature and intended scope, its purpose, and the degree of harm it threatens to inflict on living subjects who deserve moral consideration. This kind of investigation will be taken up later, but in concluding this chapter let me just emphasize how widely it is still assumed that legal violence is required both as the kind of negative reinforcement most effective in modifying human behavior, and as the only way the demands of justice can be met. Consequently, in any defense of the superiority of nonviolent alternatives in living and interacting with others, we also must show, first, that strategies of negative reinforcement generally, and legal violence especially, are not nearly as effective in achieving worthwhile goals as is often thought, and second, that the requirements of legal and moral justice can be fulfilled with much less violence than what people have become habituated to in many societies.

FURTHER READING

Section 1

William Clifford, "The Ethics of Belief," originally published in *Contemporary Review*, 1877, reprinted in *The Ethics of Belief and Other Essays* (New York: Prometheus Books, 1999).

Larry May, Shari Collins-Chobanian, Kai Wong, editors, *Applied Ethics: A Multicultural Approach*, third edition (Upper Saddle River, NJ: Prentice Hall / Pearson Education, 2002).

James Rachels, *The Elements of Moral Philosophy*, third edition (New York: McGraw-Hill College, 1999).

Section 2

Carl Cohen and Tom Regan, editors, *The Animal Rights Debate* (Lanham, MD: Rowman and Littlefield, 2001).

Larry May, *The Morality of Groups: Collective Responsibility, Group-Based Harm, and Corporate Rights* (Notre Dame, IN: U of Notre Dame P, 1987).

Ian Shapiro and Will Kymlicka, editors, *Ethnicity and Group Rights*, NOMOS XXXIX (New York: New York UP, 1996).

Donald VanDeVeer and Christine Pierce, editors, *The Environmental Ethics and Policy Book* (Belmont, CA: Wadsworth, 2003).

Section 3

Mary Midgley, *Can't We Ever Make Moral Judgments?* (New York: St. Martin's Press, 1991).

William M. Sullivan and Will Kymlicka, editors, *The Globalization of Ethics: Religious and Secular Perspectives* (New York: Cambridge UP, 2007).

Section 4

Alfonso Gomez-Lobo, *Morality and the Human Goods: An Introduction to Natural Law Ethics* (Washington, DC: Georgetown UP, 2002).

John Stuart Mill, *Utilitarianism* (Oxford: Oxford UP, 1998); originally published 1861.

Nell Noddings, *Educating Moral People: A Caring Alternative to Character Education* (New York: Teachers College Press, 2002).

Onora O'Neill, *Constructions of Reason: Explorations of Kant's Practical Philosophy* (Cambridge: Cambridge UP, 1989).

John Rawls, *A Theory of Justice* (Cambridge, MA: Harvard UP, 1971).

United Nations Universal Declaration of Human Rights (New York: United Nations Department of Public Information).

Section 5

Gerald Dworkin, editor, *Morality, Harm, and the Law* (Boulder, CO: Westview Press, 1994).

CHAPTER 2

Violence, Nonviolence, and Conflict

SECTION 1: THE NATURE OF VIOLENCE

Violence is one of those concepts the meaning of which most people assume they understand, until they are asked to give a definition of it that is precise, thorough, and consistent. Then things get more complicated and easily confusing because the word itself is commonly, and appropriately, used in so many different ways. We talk about the "violence" of a thunderstorm, "violent" sports, doing "violence" to the language, as well as "violent" crime and the organized group "violence" constituting the central feature of war. Still, at least etymologically there is a common thread here, as both "violence" and the related verb "to violate" can be traced back to the Latin (*violare, violentus, vis*), referring to the exercise of force against someone or something in a harmful manner. Also, when we move from descriptions of usage to value judgments we have to recognize the commonly shared belief that, from the position of those on the receiving end anyway, violence is generally a bad thing rather than a good thing. Of course, it is this underlying judgment that has always motivated the pursuit of strategies for avoiding or minimizing violence in human affairs, and which is presupposed in almost all ethical evaluation of the possible justifications for that kind of "evil" by moral agents.

In order to stay on task in the exploration of nonviolent, peace-enhancing approaches to living socially and resolving conflict, I will use a fairly simple definition of violence that I believe is neither too narrow nor too broad (we will put aside our concerns about violent storms or the wanton abuse of language from now on), and which treats as essential the relationship between the perpetrator(s) attributable with varying degrees of moral responsibility, and the recipient(s) deserving of some degree of moral consideration. Thus: Violence is the direct or indirect infliction of injury on someone or something by some agent; and, "injury" here refers to a continuum of harm, damage, or hurt to someone against his or her will or in some other way contrary to the recipient's interests, ranging from that which is immediately life-threatening, through different degrees of debilitation, suffering, and loss, to a point of insignificance in the thwarting of desires.

In unpacking this definition, let me first point out, again, that it is important to identify the agent of violence in real life cases, in other words, the individual or group responsible for the infliction of injury. Agents' harmful actions can be voluntary and intentional in the sense that they know what they are doing, and they deliberately aim at injuring (as in military combat). Actions can be voluntary and unintentional (an assassin kills the wrong person), they can be nonvoluntary and intentional (when someone in a psychotic rage assaults other people believing them to be demons), and they can be nonvoluntary and unintentional (when an intoxicated person passes out while driving a car and it plows into a crowd of people). Second, in thinking about "someone or something" as the recipient of this injuring behavior, it seems most productive to take a more holistic, less reductionist approach, so that we don't exclusively focus on damage to individual human beings and their personal material possessions. Although the interests of flesh and blood human persons in avoiding hurt to themselves will be given primary consideration here, nonhuman living beings too can be victims of violence by morally culpable actors. Further, in a number of cultural worldviews past and present it is believed that the webs of relationship constituting whole communities are vulnerable to injury as well, and thus worthy of moral standing in their own right. This would include not only particular human communities but also the natural "biotic communities" made up of different species, local ecosystems, and possibly the whole biosphere itself.

Third, including both direct and indirect infliction of injury in this definition needs some explanation, since usually when we think of one party treating another party violently we tend to focus only on cases of direct assault, immediate forcible hurt, etc., especially when we look at the situation from the recipient's standpoint. The question that has to be answered then is whether someone can be an agent of violence indirectly, as distinct from being in the lesser though still problematic role of accessory to some other agent's actions. Although admittedly the boundaries between the kind of indirect agency I have in mind here and being either an accomplice or a passive observer will have some gray areas, and even though these latter roles also often imply moral failure in their own way, I believe we should answer this question in the affirmative. When civilian government officials order a nation's military personnel into combat in which they themselves do not directly participate, for example, those officials are still intentionally and knowingly causing injury to other people, using as their means the men and women making up the military force. Similarly, in coordinating the execution of a convicted murderer, a prison warden may never wield the physical implements of death, but he or she will be one of the agents whose voluntary actions lead to an intended lethal outcome, so that even if the warden doesn't directly kill, he or she indirectly kills that prisoner. Maybe less obviously but quite as accurately, we can also characterize as the indirect infliction of injury the actions of citizens in successfully pressuring government officials to carry out violence against someone, as in either of these other cases. That is, individually and collectively people in an organized society become perpetrators of violence themselves in this indirect sense whenever they positively do something to effectively instigate or support the carrying out of direct violence by others (as opposed to merely refraining from action, as in the passive inattention or indifference that also could imply its own kind of culpability).

Finally, the concept of injury itself is essential to the definition of violence on which I will rely, and it too is not without its possible ambiguities. For example, though "injury" is derived from the Latin *in* ("against") and *jure* ("law"), implying a moral or legal wrong done against someone, many people think that killing a murderous assailant in self-defense, or a state's forcible repelling of an invading army, while definitely causing damage to the aggressing party, is not wrong. Of course, we could limit the range of what counts as injury to "wrongful harm" and distinguish it from "justified harm," as has been common in legal discourse over the years, but that seems too narrow a characterization to illuminate adequately the nature and variety of violent encounters under investigation here. So, I will stick with the broader definition of injury above and emphasize, on the one hand, the more obvious idea that injury to someone or something is a matter of degrees, that is, in any particular case there is a greater or lesser amount of harm, damage, or hurt inflicted. On the other hand, the focus is on infliction of harm against someone's will, without their permission, or somehow in opposition to their interests. This will allow us to exclude the normal practices of dentistry, and participation in sports such as hockey and rugby played within the rules, and allow us to include possible instances of justified harm to others contrary to their preferences. At the same time, however, if we use concepts like "permission," "consent," and "self-interest" to identify a line between injurious and non-injurious hurt, we also have to acknowledge less clear cases such as professional boxing (where the voluntarily agreed upon goal for both boxers is to inflict more damage on the other than one receives), masochism, and suicides by rationally competent persons. We can treat these as borderline cases or as the

kinds of exceptions that "prove the rule," but they do raise important conceptual and practical questions about the difference between the psychologically
functional/competent and dysfunctional/incompetent giving of consent, and
between perceived self-interest and actual self-interest. And as will be shown,
these concerns are connected with, even though distinct from, the possible justifications for someone's willingness to suffer unwanted injury at someone else's
hands in specific circumstances.

In Chapter 1, the overview of ethical analysis I provided centered around
the evaluation of actions and policies as right or wrong, and throughout this
book the moral issues regarding violence and nonviolence will be mostly of that
sort. But in thinking about what violence and nonviolence are, and how they
appear in human affairs, it would be unrealistic to ignore the ways in which
they are manifested in an individual's character as well. Again, throughout
history moral character development, how a person becomes more virtuous
or vicious and how much choice she or he has in this, has been a concern not
only for philosophers but in organized social life generally, primarily because
whether one's character is good or bad has a lot to do with how one will predictably treat others in the same community. When somebody is said to have
a "violent personality," or when someone tells us "I don't get mad, I just get
even," we usually have a pretty good idea of what is meant, not only regarding that individual's likely conduct but also the character traits that predispose
him or her toward such conduct, and we adjust our behavior accordingly in
response. And, since we can and do make decisions about what kind of moral
character people *ought* to develop in themselves as well as which strategies
of an accompanying moral education are appropriate (whether or not we are
determinists regarding the influences on human choice), we can also critically
inquire into the place of violence and nonviolence in the domain of personal
vice and virtue. For example, does the virtue of courage necessarily include a
willingness to use violence in the face of danger, or is courage more robustly
exemplified by those who confront the threat of harm nonviolently? Is citizens'
patriotic enthusiasm for the massive infliction of injury by their state's military
forces on peoples in other lands, much more of a vice than part of civic virtue? These kinds of questions in fact have been addressed by a number of the
philosophical and religious positions to be discussed later, and most systematic
advocacy of nonviolence in conflict resolution ultimately relies on a belief in
the human capability of being or becoming a nonviolent person, that is, with
respect to who one is and not only what one does.

In the "peace and justice" literature of recent decades it has become standard to refer to three different types of violence, and I too find this conceptual

approach useful in conjunction with the baseline definition I have offered. Physical violence of course is the kind most people identify first when they think about the infliction of injury on someone, and most often when the maximization of nonviolence in human relationships is argued for, it is this kind of violence that is being rejected. Physical damage and hurt is easy for almost everyone to visualize, and even though bodily pain itself cannot always be clearly and accurately expressed by the sufferer to external observers (enough pain makes anyone incoherent), we naturally sense the vulnerability of our own bodies to hurt and recognize the destructibility of other material things we value, so when we see, hear, or read about physical harm to others it doesn't take much effort to imaginatively put ourselves in their place and respond with aversion.

Psychological violence is often distinguished from physical violence as a second type, though this distinction is not usually intended to imply any metaphysical commitments to either the reducibility or irreducibility of mental states to physiological states within the human person. The idea here is that people can be damaged emotionally and cognitively by the actions of others, even if in particular cases they are not killed, maimed, tortured, or disabled in any immediate bodily manner. Certainly physical violence, and even threats of physical violence, often are causally linked with psychological violence, but the nature of injuries of the latter type are generally experienced as different from the damage to body tissue associated with the former. So, for example, constant verbal abuse of someone, various instances of humiliation, betrayal, and deception, strategies of terrorizing people into compliance, etc., all can be understood as involving greater or lesser degrees of psychological injury even if, as is said, "not a hand is laid on" any of the recipients. In these cases someone is hurt by someone else, and the hurt can be more or less debilitating, so the leading moral question once again will be, "When, if ever, is such violence justified, and when is it morally wrong?"

A third type of violence, often identified as a major obstacle to the achievement of a more peaceful and just social world, is called "institutional" or "structural" violence. What this concept aims to illuminate are the ways in which certain groups of people are more vulnerable to, and more often victims of, physical and psychological injury because of their location within a stratified, or hierarchically structured, society. That is, if as a result of people's economic class, race/ethnicity, sex, religious affiliation, sexual orientation, or age, they have more or less social power, status, and access to resources, and greater or fewer life choices, then in effect they exist at different levels in a social hierarchy, and in such societies those at the bottom are generally more vulnerable to violence than those at the top. In any particular society, which of these sub-group variables has been most significant in the evolution of the dominant stratification pattern can vary to some extent, and researchers still disagree sometimes on whether, for example, class, or ethnicity, or sex (or an equipotent combination of these) is more causally foundational. In any case, in referring to institutional/structural violence what is meant are not acts of violence *per se*, but the socially constructed (and thus changeable) conditions that set up some people as more likely recipients of violence because of their relative lack of social power and protection.

The nature and empirical reality of institutional violence has generated more controversy than the concepts of physical and psychological violence, and the main criticisms of its explanatory usefulness have been of two sorts. On the one hand, there are those who deny that at least modern politically democratic societies are in fact stratified by group with respect to social advantages and disadvantages, and argue instead that differences in social status, wealth, etc., are essentially *individual* differences of merit and personal ambition on a competitive "level playing field." On the other hand, there is the concern that since in human society it is people who do violence, not some thing called a "social structure," discussions positing the effects of structural violence muddle the concept of agency. Again, this is especially relevant if we want to attribute moral responsibility for violent actions and policies, and demand social change in the direction of nonviolence and meaningful peace, but it is also important just for the sake of consistency in the definition of violence itself.

A thorough response to these criticisms would take another book, so I will confine myself to pointing out, first, that the denial of group stratification and its causal relevance in the incidence of violence in a society amounts to the denial that people are regularly and in culturally conditioned ways treated better or worse by others because they are rich or poor, male or female, heterosexual or homosexual, or because of their racial/ethnic identity, religious affiliation, or age. Since the evidence against such a myopic belief is overwhelming, I don't think it is worth taking seriously here except in terms of its ideological role in supporting the economically, culturally, and legally privileged groups in many societies, where those groups' superior status and power is protected in part by denying that they have superior status and power.

Secondly, there is nothing unintelligible about describing a national legal system, or cultural mores, or a regional economy as reinforcing, legitimizing, or leaving some groups of people relatively unprotected against the violence directed at them by other people because of that group membership. The agents of direct and indirect infliction of injury here are not the systems, mores, or economic "forms" themselves, since these are more accurately seen as the outcomes of choices made by morally responsible parties at some earlier point in time. Structural features of an organized society, however, are reducible to sets of more or less codified, habitual relationships and expectations between flesh and blood human beings, each with his or her own unique biography of course, but all inescapably identified by the various socially defined roles they fill and the social stereotypes they instantiate. And, as these personal characteristics (being a parent or child, a woman or man, unemployed or a company CEO, of one racial group or another, Muslim, Jewish, Christian, or Hindu, etc.) are valued differently, this again is reflected in economic, cultural, and governmental practices that greatly influence, for example, where people can afford to live, what educational opportunities and means of livelihood they have available to them, and how much protection, aid, and respect they can expect from others in their community. Just to take the case of modern industrialized societies, official and scientific records over the last few centuries always have indicated a strong connection between some of these social "types" and being a recipient of violence. Most consistently, if a person is very poor it is more likely he or she will suffer violence from any of a number of sources; if that person is also female that likelihood increases; and in western societies (as well as in nonwestern societies during the era of European colonial occupation) if that person was racially identified as non-white the likelihood increased further. One final point on the conceptual and heuristic value of "institutional violence": It expands the range of moral accountability, and allows us to identify as perpetrators of at least indirect violence all members of a particular stratified society who actively support the economic, political/legal, or cultural *status quo*, especially when they are aware that doing so contributes to the disproportionate violence experienced by those in the less powerful, less privileged, less valued groups in that society (and where "being in denial" about this state of affairs is no excuse).

The definition of violence and the three types, or dimensions, of violence explained above will be used henceforth to investigate the causes, socially scripted interpretations and justifications, and avoidability of this sort of human activity within three often overlapping arenas. As I have already referred to them in passing, we can distinguish loosely the interpersonal, inter-group, and international spheres wherein the dynamics of physical, psychological, and institutional violence are played out. Of course, interpersonal infliction of injury is the most immediate, and can be unilateral, as in a murder or robbery, or reciprocal, as in a bar fight or hand-to-hand military combat. By inter-group violence, I mean violent strife (again, more or less one-sided) between groups typically within one political state or common region, as in urban gang wars, the former racial segregation practices in the US and South Africa, "ethnic cleansing" efforts in the Balkans and Sudan, clashes between Hindus and Muslims in India, and most civil wars. International violence, on the other hand, involves organized group violence intentionally directed across national boundaries with varying degrees of geographical extent and impact. This includes war between political states, invited and uninvited multinational military interventions in local conflicts, and terrorist attacks on a population by foreign organizations (as distinct from "domestic terrorism"). It also includes the international sex slavery business, the weapons trade, and economic policies coercively imposed by more powerful states on less powerful states predictably enriching the former while causing more widespread suffering in the latter.

SECTION 2: THE NATURE OF NONVIOLENCE AS A STRATEGY OF CONFLICT RESOLUTION

Although nonviolence can be defined categorically as the intentional avoidance of harm to any living thing, a definition employed in traditional Indian Jainism, for example, I will treat it primarily in a more limited way as a strategy for dealing with conflict in interpersonal, inter-group, and international situations. In this context, nonviolence is first and foremost a choice of conduct in the interaction with others, whereby one voluntarily refrains from inflicting injury on someone or something as a means of overcoming the resistance presented by that other to one's own will. It is unrealistic to think that we can or should avoid conflict completely in our lives, but it is also unrealistic to believe that the use of violence is a necessary or inescapable response to, or often the best means of resolving conflict. In fact, from the day-to-day disagreements we can have with other individuals, to the competing interests of various groups within a heterogeneous society, to international policy disputes over trade, resource control, immigration, or environmental protection, in the majority of cases the parties in conflict do not resort to physical or psychological violence to further their aims. Since most conflict in human affairs already is (and almost always has been) dealt with nonviolently, and assuming that injury taken by itself is a bad rather than a good thing, the practical issues to address are, again, what justification there could be for ever choosing violence as a means of "getting our way" and also, what it would take to significantly reduce further the instances of such violence, within the range of human capability. Further, the implication here is that violence is an aberrant or unusual response to conflict situations rather

38

than a desirable or normal response, so that if people become accustomed to thinking of it instead as normative and an everyday feature of life, usually this would be a strong indicator of something seriously wrong with the patterns of human interaction within that particular social environment.

Many nonviolentists have argued for years that efforts to reduce violence in human relationships at both the local and global levels must start with people's attitudes about this generally undesirable phenomenon and its nonviolent alternative. For example, for those people conditioned to be in constant fear of violent attack in their everyday lives, and who also subsequently reject as ineffective and even more dangerous to themselves nonviolent approaches to dealing with that perceived threat, there are at least two ways to challenge their beliefs. On the one hand, it may well be that their social world is in fact a lot less dangerous to them than they think it is, and they have overestimated the likelihood of their being victimized by violent "others." Although unfortunately this is not always the case, many different studies in various societies have shown that people are often much more fearful of violence from non-acquaintances than the facts warrant, and this lack of correspondence between belief and reality needs to be brought to light. On the other hand, even where and when the threat of violence is not overestimated, the assumption that violence is the best defense against violence can be shown to be false often, especially if long-term consequences are taken into account as well as more immediate outcomes. In addition, if both the fear of violence and its concomitant acceptability in the name of self-protection are cultivated and reinforced by those in positions of power in order to better control the rest of the community, then widespread criticism of this kind of social manipulation is crucial too if the belief in the ubiquity of violence is not to become a self-fulfilling prophecy.

If the basic idea of nonviolence is understood negatively, as refraining from the inflicting of injury in conflict situations, its conceptual range needs to be expanded in order to see more clearly its connections to the vision of a truly peaceful and just society. That is, not only is nonviolence a conduct or policy choice on the part of moral agents, but it can also characterize states of affairs that result from such choices as a positive experience, especially when actors come to know of and eventually rely on the nonviolent intentions of each other in their interactions. So, we can talk meaningfully about a nonviolent social world, where nonviolence is the predictable and normative strategy of conflict resolution, and where in a mutually reinforcing way fear of others also is typically reduced, trust is increased, and conditions are created for social relations of enhanced mutual respect, cooperation, and equity. For most people committed to a "peace and justice" agenda these days, nonviolence thus is the foundation for a truly just social order and, in consequence, a lasting peace among human individuals and groups. And, regarding the assessment of moral character, in the same way that we can understand what it means for someone to have a "violent nature," so also we can make sense out of the contrasting ideal of a "nonviolent nature," as a person's habitual aversion to injuring others integrated with the positive tendency of concern for others' well-being.

In the long and diverse history of thought regarding nonviolence and why it is *normally* preferable to violence in human affairs, it has been common to distinguish between nonviolent approaches to *initiating* action that affects others' interests, on the one hand, and to *responding* to threatening, injurious, or wrongful actions initiated by others, on the other hand. This also coincides with the distinction between aggression and defense against aggression which, as will be explained in Chapter 5, is central to most attempts to morally justify war when it is defensive, and condemn it when it is aggressive, even though determining the difference in particular cases is often not as straightforward as is portrayed in most nationalist and militarist rhetoric (e.g., when what "they" do is aggressive, while "we are only defending our interests"). Whether in interpersonal, inter-group, or international contexts however, when the goals, desires, or policies of various parties come into some kind of recognizable conflict, whoever takes the initiative in dealing with this situation can and often does employ first the nonviolent strategies of negotiation and diplomacy, with the hope of arriving at mutually beneficial agreements that will resolve the problem without anyone's injury. This may involve one or more of the parties giving up their original aims, or modifying them in a spirit of compromise and mutual accommodation in light of the higher value placed on "getting along" and "maintaining the peace" than on "having one's own way" at all costs. In many cultures the skill at using these strategies in conflict resolution is itself highly valued, and those with reputations as successful mediators, negotiators, and peacemakers often have been treated as some of the very most important members of the community.

In the other type of circumstance, where actors are faced with the choice of how to respond to actual or potential injury resulting from others' actions, negotiation and diplomacy are also viable options in many cases, particularly when there are prior recognized agreements in place, or legal codes, or traditional practices that can be appealed to, in order to "right the wrong" done. At least as first steps in the protection of legitimate interests against violation, nonviolent diplomatic efforts are generally (though not always) viewed as noncontroversially preferable, but nonviolent strategies of defense against violence have been more widely criticized and rejected in favor of violent reaction when they do not quickly succeed. This is where nonviolentists always have had a more difficult case to make, when arguing for patience and further nonviolent response to the apparent willingness of others to continue their violence, and this is why historically more thoroughgoing and consistent versions of nonviolentism in conflict resolution have gained the reputation of being so radical, socially subversive, and even immoral. The ancient psychology behind the principle of *lex talionis* ("law of retaliation") still exerts a powerful influence today, as the desire so enthusiastically expressed by many to repay injury with injury, and yet because of the cycles of violent revenge it feeds, it remains one of the biggest obstacles to solving effectively interpersonal, inter-group, and international problems.

In spite of varying degrees of social unpopularity then, different nonviolence advocates have recommended different, sometimes overlapping approaches to dealing with physical, psychological, and institutional violence in ways that avoid or minimize significant injury to the perpetrators/aggressors, besides negotiation and diplomacy as usually understood. Briefly, these include nonresistance, passive resistance (or active noncooperation), nonviolent direct action, civil disobedience, and pacifism.

1. Nonresistance is typically defined as the simple refraining from any kind of physically assertive resistance to aggression, violence, or harm by others, though more positively it can involve the open willingness to comply with the aims of those threatening injury. One can argue for this strategy as the best way to avoid making the situation even worse for those being victimized, or as an effective means of causing the victimizers to "change their minds" about what they are doing, or just as the morally superior response demanded by some higher (usually divinely originated) principle. Those in law enforcement often recommend this for individuals confronted by attempts at armed robbery, or by the drunken lout who wants to start a fight, for example. At the political level some also have advocated this approach as the best way to deal with unjust legal systems, as well as with an aggressive attack by the military forces of another state.

2. What has been called passive resistance is a nonviolent strategy emphasizing noncompliance with the demands of violent aggressors, oppressors, or other violators of the legitimate interests of vulnerable subjects. As such, the degree of literal passivity or activity will vary in particular instances, and your behavior might be more passive by actually doing what a bully tells you to do, for example, than by standing up to him/her and saying "No." Still, some nonviolentists have not liked the implications of weakness, unassertiveness,

or mere quietism that might be associated with the word "passive," and so prefer something like "active noncooperation" instead (although mountains are passive too, and yet immovable). In any case, the idea here is that instead of provoking or initiating a confrontation in a situation with the perpetrators of injurious actions or policies, those engaging in passive resistance just refuse to obey or go along with what those actions or policies require in response. This kind of resistance has been a feature of larger social movements historically as well as being practiced on a more individual basis, and also can be more overt or covert. So, refusing to pay your taxes because of your government's military aggression against others, refusing to obey the commands of military occupation forces, illegally hiding political refugees in your home, and refusing to comply with the demands of neighborhood extortionists all would be categorized conventionally as cases of passive resistance even though action is in fact taken in each instance. They also all involve nonviolent noncompliance in response to those who already have initiated or threatened some kind of violence.

3. Nonviolent direct action is similar to passive resistance in that it too essentially includes noncompliance in the struggle against the coercive violence of others, but it is also different because it is much more proactive than reactive, always overt, and usually an organized group action rather than a method employed by individuals on their own. Most often this strategy has been recommended as a way to bring about progressive, humanitarian change in an oppressive, unjust social system characterized by extensive institutional violence, especially with respect to its legal codes. The proactive orientation, as implied by the concept of direct action, can be seen in practitioners' efforts to initiate confrontations with the agents of this oppressive system, on behalf of those suffering injury resulting from their subordinate positions within it. Here then, social activists "take it to" those in power (economically, culturally, or politically), but they do so nonviolently, even if violently attacked by police or mobs who want to maintain the social *status quo*. They do this in order to call attention publicly to the unjustifiably harmful consequences of the laws, social practices, or policies they seek to do away with. Legal and illegal protest marches, the occupation of public or private buildings or land, the disruption of stockholders' meetings for the purpose of criticizing companies' labor practices, and publicly enacted group vigils, are widely recognized examples of nonviolent direct action. They all aim, first, at forcing the perpetrators of direct and indirect violence to react in publicly visible ways (further highlighting the injustice of their position), and second, at encouraging those in power to make the desired changes.

4. Civil disobedience is the act of openly disobeying a specific law (not the rejection of law in general) judged upon careful analysis to be morally unjust, with an acceptance on the part of the actor of the legal penalties for her/his disobedience. The point once again is to call attention to that law's injustice and the need for it to be changed, in this case by one's demonstrated willingness to suffer legal punishment in order to force such change. Civil disobedience is thus a tactic compatible with both passive resistance and nonviolent direct action, but not limited to the usual goals at which they aim. Its distinguishing features are its intentional, publicly visible illegality based on the ethical critique of the specific law to be broken, along with the refusal to evade or contest the legal consequences of one's actions. In modern history the philosophical debate about the moral justifiability of civil disobedience itself, and the extent of the obligation to obey the laws of one's society, has been associated with thinkers such as Henry David Thoreau in the nineteenth century, and Mohandas Gandhi and Martin Luther King, Jr. in the twentieth century, but this issue can be traced back to ancient times as well. For example, in Plato's dialogue *Crito* Socrates concludes that he must abide by the laws of Athens even though it will lead to his wrongful execution; in Sophocles' tragedy *Antigone* he presents the main character's dilemma of having to choose between the laws of the state and divine/moral "law"; and in the fourth century, Christian philosopher Augustine asserted in *The City of God* that an "unjust law is no law at all."

5. Pacifism is sometimes defined by its critics as the complete rejection of all physical violence always, whether it is aggressive or defensive, but the large majority of those who identify themselves as pacifists disagree with that kind of absolutist characterization. They instead define it as the general, though for many the non-categorical, opposition to war, without ruling out possible instances of justified violence in defending oneself or another vulnerable person against violent assault (say, against a would-be murderer or rapist). I will describe the range of pacifist views more thoroughly in Chapter 5, but as a nonviolent approach to conflict resolution pacifism can be seen as a policy adopted by a government (or some other political organization) in its relations with other states and with other domestic or foreign organized groups, whereby military violence is avoided even if other means of coercion are used, such as economic sanctions or appeals to international tribunals. On the other hand, individual citizens can express their pacifist, anti-militarist beliefs regarding what governments should and shouldn't do by employing some of the other strategies above, and in the history of anti-war activism there have been countless cases in many countries of people courageously engaging in nonviolent direct actions, active noncooperation, civil disobedience, and other methods

to pressure politically and economically powerful elites to change their war-making ways.

Finally, a topic that is related to the discussion of nonviolent responses to violence but not originally a product of that discussion has to do with what is often called restorative justice. This refers to a way of dealing with wrongs done to people by others within their community, whereby offenders are confronted with their personal responsibility in causing harm to someone and subsequent necessity to make some kind of restitution to the victim. Although in North American history this goes way back to a variety of practices used in many indigenous societies, in the last few decades the principles of restorative justice have been applied in different countries around the world primarily as either supplements or alternatives to the standard legal responses to crime. The relationship between restorative justice and retributive justice is something I will return to later, but for now it will suffice to say that proponents of the former see it as offering significant improvement to existing criminal justice/corrections systems rather than as a complete replacement of the latter. They argue that institutionalized retribution for crimes against persons and property has its place in the legal effort to "right wrongs" and prevent future crime, but that the near-exclusive focus on punishment regularly has been counterproductive in working toward these same goals. When the legal processes center around what kind of penalties to inflict on those convicted of crimes, the tendency has been to treat crime itself more as a violation against the state and overlook the basic fact that it often injures flesh and blood persons directly or indirectly, as well as the internal integrity of a community. Both offenders and victims then typically end up in more passive roles *vis-à-vis* state agencies; restitution for those actually harmed is minimal at best; and the need for successful reintegration of most offenders back into their communities is downplayed by those who emphasize being "tough on crime" while forgetting that crime violates the peace of a whole community which must be somehow restored for the good of all, not just for those who have not yet been victimized. In fact, advocates of restorative justice often point out how much tougher it can be for offenders to be forced to actively participate in "making right" in some meaningful reparative manner the wrongs they have perpetrated, and to be held directly accountable to the victims they personally have harmed. Specific strategies for repairing the harm done by crime, such as victim-offender mediation, victim impact panels, community service for offenders, etc., are not equally effective in all cases, but more research in the field of corrections is showing that restorative justice programs can reduce crime in various social environments, assuming that some kind of viable community exists or can be created in the first place.

FURTHER READING

Section 1

Hannah Arendt, *On Violence* (New York: Harcourt Brace Jovanovich, 1969).

Linda Bell, *Rethinking Ethics in the Midst of Violence: A Feminist Approach to Freedom* (Lanham, MD: Rowman and Littlefield, 1993).

Claudia Card, *The Atrocity Paradigm: A Theory of Evil* (Oxford: Oxford UP, 2002).

Deane Curtin and Robert Litke, editors, *Institutional Violence* (Amsterdam: Rodopi, 1999).

Angela Y. Davis, *Women, Race and Class* (New York: Random House, 1981).

Andrea Dworkin, *Pornography: Men Possessing Women* (New York: Penguin Books, 1989).

Bruce B. Lawrence and Aisha Karim, editors, *On Violence: A Reader* (Durham, NC: Duke UP, 2007).

George Orwell, *1984* (New York: Harcourt Brace Jovanovich, 1949).

Section 2

Augustine, *The City of God* (New York: Image Books, 1958); originally written between 412 and 427 CE.

David Barash, editor, *Approaches to Peace: A Reader in Peace Studies* (New York: Oxford UP, 2000).

Diana Francis, *People, Peace and Power: Conflict Transformation in Action* (London: Pluto Press, 2002).

Philip Hallie, *Lest Innocent Blood Be Shed: The Story of the Village of Le Chambon and How Goodness Happened There* (New York: Harper Collins, 1979, 1994).

Tom H. Hastings, *Nonviolent Responses to Terrorism* (Jefferson, NC: McFarland and Co., 2004).

Robert L. Holmes, editor, *Nonviolence in Theory and Practice* (Belmont, CA: Wadsworth, 1990. Republished by Waveland Press, 2001).

Krishna Mallick and Doris Hunter, editors, *An Anthology of Nonviolence: Historical and Contemporary Voices* (Westport, CT: Greenwood Press, 2002).

Tony F. Marshall, *Restorative Justice: An Overview* (London: Restorative Justice Consortium—Social Concern, 1998).

Plato, *Crito*, translated and published in *The Last Days of Socrates* (New York: Penguin Classics, 1969). Originally written early in the fourth century BCE.

Gene Sharp, *The Politics of Nonviolent Action*, Volumes 1-3 (Boston: Porter Sargent Publishers, 1973).

——, *National Security through Civilian-Based Defense* (Omaha, NE: Association for Transarmament Studies, 1985).

Mulford Q. Sibley, editor, *The Quiet Battle* (Boston: Beacon Press, 1963).

Sophocles, *Antigone*, translated and published in *The Three Theban Plays* (New York: Penguin Classics, 1984). Originally written in the middle of the fifth century BCE.

Henry David Thoreau, *Walden, and Civil Disobedience*, edited by Owen Thomas (New York: W.W. Norton, 1966); "Civil Disobedience" originally published 1849.

Mark S. Umbert, Robert B. Coates, Betty Voss, editors, *Restorative Justice Annotated Bibliography* (St. Paul, MN: Center for Restorative Justice and Peacemaking, June 2003).

CHAPTER 3

The Relevance of Human Nature

SECTION 1: THE CONCEPT OF HUMAN NATURE

If we believe that interpersonal, inter-group, and international human relations should become much more nonviolent, peaceful, and just, we are already logically presupposing that such an outcome is possible (again, recognizing the "ought implies can" principle). But is it, really? Throughout recorded history there have been plenty of thoughtful people who believed that humans were not in fact capable of getting along with each other nonviolently for any length of time, and unfortunately quite a bit of evidence exists to justify their pessimism. If the pessimists are right, however, the plausibility and even intelligibility of the demand for a truly peaceful world is thrown into serious doubt, since if a goal is impossible to achieve it makes no sense to claim that it should be achieved. So, we do have to decide whether a pessimistic or optimistic view is more convincing regarding the human potential for living habitually nonviolent social lives, before we can decide what can be reasonably expected from peacemaking efforts around the world.

Philosophical discussions of "human nature" have been wide-ranging over the millennia, and of course not always primarily focused on questions of peaceful social relations. Philosophers have dealt with metaphysical issues involving, for example, the reality of the individual human body, the existence of a mind or soul and its possible distinction from the body, the continuity of personal identity, whether human free will exists, and whether there are any essential, exclusive, and fixed properties defining the type "human." Although the various solutions offered to these philosophical puzzles have often informed different perspectives on violence and nonviolence, historically there has been no consistent or uniform connection established between metaphysics/ontology and social theory. When philosophers do attempt to justify their conclusions in the social and moral domain by appeals to human nature, usually they point to psychological characteristics which are considered universal in normal, functional members of *homo sapiens*, and which determine the limits of human interaction and relationships. This approach has included positions taken on whether humans are essentially social or non-social beings in the first place; whether they are capable of altruism as well as egoism; whether hierarchy is ineliminable in social relationships and egalitarianism only a temporary aberration; whether or not humans have a basic tendency to fear and hate those who are different from themselves; and whether there are significant differences between men and women (essential or only socially conditioned) in the propensity for and response to violence.

In this chapter I too will focus more on the concept of human nature understood in terms of species-wide mental and emotional capacities, needs, desires, and aversions, and the range of value judgments arising from this psychological/biological foundation. The metaphysical connections between human beings, and between humans and other living beings, will also appear in some of the accounts to be described here as well as in the next chapter. But rational reflection about human nature is relevant, again, to the extent that it helps us decide what kind of realistic chance there is that people can create a social world in the foreseeable future which, radically more so than at present, is characterized by nonviolence, meaningful and sustainable peace, and true social justice.

SECTION 2: HUMANS AS GOOD BUT CORRUPTIBLE

In a number of intellectual traditions around the world you can find philosophers who have argued in one way or another that human nature is essentially good, and that human evil or wickedness, including propensities for violence and cruelty, is the result of some sort of failure to actualize that natural, species-defining goodness. Though it is not always clear what is meant by "good," typically the reference is to internal attributes of the individual judged to be desirable in the development of a virtuous character. For example, it has been argued that all functional humans possess natural capacities both for reason and for sympathy toward others, and these are valuable ("good") potentialities of the self because when adequately cultivated they can contribute significantly to personal and societal flourishing while reducing the reliance on violence to achieve ends.

One influential account of the basic goodness of human nature was put forth by the ancient Chinese philosopher Mencius (c. 371-289 BCE), also known as Meng tzu (or Mengzi). He was a follower of Confucius (551-479 BCE), also known as K'ung Fu Tzu (or Kung Fuzi), but developed Confucian doctrines into a distinctive system of his own, in some ways at odds with the views of some other Confucian philosophers. He argued that there are inherent capacities for moral goodness with which all humans are equally endowed, and these can be more or less developed over the course of our lives. If a person pursues evil then, or becomes more vicious than virtuous, it is the result of external conditions and not original to her or his nature. Mencius claimed that human nature is "originally" good in the same way that water naturally flows downhill, and as water nonetheless can be made to move uphill by thwarting or redirecting its natural tendency, so also we can be made to do evil by forces that thwart or distract us from actualizing our natural goodness. In explicating his view of the connection between human nature and morality, Mencius said that there are four innate "feelings" in humans that will, with proper nurturance, lead to the development of the four most important personal virtues. These are the feelings of "commiseration," "shame and dislike," "deference and compliance," and "right and wrong," and if someone somehow does not have these feelings as part of her/his "original nature," that individual is not really human. Together, these feelings are called by Mencius the "Four Beginnings" because they are the "beginnings" of the four virtues, respectively, of "humanity" or "benevolence" (*jen*), "righteousness" (*yi*), "propriety" (*li*), and "wisdom" (*chih*).

Mencius believed that the best society was one that exhibited the most harmony, social order, security, and prosperity. He shared these values with earlier thinkers (including Confucius himself), and many later philosophers in Chinese history followed him in this respect. In addition, it was a common assumption in traditional Chinese philosophy that the moral character of political rulers had a crucial "trickle down" effect on the rest of society. This meant that a morally exemplary ruler (sometimes identified as a "true king") would be most likely to maximize harmony, order, security, and prosperity for everyone in the kingdom, as well as improve the general level of virtue. On the other hand, a self-serving, morally evil ruler (often seen as a "mere despot") would be the primary cause of social strife, disorder, insecurity, and material deprivation. So for practical reasons it was most important to Mencius that rulers nurture in themselves the "Four Beginnings," or "recover" this natural source of goodness if they had been led astray by bad influences, since the more humane, righteous, proper (in the sense of having respect for and sensitivity to the demands of particular social situations), and wise a ruler was, the more those virtues would characterize and orient the whole society. And of course, the more those four virtues permeated all social relations, the less violence there would be, and the more peaceful and mutually respectful interpersonal and inter-group interactions would become.

Mencius did seem to presuppose that even the most harmonious and virtuous society would be hierarchically organized, however, within the family as well as within the larger role-differentiated community, by age, sex, and class. He also apparently took it for granted that no matter how internally peaceful one state was, there always existed the possibility of external enemies which even a virtuous political ruler might have to defend against with military force. Still, for Mencius all humans are naturally capable of treating all other humans humanely, compassionately, and respectfully, because we naturally recognize each other as valuable fellow beings when our moral "vision" has not become too clouded by vice. Thus almost all enmity, war, oppression, and indifference to the needs of others are explainable as the result of externally caused and often contagious dysfunction, corruption, and perversity in human character development.

If we shift our focus from ancient China to modern Europe, and from the Confucian humanism of Mencius to the humanism usually associated with the western philosophy of liberalism, we can identify both theistic and secular versions of the belief that humans should actualize their natural potential and thereby improve themselves as individuals and as societies. One British philosopher who in many ways represented the optimism of eighteenth-century liberalism was Mary Wollstonecraft (1759-97). Her views were based on a Christian humanism that assumed the special status of humans as alone created in the image of God, and assumed as well our naturally endowed faculty of reason by which "the Deity" expected us to govern our lives and achieve moral progress. Wollstonecraft also argued for a variety of liberal positions often viewed as quite radical during that era, though more commonly accepted by western intellectuals today. For example, given that the "perfectibility of reason" is part of the divine plan for humanity, she maintained that reason itself should be recognized as the final authority in human affairs instead of some merely customary, arbitrary social power, and that every person's natural reason be allowed the freest rein possible for its fullest development. In her account this also meant that the ability to exercise our natural liberty was required if our rational potential was to be realized and effectively applied to the advancement of human civilization. And, in turn this implied that all forms of social and governmental tyranny (no matter how "traditional") imposed on the essentially rational, self-determining human individual were to be rejected, not only because they infringed on our "natural rights" and compromised our natural equality of worth as humans, but also because they too were unacceptable obstacles in the path of historical progress.

Wollstonecraft argued further that the development of reason was necessary both for the individual's acquisition of knowledge about the world, and for the cultivation of moral virtue, understood here as the predisposition to judge and act in accordance with objective moral truth. Since the usual liberal emphasis on maximal personal liberty in a society permeated by the values of tolerance, mutual respect, non-aggression, and collective improvement presupposes citizens who are adequately rational, knowledgeable, and virtuous, she pointed out that an extensive educational system accessible to all community members was crucial if these social values were to be brought to life in any meaningful way. Without appropriate education, a person's character tends to be conditioned instead by the external forces of blind custom, prejudice, threats of violent coercion, and submission to arbitrary authority, so that individual and social decision-making more often are grounded in unreason, ignorance, and vice. In Wollstonecraft's estimation, the evil institution of slavery as well as the socially conditioned decadence of the professional military class were two prime examples of the outcome of inadequate moral education and socially accepted irrationality. But she became most well-known by the end of her life and in subsequent intellectual history for her arguments that the humanistic, liberal vision of human nature and the good society applied equally to women as well as men. As she demonstrated thoroughly, this implied that the traditionally enforced dependency, subordination, and exclusion from opportunities for intellectual and moral self-actualization of the female half of the European population were also major obstacles to *human* progress that must be removed.

In contrast to Wollstonecraft's theistic orientation, a nineteenth-century German philosopher who formulated an explicitly atheistic version of the liberal view of human development was Ludwig Feuerbach (1804-72). He maintained that all religious belief in divine beings was the product of the historical quest for knowledge and emotional affirmation of the human essence itself, as well as its place in the natural world. Emphasizing the extensive capabilities of intellect and imagination distinguishing the human species from other animal species, Feuerbach pointed out that, especially within the western monotheistic religions, the concept of God was a completely anthropomorphic projection of what was most valuable and fundamentally defining in human nature. That is, rather than being created in God's image, humans create God in their image as a conceptual fiction which is then endowed with eternal existence, as well as with all other "powers" of essential human nature freed from the limitations of their expression in flesh and blood individuals.

The human understanding of God, then, is just an inverted, alienated understanding of our own "species nature," and the belief in our "original sin" of being imperfect in comparison with God is just the "mystified" consciousness of the distinction between the human essence as such and our individualized existence. So, for Feuerbach there are no theological truths, only anthropological truths misunderstood and expressed in distorted, "upside-down" theological forms. And, one of the primary goals of human history is the final recognition of this fact and the subsequent redirecting of devotion, care, and moral commitment away from the fictional divine world to the materially real world of human relationships. In effect, religion will just be outgrown eventually, as a more childlike stage in the developmental life of the species.

Feuerbach's optimistic account of human nature was based in part on his arguments for the inevitability of human progress, as it is manifested both in scientific achievement and in the gradual de-alienation (i.e., naturalization) of "religious consciousness," but also in part on his view of that "species essence" itself. Giving his own interpretation to a rather ancient model of the type human, Feuerbach asserted that the combination of "Reason, Will, and Affection" constituted the true "nature of man," as the "divine Trinity" de-mystified and brought down to earth where it finally will be understood as the proper object of collective glorification. These three essential attributes, as the powers of thought, will, and love, are perfections of the species when defined as the totality of their manifestations over historical time, and are ends in themselves in the universal human project of self-actualization. Once people have transformed their "consciousness of God" into the "consciousness of the species," and come to recognize more completely the human essence and its inherent value in themselves and each other, a real, this-worldly human fellowship will naturally result. Thus, the fear, hatred, and alienation that lead to violent conflict and oppression in human affairs are developmentally understandable but historically surmountable outcomes of "false consciousness," while peaceful, secure social living characterized by mutual affirmation, support, and love among all peoples is the outcome of a "true consciousness" of our essential nature and our basic need to actualize it in all our relations.

The American pragmatist philosopher John Dewey (1859-1952) expressed a more qualified optimism in various writings on modern civilization, especially emphasizing the potential of democracy for human self-improvement. He viewed as overly romantic some of the eighteenth- and nineteenth-century accounts of an inevitable unfolding during "the modern age" of an enlightened and essentially good human nature. But in keeping with the liberal humanist tradition he did believe that modern advances in science, technology, and political democratization greatly increased the likelihood of self-actualization and social flourishing on the part of more people worldwide. Dewey's assessment of the possibilities of material and social progress in human history was functionalist and naturalistic in orientation, with his investigative starting point usually being the individual person as a self-adjusting, sentient organism in dynamic interaction with an environment. As we are social creatures, however, he believed that personal development is inseparable from some measure of collective experience and cooperative action, so that successful living depends on the extent to which mental and emotional human capabilities are encouraged and employed in healthy ways within the different spheres of an organized social world.

From this standpoint, while oligarchy and authoritarianism have characterized most societies in history, they only allowed for a sub-optimal "development of human personality," and at best only for the privileged few at the expense of the many. The "democratic credo" on the other hand, is based on "faith" in the natural human ability for individual and collective problem-solving; in the fact that every member of society can make a positive contribution to the common good if given a proper chance; and in the value of equality of opportunity as well as before the law. In Dewey's works the "democratic ideal" appears then as a whole "way of life" and not only as a form of government, whereby every mature person participates in the decision-making relevant for all social institutions affecting his or her own life. What Dewey primarily had in mind here was the increased democratization of family and religious life, education, and the work world, beyond the recommendation for more active participation and less apathy by citizens in governmental affairs. He viewed political democracy as a crucial means (but only as a means, rather than an end in itself) for facilitating the establishment of this kind of wider social democracy, and in turn the latter would provide a more secure foundation for the continuation and vitality of the former. Since most interpersonal, inter-group, and international violence is the direct or indirect product of habitual relations of dominance and subordination, and the concentration of power and resources in the hands of some groups to the detriment of other groups, the more social democracy succeeds around the globe the greater will be the empowerment potential of all individuals, and the more widely violence itself will be recognized as the maladaptive and counter-productive strategy of conflict resolution it increasingly has become.

SECTION 3: HUMANS AS EVIL BUT CONTROLLABLE

In contrast to the position that a human being is basically good but can be led astray by corrupting external influences, other philosophers have maintained that humans naturally tend toward evil but are susceptible to conditioning and external control so that at least some social goods can be achieved in spite of ourselves. Those across the centuries and in different societies who have argued for this view of human nature typically have agreed that these social goods have to do with maximal social order, security, and prosperity, and minimal armed conflict. But again, the concept of "evil" itself has not been uniformly employed in the assessment of human potential, nor have all these thinkers been equally hopeful about the possible outcomes of social conditioning strategies.

Another ancient Confucian philosopher who pretty much took the opposite view from Mencius on this question was Hsun Tzu, or Xunzi (c. 300-230 BCE). Whereas Mencius traced the typical Confucian virtues of humanity, righteousness, propriety, wisdom, and following the Mean to their sources in natural human feeling and beyond that to the Way of Heaven itself, Hsun Tzu saw their development in an individual as the result of teaching, law, discipline, and personal effort against natural impulses. He regularly challenged the views of Mencius directly, and although he agreed that humans could achieve moral goodness and create good societies, he argued that it was only by allowing themselves to be transformed by means of social control, contrary to their originally "evil" starting point.

Hsun Tzu defined "goodness" in human affairs as "true principles and peaceful order," and as such it must be learned, while "evil" refers to "imbalance, violence, and disorder," and is the inevitable consequence of the unchecked expression of our "inborn nature." By characterizing human nature as evil, then, he meant that all people are born selfish, grasping, and lacking in both sympathy for others and internal restraint of their appetites, so that if left to themselves they will only be motivated by egoism, greed, envy, and hostility toward others. To avoid the social chaos and general misery that would result from the uncontrolled self-development of individuals, Hsun Tzu argued that intentional, methodical "moulding" of personal character must be instituted society-wide, and this is where he relies on the central distinction between human *nature* and human *activity*. His use of the concept of "activity" (*wei*) included the sense of creating or constructing something, as in the making of an artifact (*wei* also often referred to the "artificial"). Thus, an originally egocentric, anti-social, disorderly nature had to be *acted* on, or *worked on* with the aim of *making* the individual self-disciplined and sincerely appreciative enough of propriety and righteousness so that he or she could fit into and contribute to the maintenance of a harmonious social order. Of course, this view is not entirely pessimistic about the possibility of people living nonviolent, peaceful lives characterized by self-restraint, "deference," and "compliance," but for Hsun Tzu it all depended on the "civilizing influence" of "teachers and laws," orchestrated by wise rulers and independent of any divine guidance.

A more thoroughly pessimistic view of human nature and its capacity for violence can be found in the works of the early modern British philosopher Thomas Hobbes (1588-1679). He believed that the physical science of mechanics as it was being developed during his time could provide the basis for a science of society as well, so that all human interaction could be explained in terms of the actions and reactions of bodies in motion. Thus, for him all "voluntary" actions of human individuals were either motions toward objects that cause them, called "Appetites" or "Desires," or motions away from objects that cause them, called "Aversions." All emotional responses and all valuing or disvaluing of anything in experience then also are only species of desire or aversion, implying that "good" and "evil" themselves are merely conventional terms for essentially subjective judgments about this or that object of potential gratification or fear.

Hobbes argued that this mechanistic account of human conduct and motivation meant that all voluntary actions are unavoidably self-centered, in other words egoistic, and that a truly altruistic action is in effect mechanically impossible. Humans have no natural sympathy or empathy for others, neither do they have any internal inhibition preventing them from harming someone else as long as they perceive it to be in their self-interest to do so, and they think they can get away with it. For every individual, other persons are either obstacles or mere means to be exploited in the pursuit of selfish ends, so we are fundamentally nonsocial, atomistic beings driven by self-preservation, self-aggrandizement, fear of each other, and the desire for power (which Hobbes defined as the "present means to obtain some future apparent good"). Conflict, enmity, and violence are inherent in human relations, so in a social environment with no agreed upon, enforceable rules restraining our behavior we would exist in a general "condition of war" of everyone against everyone else, according to him, where all lived more or less equally in a state of constant fear "and danger of violent death."

Although this "state of war" characterizing what Hobbes called the "state of nature" is the likely outcome if people in any locale were to be governed by their "passions" alone, he pointed out that such life conditions are recognized as aversive by most intellectually functional humans, and their natural capacities for reason can be used to avoid this worst possible scenario. As a social contract theorist he treated a legitimate organized society, or "Commonwealth," as an artificial product of a set of rational agreements between self-interested individuals who are concerned primarily with their own safety from the predations of others. More specifically, the only viable "Commonwealth" in his estimation was created by an original agreement to set up a "common power" over all would-be members, which as "Sovereign" would make and enforce with threat of punishment laws forcing people to get along and respect each other's "persons and property." Hobbes also believed that the power of the "Sovereign" in relation to all "Subjects" in the "Commonwealth" had to be absolute in order to achieve the two-fold aim of maximizing personal security for everybody, and avoiding the degeneration into a "state of nature." So justice (as "the performance of covenants made," based on a distinction between "mine" and "thine"), civil peace, and nonviolent conflict resolution could all be maintained within the state, but only through the legal threat of harm to rule-breakers by a government with enough coercive power to effectively carry it out.

As unflattering as Hobbes's account was of human motivation and trustworthiness, the portrayal of our natural condition offered by another nineteenth-century German philosopher was even more grim. Arthur Schopenhauer (1788-1860) adapted the epistemology of Immanuel Kant (1724-1804), on the one hand, and aspects of Buddhist and Hindu metaphysics, on the other hand, in his development of an explicitly pessimistic theory of human existence and its place in the cosmos. He argued that the primal, creative force underlying all of reality was a dynamic, impersonal, nonrational, formless, purposeless "World Will," and that all particular phenomenal things were only its transient manifestations. This meant also that the human individual is an incarnation of the World Will, and that each person's will is the real driving force in his or her daily life, whether or not it is recognized or admitted in one's own self-conscious experience. The individual "will" here refers to all of our urges, instincts, and desires (active and reactive), which are the actual motivating factors behind most of our behavior, and which often operate at a subconscious or only semi-conscious level. Contrary to the common philosophical view that humans are capable of self-mastery (including control of their violent impulses) as well as accurate understanding of themselves and their surrounding world, *because* the will normally is subordinated to the intellect, Schopenhauer tried to show instead that the intellect was really only the "servant" of the will. He used the image of a strong, blind man carrying a weak, sighted man on his shoulders, to describe how intellect can provide some guidance for the will in fulfilling its wants, and yet how little control reason typically exercises in a person's conscious existence.

Given that human life is just one more random epiphenomenon of the World Will, and thus in itself has no meaning, value, or purpose, and that our normal condition is one of "enslavement to the will" and to its unceasing but ultimately pointless demands, Schopenhauer believed that people generally struggled through life in unhappiness, discontent, and fear. Unsurprisingly then, he rejected as illusory the hopeful liberal humanism of his era, and saw the many different organized movements to bring about social progress as more likely to increase human misery, and only make a hopelessly bad situation worse. In keeping with the Buddhist view that life is suffering, suffering is caused by desire, and the way to stop suffering is to stop all desire (the first three of the "Four Noble Truths" in traditional Buddhism), he thought that somehow stilling one's own will was the only way to escape one's psychological bondage. Even suicide, though understandable, was in the end pointless as well in his view. The rare person who could sustain this kind of "will-less" living would be a "saint," and certainly Schopenhauer never thought he would attain this status himself. For most individuals, including him, the best they could achieve would be brief periods of respite from the restless proddings of the will, which could result from the disinterested contemplation of art. Other than this very temporary "metaphysical solace" found in aesthetic experience, or the much more unlikely possibility of becoming a "saint," he saw little reason to think that real peace was possible for the human animal, either in terms of inner tranquility or social relations.

Although modern liberalism, with its humanist presuppositions, continued to influence a great deal of intellectual discourse during the twentieth century, there was always significant opposition to this philosophy around the world. Especially in the more conservative expressions of various doctrinal religions there was (and still is) a wide-ranging rejection of the general belief in the natural capacities of humans to engage in effective problem-solving, "do the right thing," and improve their lives personally and collectively, without coercive intervention by any "higher powers." One such anti-humanist account can be found in the writings of the Islamic scholar Abul A'lā Maudūdi (1903-79), who lived in India and eventually Pakistan, and who was primarily interested in working out the political implications of Islam. In direct contrast to the "faith" in human nature implied by the "democratic credo" championed by Dewey, Maudūdi argued that the vast majority of people are "incapable of perceiving their own true interests" because of their basic weakness and short-sightedness, and thus are incompetent to manage their own affairs without the divine guidance revealed specifically in the Qur'ān (Koran).

Maudūdi pointed out that the basic principle in Islam is that humans must surrender all authority over themselves and each other to God (*Islam* itself being an Arabic word meaning "submission," while a *Muslim* is "one who submits" to God). When this principle is applied to a politically organized society it means: (1) that God (Allah) should be the true sovereign of the state while "all others are merely His subjects"; (2) that God should be the true source of law in the state, and that this "law laid down by God through His Prophet" Muhammad (c. 570-632) in what became the *Qur'ān* must not be altered by humans; and (3) that a government following these guidelines receives its legitimacy and its right to demand obedience only insofar as it acts as the enforcer of divine laws. In his lifelong advocacy of the establishment of Islamic states wherever there were large populations of Muslims then, he envisioned such a state as a theocracy (though in his account different from and superior to the theocracies that have appeared in Christian history), and as "the very antithesis of secular Western democracy," given the latter's reliance on the false ideal of popular sovereignty.

Along with the view that a well-constituted Islamic state has no real legislative authority, only the executive authority to interpret and carry out the laws "revealed by God," Maudūdi's position is that the state not only has the obligation to protect its people from both external dangers and injuries to each other, but also to facilitate the moral development of all social members so they might flourish together. This too is spelled out in Qur'ānic law, which covers most aspects of personal life as well as institutional organization. So, he argues that in order to fulfill its function of executing the will of God, the Islamic state must be "universal" in its scope of activity, that is, "totalitarian" in its thorough intrusion into individuals' lives for their own good. And again, the underlying assumption about human nature here is not so much that we are fundamentally vicious, anti-social, and violent, but that we are not independently capable of creating the social conditions for secure, peaceful, prosperous living, needing instead to acknowledge our total dependence on divine law and its enforcement by "proper" authorities, if we are to achieve these perennial human goods.

SECTION 4: HUMANS AS INHERENTLY NEITHER GOOD NOR EVIL, BUT EDUCABLE

As long as there have been commentators on human nature who presented either optimistic or pessimistic accounts of our basic capabilities for living nonviolent, peaceful, socially just lives, there have been others who saw the human condition as being in itself neither good nor evil. Although such thinkers have taken a more neutral view of the starting point for the moral direction of essential human tendencies, they of course have not always been "agnostic" about the existence of a human "essence" in the first place, nor have they been neutral regarding the moral goals people can and should reach. Much more so than the prior two general characterizations of human nature, this approach typically emphasizes the developmental interaction between inherent features of the human person (for example, rationality and desire) and environmental factors. Depending then on socialization practices within any given community as well as access to material resources, and the extent of the institutional violence structuring human relations, an individual will be seen as more or less likely to become strongly inclined toward non-threatening, respectful, and caring interaction with others.

Plato (429-347 BCE) has been the most influential ancient western philosopher to struggle with the question of how a just society might exist, given a human nature that is originally neither good nor bad in itself. Even though in his various writings he took somewhat different perspectives on what it is essentially to be human, and how that mattered in living our lives as we should, the account he offers in *The Republic* is the one most often cited in discussions of the Platonic view of the self and its capacity for virtue and vice. Written in dialogue form, the overriding theme in *The Republic* is the nature of justice itself and how it can be manifested in human affairs. Plato set up his analyses here mainly by having the character Thrasymachus put forth a very cynical view of justice based on very pessimistic assumptions about human nature, which Socrates (representing Plato's own position) then attempts to refute throughout the rest of the book. Thrasymachus argues, on the one hand, that in any society the terms "justice" and "injustice" in fact are defined by those with the most power, to justify their own egoistic actions and control the actions of others, so quite literally in his view "might makes right." On the other hand, beyond this more positivistic account of the significance of moral discourse he argues that a prudent person should pursue injustice as much as is possible without getting caught, all the while demanding justice and self-restraint from others. Since "injustice" in this context refers to getting more than one's proper share of life's goods and taking unfair advantage of others in the process, Thrasymachus portrays the ideal human life as one of successful hypocrisy coupled with unlimited power to act unjustly with impunity.

To show that this "realist" account of human motivation and "the good life" is wrong, Plato has Socrates describe both a politically organized society (a *polis*) and the human "soul" (or *psyche*), and the analogous conditions under which each functions well or badly. His aim is to prove not only that everybody is better off and happier living in a just society as opposed to an unjust society, but that the truly prudent individual would seek to become a thoroughly just person for the sake of his or her own inner well-being. Thus, "the state" is seen as having three basic functions: the legislative, executive, and productive, which in a well-organized society ought to be carried out by three distinct classes, respectively, the rulers, the military (also variously translated as "auxiliaries," "administrators," and "guards"), and the craftsmen/producers. Plato believed that individuals had different natural aptitudes that suited them for participation in one of these social functions more than the others, but without a well-defined division of labor based on insightful utilization of people's natural tendencies, excellence in the fulfilling of any of these functions was impossible, and discord, chaos, and social insecurity much more probable. There were the same three necessary functions in the human soul, and in a healthy, well-developed person they corresponded to the three distinct elements of reason, the will or spirit, and the appetites (or desire). In other words, reason should be the ruling element in the soul, the will should carry out the dictates of reason regarding what is good or bad for the whole person, and the appetites should be granted their proper domain rather than being merely suppressed, but also conditioned by and subordinated to reason. To the extent that this psychological division of labor didn't happen, the soul was more dysfunctional and, lacking internal harmony, the person was more unhappy.

The virtues most relevant both for the creation of a "good society" and the development of a "good soul" in Plato's estimation were wisdom (characterizing the rulers in the state and the rational element in the soul); courage (possessed by the class of executors in carrying out the policies of the rulers, and by the "spirited element" in the soul carrying out the demands of reason, in spite of adversity); temperance (conditioned acceptance of the proper decision-making hierarchy—a true self-mastery in both the state and the soul); and justice itself (as clear, mutually reinforcing division of labor, specialization of function, and internal order) treated often by him as the sum of moral virtue. But these virtues did not just appear as a matter of course in either the state or the person; they were achievable, but they required intentional inculcation and the right environment, neither of which could be counted on in the human world as he saw it back then. This meant that good character was the result of good education practices, and the beneficial consequences of both the community and the individual becoming virtuous, that is, just, were obvious to Plato. Certainly peace, prosperity, and security within the state would be maximized, aided further by the fact that psychically healthy and thus happy individuals also make better community members. And, although Plato himself didn't seem to believe that one state becoming just would lead necessarily to a reduction of armed conflict with other states, it is fair at least to speculate about his version of personal and social justice contributing to efforts at nonviolent conflict resolution in international relations then and now.

Karl Marx (1818-83) was another nineteenth-century German philosopher, whose account of the human potential for creating more or less peaceful, prosperous, and egalitarian communities has informed much of the thinking in the international communist movement over the last century and a half. Though his views on human nature have been interpreted in many different ways over the years both by his defenders and detractors, he himself usually avoided any kind of abstract "essentialism" regarding the type human. In part this was because of its ahistorical, static, and thus distorting implications for social change, and in part because he saw it as an unhelpful distraction from his project of carrying out an empirical yet critical study of sociological phenomena and the chances for significant social improvement. As early as 1845 he had rejected the traditional philosophical focus on some fixed essence inhering in the isolated human individual, arguing instead that our "species nature" was really only usefully comprehended as a dynamic and historically variable "ensemble of the social relations." That is, as humans create their own social circumstances over the generations in response to a variety of factors in their physical environment, modifying that environment as well in the process, they also in effect create themselves as determinate versions of *homo sapiens*. This never-ending dialectical interplay between objective social and material life conditions on the one hand, and human subjective tendencies and capabilities on the other hand, was always at the foundation of Marx's social analyses. By emphasizing it he was able to provide a framework for explaining most historical change and for assessing the potential for human flourishing in any specific time and place.

Of course Marx acknowledged a general biological commonality among all humans, including the fact that we are irreducibly social animals whose psychological traits are universal in all functional members of the species (for example, our natural capacities for self-consciousness, empathy, and language). He also maintained that, much more so than any other species, humans are technological or "tool-making" animals, which not only makes them the most adaptable and creative vertebrates on the planet, but again, compels them to transform their natural environment in accordance with their varying needs and interests. Like many modern western philosophers, then, Marx still assumed that humans were a special species distinct in many ways from all the rest of "Nature" even though his account was more naturalistic than most at the time. And, in good modernist fashion he also interpreted human history in developmentalist terms, in light of what he took to be the mutual causality of technological and social progress. What he did not assert, however, was that there is some universal natural goodness in humans that only requires the removal of external impediments in order to manifest itself; nor did he think, for that matter, that there is any inherent, ineliminable viciousness requiring regular suppression by external controls in order for people to live well.

The general theory of society formulated by Marx and his collaborator Frederick Engels (1820-95) became known as "historical materialism" by the end of the nineteenth century (though they themselves usually referred to their theory as the "materialist conception of history"), and not entirely unlike Plato's account, it pointed to the division of labor as the basic principle of all large-scale social organization. This principle also could account for most social change and stability over time, and at least in recorded history divisions of labor had evolved into fundamentally antagonistic divisions between economic classes in most societies. In this historical materialist approach, all such "class societies" are constituted by a dominant class in conflict with various subordinate classes over the ownership, control, and exploitation of technologies, natural resources, and sources of labor. This dynamic creates the economic "base" of a society, upon which there subsequently develops an institutional and ideological "superstructure," including government and law, religion, socialization practices, and other cultural norms. These are all reflections in one way or another of the underlying class relations, and normally reinforce "ruling class" power and interests. In the Marxist tradition then, it is the nature of class society itself and its structural antagonisms that provide the fertile ground necessary for the occurrence of most interpersonal, intergroup, and international violence, as well as all social injustice, rather than any trans-historically fixed human nature. It follows that the most sustainable way to radically increase the chances for nonviolent, peaceful living in social relations of mutual respect and material support is to outgrow class society and create egalitarian classless societies instead, first regionally and eventually worldwide. Consequently, the critique of capitalism is also implied by this historically grounded "class analysis." Capitalism is viewed in Marxist theory as only the most recent globally predominant form of class society, driven by its own internal but ultimately unsustainable dynamic of relentless expansionist competition to accumulate ever more private capital, by means of commodity production and the exploitation of paid labor.

In his investigations of the possibilities for human social improvement, Marx moved away from philosophical speculation and toward a critical social science based on empirical observation. Since his time more and more western intellectuals have advocated extending the scientific study of *homo sapiens* to all questions at all susceptible to empirically testable answers, and in the twentieth century the science of psychology especially made great strides in this direction in explaining human perception, motivation, and behavior. The American psychologist B.F. Skinner (1904-90) contributed significantly to this trend, and his name remains one of the most well-known in the history of behavioral psychology. He always took a hard line against psychologists' efforts to study unobservable inner mental states of individuals, arguing instead that the scientific focus should be exclusively on observable behavior and its causal connections with environmental variables. This thoroughly positivistic approach, which at least methodologically presumes that human beings *are* what they *can be observed to do*, was taken consistently by Skinner and many other behaviorists as they researched strategies of "behavior modification" subsequently applied to a wide range of social situations in which the control of people's actions was considered important, for example, within schools, correctional institutions, and the workplace.

Since in Skinner's estimation human predispositions to conduct themselves in one way or another are just products of behavioral conditioning, "human nature" is originally neutral with respect to our inclinations toward violence and hostility, or nonviolence and amicability. This means that with an adequately developed "science of behavior," people are finally in a position to decide collectively whether they want to live in a more violent or less violent social world, and actually bring about that world through an extensive program of behaviorist social planning. Skinner was a determinist regarding the age-old philosophical question of whether humans were essentially free (where "freedom" was defined basically as the ability to choose otherwise than how one in fact chooses in a particular instance), as he viewed all conscious choices as being caused by factors beyond the immediate control of the person choosing. But he also pointed out that many of our choices in daily life are enacted successfully without perceivable constraints contrary to our will or desires, so that we often *feel free* even if all our choices are in fact causally determined. This is because the experience of coercion or the thwarting of choice against the wishes of the actor represents only one kind of causal force. As Skinner emphasized, the other, and ultimately more effective, kind of causal control affects the *motivations* to choose in one direction or another, so that people are caused to *want* to think or act in certain ways, and when they then do so, they feel unconstrained and unfrustrated. This also is in essence the principle of "positive reinforcement," the employment of which he advocated as necessary in large scale social planning if people really do want to maximize their chances for peace, prosperity, happiness, and *experienced* freedom from coercion.

As Skinner explained it, a positive reinforcement strategy would aim at controlling people's behavior by rewarding them for socially desirable actions, either by creating situations they like or removing situations they don't like, increasing the likelihood that they will repeat those actions. Unfortunately, for most of human history up to the present the opposite strategy of "negative reinforcement" has been used much more often to control people, and for the most part ineffectively according to Skinner. This involves attempts to reduce the likelihood that undesirable behaviors will be repeated by removing situations people like or creating situations they don't like, in other words, by punishing or threatening to punish them. Not only all punishment but all war then, and any other violent strategy of conflict resolution aimed at modifying another party's actions, are at bottom just efforts at negative reinforcement, which Skinner acknowledged can have some short term success. But they fail in the long run because they don't really change the other party's motivation to act differently; such efforts at best can only thwart this or that particular undesirable action, easily deluding their proponents into dramatically overestimating their overall effectiveness.

The twentieth-century French philosopher, novelist, and playwright Jean-Paul Sartre (1905-80) also treated basic human tendencies as originally neutral regarding violence and nonviolence, war and peace, and morality in general, but at the same time he was skeptical of most determinist explanations of human choice. As one of the most influential existentialist writers of the last century, Sartre was interested primarily in how self-conscious persons, biographically unique though all sharing the "human condition," interpreted their own individual existence and made their own lives meaningful. He didn't deny that there were many different causal influences (external and internal) on an individual's life situation, but he argued that all functionally conscious people have to choose how to respond meaningfully to their circumstances and options in any case, and in this sense they are fundamentally and inescapably "free." As he pointed out, however, this freedom is somewhat paradoxical since one cannot choose *not* to be free as long as one is alive and capable of voluntary behavior. The human person is "condemned to freedom," and even trying to avoid choosing in a particular situation is itself a choice.

The version of human-defining freedom investigated by Sartre and most other existentialist philosophers actually had little to do with the traditional problem of "free will," since even if determinism were true, the subjective experience of individuals would be the same in terms of their needs for meaningfulness, personal significance, and justification for life choices made. On the other hand, this account of existential freedom does to some extent share with other philosophers' beliefs in free will the implications for *personal* responsibility for one's actions. And for Sartre, this brought up another problem with determinism, insofar as it allows people to deny responsibility for their own lives and make excuses, blaming other causes instead for "making" them choose the way they do. As he put it, we exist "without excuse," choosing and re-choosing (that is, continually reinventing) whatever intelligibility and value our actions and lives have, and yet we have no ultimate justification for our choices. Especially in a world without a god (which Sartre, though not all existentialist writers, assumed was the case) to set up "eternal values" and guidelines for us, we simply are "abandoned" to our fate as responsible for all meaning, with no objective justification for our past and no guarantee of "correct" choices in our future, and it is the recognition of this human predicament that causes the "anguish" from which so many people flee by more or less imaginative paths.

For Sartre, this "ontological condition" of freedom and responsibility, grounded in the nature of human consciousness itself, did not constitute any kind of fixed, general human essence of which living individuals are merely instantiations, nor was it to be confused with political liberty or economic "self-reliance." Again, it implied more an unavoidable "situation" of self-creation for all conscious persons, summed up in his claim that "existence precedes essence." That is, human individuals exist first and then throughout the course of their lives they create their own personal essence (which in effect is also to create individually an image of what humanity is itself), so that who a person is "essentially" is just the ongoing sum of the choices made thus far in his or her life. And although the ethical implications of all this are admittedly ambiguous, as the existentialist and feminist philosopher Simone de Beauvoir (1908-86) explained more thoroughly, there are some basic moral values that seem to recur in Sartre's account. Most obviously, this freedom of self-creation characterizing conscious human existence is itself of axiomatic value, and along with this there is attributable to human subjectivity generally a fundamental "dignity" or inherent worth. Also, since existential freedom is always lived out in the context of relations with other humans, conduct that negates or debilitates their freedom by definition "dehumanizes" them and thus is to be avoided or fought against, while conduct as much as possible consistent with their humanness is required. For both Sartre and Beauvoir particularly, these humanistic values did then point to the need for political activism (nonviolent or violent, as the situation required) in the name of social justice and against all social forces and policies that oppressed, exploited, and in other ways significantly diminished individual human lives.

SECTION 5: BIOLOGY AND ENVIRONMENT

One of the more notable features of modern intellectual history has been the increasing reliance on the empirical sciences to generate answers to questions previously assumed to be the domain only of philosophers and theologians. In the multifaceted study of human beings this trend has continued of course, as in the above-mentioned development of the science of behavioral psychology. But while Skinner's behaviorist approach focused almost entirely on the environmental conditioning of the individual human organism, research in biological science for well over a hundred years has been trying to determine the basic physical constitution of *homo sapiens*, how that biological nature is genetically transmitted through successive generations, and how it is itself manifested in behavioral possibilities and limitations. Within the framework of evolutionary theory, the theory of genetic inheritance especially has been applied ever more widely to the understanding of human thought, feeling, and conduct. Accordingly, any discussion these days of human nature and our propensities for violence or nonviolence must also acknowledge the accumulated evidence regarding our biological heritage and its causal role in who we become and what kind of lives we are capable of living. Although the relationship between environmental factors and genetic factors has often been interpreted in popular culture as a conflict of explanation between "nurture and nature," there seems to be growing scientific agreement that, in general, our situation as living organisms involves the complex interplay between these two types of phenomena. That is, relatively invariant genetic predispositions are "triggered" by more variable environmental stimuli, leading to different but in principle predictable specific outcomes.

Naturally a full summary of current research in human biology, from studies of brain functioning to work done on the human genome itself, is well beyond the scope of a book like this. But I think we can see at least how the age-old concern about our inherent capacity for creating a better or worse social existence would be addressed from the standpoint of contemporary biological science. In the first place then, we have to understand something about our own natural history as a species of animal on this planet. This in turn means understanding the principle of natural selection as the central hypothesis of the general theory of evolution, the most empirically defensible scientific (as distinct from religious) theory available for explaining the appearance and disappearance of earthly life forms over very long periods of time. To use the description of Charles Darwin's (1809-82) original formulation offered by Stephen Jay Gould (1941-2002), the principle of natural selection follows logically from three now well-verified biological facts: (a) Organisms tend to produce more offspring than can survive, though not in every individual instance; (b) offspring vary among themselves; (c) some of this variation is inherited by future generations. From these facts we can infer justifiably that survivors in every species of living thing *on average* (and obviously not in every case) will tend to be those individuals possessing variations best suited to local environments, which themselves are subject to a variety of changes. We can thus infer as well that the offspring of survivors will *tend* to resemble their successful parents, and that the accumulation of these "favorable" variations through time will create evolutionary change. As Darwin himself emphasized, however (though rather ambiguously in some of his writings), this concept of natural selection does *not* in itself imply any general "progress" in natural history, defined as an overall comparative improvement in life forms, nor can we read into it any distinction between "higher" and "lower" types of organisms. Factually, there is only inter- and intra-species difference, and more successful or less successful adaptation over the generations to changing local environments.

Because humans probably always have been social animals (in contrast to, say, tigers or orangutans), applying natural selection to our natural history also requires efforts to explain the patterns of social organization and behavioral norms within communities. In recent years this concern has led to more and more research connecting the sciences of biology, psychology, and anthropology, guided by the idea sometimes referred to as "gene-culture coevolution." What is asserted here is that in addition to human genetic evolution, there is a distinct though inseparably linked track of cultural evolution (again, not necessarily "progressive"), which on the one hand can be seen as the ultimate product of our genetic heritage. On the other hand, it creates a whole other environmental dimension to which our genetic predispositions are more or less sensitive, well beyond what most if not all other social animals have to respond to in their natural environments. Advocates of this gene-culture coevolution thesis point out that it does not imply a strict genetic determinism, whereby particular gene combinations dictate particular cultural forms or conventions (for example, resorting to blood sacrifices in times of material hardship for a specific community). As

Edward O. Wilson has argued, what it implies instead is that "complexes of gene-based epigenetic rules predispose people to invent" such culturally scripted, socially reinforced, but historically changeable responses to collectively perceived environmental exigencies.

Even though in the view of Wilson and other like-minded scientists cultural traits tend to be passed on over the generations in a manner analogous to genetic traits, that is, by reproductive success plus (variably defined) successful adaptation to local environments, they also emphasize that much is still unknown about the complexities of gene-culture causal interaction, and that at least since Neolithic times (starting about 10,000 years ago) the pace of cultural evolution/adaptive change has clearly outstripped our genetic evolution. This apparently large incongruity in the rate of change in part means that most likely humans still have the genetic makeup, and thus the same biological nature, that they had more than 40,000 years ago. It also means that, given the reciprocal rather than merely unilateral causality characterizing the gene-culture relationship, and given the fact that all culture is created by people themselves, we are not simply and hopelessly at the mercy of a fixed genetic formula for humanness in our attempts to effect social change and exercise some control over our destinies.

The causal role of genetic inheritance in human behavior and social conventions as well as, more obviously, our anatomy and physiology, has been pointed to most often in modern capitalist societies to justify recurring versions of "social Darwinism," the belief that relations of dominance and subordination between individuals, ethnic groups, nation-states, classes, and the sexes, are natural *and therefore appropriate* outcomes of natural selection and the "survival of the fittest." This use of biological theory to rationalize social oppression portrays the tendencies for competition, conflict, egoism, and fear as the predominant ones in human society, and treats the contrary potentials for cooperation, altruism, and peaceful mutuality as marginal at best, if not actually dangerous when advocated as desirable social norms. But as the contemporary moral philosopher Peter Singer has argued, we can take current Darwinian theory seriously and with complete consistency work instead for the ethical goal of radically more nonviolent, peaceful, equitable, and mutually supporting social relations among all peoples. In his view we can do this not in spite of human nature, but in accordance with a better scientific understanding of it, which these days includes the recognition that cooperation and altruism are not after all aberrant or marginal, but in fact widespread in most societies, and explainable as historically transmitted though culturally diverse adaptations. Rather than misapplying Darwinism and genetics to legitimize reverting back to something like a Hobbesian pessimism about human nature (which also in its own way valorizes the principle that "might makes right"), Singer recommends using evolutionary theory to help us identify human limitations as well as possibilities as we pursue an agenda for significant social improvement. This will put us in a better position to accurately assess the biological "costs and benefits" of truly progressive policies of global peace and social justice, and in principle increase the chances for their success.

FURTHER READING

Section 2

Wing-Tsit Chan, translator and editor, *A Sourcebook in Chinese Philosophy* (Princeton, NJ: Princeton UP, 1963); Mencius, selections from *The Book of Mencius*, 49-83.

John Dewey, *Democracy and Education: An Introduction to the Philosophy of Education* (New York: The Macmillan Co., 1916).

———, "Democracy and Educational Administration," *School and Society* 45, April 1937, 457-62.

Ludwig Feuerbach, *The Essence of Christianity*, translated by George Elliot (Mary Ann Evans) (New York: Harper Torchbook edition, 1957); originally published 1841.

Mary Wollstonecraft, *A Vindication of the Rights of Men* (originally published 1790), and *A Vindication of the Rights of Woman* (originally published 1792), together in one text, *The Vindications*, edited by D.L. Macdonald and Kathleen Scherf (Peterborough, ON: Broadview Press, 1997).

Section 3

Wing-Tsit Chan, *op. cit.*, Hsun Tzu, Chapters 17, 23, in *The Hsun Tzu*, 116-24, 128-35.

Thomas Hobbes, *Leviathan* (New York: Penguin Books, 1968); originally published 1651.

Abul A'lā Maudūdi, *The Islamic Law and Constitution*, translated and edited by Khurshid Ahmad, 1955, 1960.

Arthur Schopenhauer, *The Will to Live: Selected Writings of Arthur Schopenhauer*, edited by Richard Taylor (New York: Frederick Ungar, 1967).

Section 4

Simone de Beauvoir, *The Ethics of Ambiguity,* translated by Bernard Frechtman (Secaucus, NJ: Citadel Press, 1948, 1975).

Francis M. Cornford, *The Republic of Plato* (Oxford: Oxford UP, 1975).

Karl Marx, "Theses on Feuerbach" (1845), Karl Marx and Frederick Engels, "The German Ideology: Part I" (1845-46), reprinted in *The Marx-Engels Reader,* 2nd edition, edited by Robert C. Tucker (New York: W.W. Norton and Co., 1978); 143-45, 146-200.

Jean-Paul Sartre, *Existentialism and Humanism,* translated by Philip Mairet (London: Methuen and Co., 1946).

B.F. Skinner, *Walden Two: Freedom and the Science of Human Behavior* (New York: Macmillan, 1948; Prentice-Hall, 1976).

Section 5

Charles R. Darwin, *The Origin of Species* (New York: Mentor Books, 1958); originally published 1859.

Stephen Jay Gould, *Full House: The Spread of Excellence From Plato to Darwin* (New York: Three Rivers Press, 1997); see Chapter 12.

Marc D. Hauser, *Moral Minds: The Nature of Right and Wrong* (New York: HarperCollins, 2006).

Peter Singer, *A Darwinian Left: Politics, Evolution and Cooperation* (New Haven, CT: Yale UP, 1999).

David Livingstone Smith, *The Most Dangerous Animal: Human Nature and the Origins of War* (New York: St. Martin's Press, 2007).

Frans de Waal, *Primates & Philosophers: How Morality Evolved* (Princeton, NJ: Princeton UP, 2009).

Edward O. Wilson, *Consilience: The Unity of Knowledge* (New York: Alfred A. Knopf, 1998); see Chapters 7, 8.

CHAPTER 4

Life, Death, and Moral Goals: Religious and Secular Perspectives

SECTION 1: BELIEF SYSTEMS AND VIOLENCE

The attitudes of many people about the appropriateness or inappropriateness of violence are based on the value and meaning they attach to life and death, and thus also on their understanding of their own place and moral purpose in this world. As social animals, most humans initially acquire this understanding as a result of the socialization processes they undergo by being raised within particular cultural communities. But depending on the cultural environment, and how thoroughly they have been inculcated with the worldview of their elders, individuals become more or less capable of exercising choice regarding what to believe about their own lives as they move from childhood to adulthood. For those willing to decide these "meaning of life" issues for themselves through thoughtful evaluation of various belief systems and interpretations of reality (including those they absorbed in their earlier upbringing), becoming educated about the range of options is crucial, and in this chapter I hope to contribute to that end.

More specifically, in what follows I will offer summaries of a number of historically influential systems of thought, both religious and secular, which provide different answers to these perennial human questions about life, death, and the viability of relations with others. Included here are the common themes found in religious fundamentalism (Section 3), as well as the views of three major figures in modern nonviolentism: Leo Tolstoy, Mohandas K. Gandhi, and Martin Luther King, Jr. (Section 4). For the sake of clarity and consistency I will refer to all of these conceptually organized accounts of human reality as "belief systems" rather than using the broader and often more amorphous term "worldview," so that even though a particular belief system can inform someone's general worldview, the two will not be treated as the same. Although a belief system here will be narrower than a worldview, it will be broader than a "doctrine" or a "theory" in the sense that either of these can be part of a belief system, or at most one type of belief system among others. Further, I will not treat "belief system" as merely synonymous with "ideology" either. The concept of ideology has been used (and abused) in many different and sometimes confusing ways over the past few centuries, and I would like to wade through at least most of this theoretical mess by emphasizing the essentially political function of "an ideology" in conditions of group conflict and "vertical power" relations. For example, a religious belief system such as doctrinal Christianity, or a theory of social development such as the Marxist theory of historical materialism, though not in itself ideological necessarily, can take on an ideological character or be used ideologically when some of its adherents use it as a means to justify or account for their social position over against some other group(s) with whom they are in some kind of antagonistic relationship.

Since each belief system identified here has its own intellectual tradition and internal diversity of historical expression, interpretation, and often factionalism, even a brief overview of it risks being misleading, at least from the standpoint of its proponents. To minimize this risk, and yet make these summary descriptions both manageable and productive for the reader interested in sampling from global intellectual history and assessing its current influence, I will focus on what these various belief systems have to say, *typically* in my estimation, about the following topics:

1. The existence, nature, and comparative value of both the natural world and some kind of supernatural world.
2. The nature of and moral goals associated with human relationships to: (a) divine beings; (b) other humans; (c) non-human natural beings.
3. The acceptability of intentional violence.

SECTION 2: SOME RELIGIOUS VIEWS

As I identify relevant beliefs in various religious traditions, I will leave aside the definitional question regarding the necessary and sufficient conditions constituting a religion in the first place, and just go along with the more conventional, non-technical characterizations of this or that belief system as "religious." This allows me to include Buddhism, Jainism, and Daoism, since religious ideas and practices did develop eventually out of these "philosophies of life," even though originally none of them included a central concept of a divine being, while usual academic definitions of a religion require such a concept.

Judaism

1. As the oldest of the three Abrahamic religions, Judaism was established as the religion of the ancient Israeli, or Jewish, people, and is based on the writings of the Hebrew Bible (especially the first five books, collectively called the *Torah*) and the *Talmud* (rabbinical writings also treated as authoritative, and composed much later, between 50 and 500 CE). The grounding metaphysical idea is that there is one supernatural God who created the whole natural world including humans, though humans alone among all living things were created in God's "image" and thus have a separate and special status in this world. There is no uniformly strong doctrinal emphasis on what happens to a person after physical death, on the existence of an immaterial "soul," or on concepts of an otherworldly "heaven" or "hell" where this person (in whatever form) might dwell eternally. In any case the natural, created world is not viewed typically as less valuable than some possible supernatural world, and one's natural life is not seen as a mere means for eventually attaining some "higher" state of spiritual existence.

2. Judaism teaches that the one God originally made a covenant with Abraham, that still obtains, to bless and protect the Jewish people in return for their exclusive devotion and faithful adherence to God's will (eventually formulated as "law" in the scriptures). In this sense the Jews are thought to be God's "Chosen People," not so much because they have special rights compared to other peoples, but because they have special responsibilities to God which are to be fulfilled most importantly by creating and maintaining a just society. This especially applies within Jewish communities, but again, insofar as all humans are created in the image of God there is a strong ethical imperative to treat all humans with respect and dignity, and to advocate social justice wherever it is lacking. Given this unique covenant between the one God and the Jewish people, Judaism is not an evangelistic religion, and there never has been any organized effort to convert non-Jews to its theological precepts. It was created by, and for, this one ancestrally linked ethnic group, though it is open to others who do choose to convert. In addition, the moral goal of serving God by living lives of justice, truthfulness, and mercy usually has been understood anthropocentrically, so that all non-human living things are assumed to have only

73

extrinsic value for human interests rather than the intrinsic value accorded to all humans (and of course God), even though cruelty to other animals is generally prohibited.

3. In the Hebrew Bible and the *Talmud* there is no consistent doctrine of nonviolence or pacifism espoused. In fact, a fair amount of approval is expressed for Israeli warmaking and violent punishment meted out by humans and God, usually when the collective interests of the Jewish people are somehow threatened by some other "enemy" people, or when someone has gone against God's will. On the other hand, scholars point out in these texts many recommendations for resolving conflicts before they turn violent, for attempting to convert an "enemy" into a "friend," and against over-eager, over-zealous retaliation and punishment. The recurring theme here seems to be that Jews should trust in the protection of God first and foremost, and that God is the proper judge and dispenser of retribution for human wrongdoing. Some have concluded, therefore, that whenever feasible, devout Jews should refrain from retaliatory as well as aggressive violence unless it is clear that God expects otherwise in that situation.

Christianity

1. Emerging as an offshoot of Judaism a little more than two thousand years ago, the Christian belief system included the Judaic account of the creation of the natural world by a supernatural, transcendent God, and the anthropocentric affirmation of humans' special place in that creation, even as nonetheless "fallen" beings in need of "redemption." In contrast to Judaism however, Christianity developed in such a way that great emphasis typically was placed on the possible achievement of an eternal, heavenly existence after a person's life ended in this mortal, profane world. The natural world clearly then was not as valuable as the supernatural world a human eventually could inhabit (either in bodily or bodiless form, depending on which sectarian version one believed), and often was seen merely as a temporary, material arena within which a person had to prove to God that she or he deserved the eternal bliss of heaven rather than the alternative of an eternal condition of "hell" (also variously described).

2. Christianity treats the Hebrew Bible as part of the written "Word of God," and so also accepts the moral principle that people should worship this one God and live their lives in accordance with "His" revealed will. But it diverges from Judaism concerning this relationship to the divine on at least three points. First, it asserts that the Jewish prophets' prediction of a "messiah," or "savior,"

actually came true in the person of Jesus, as the one and only incarnation of God in this world. Second, it claims that "salvation" is intended not only for the Jewish people but for all humans who believe that Jesus was in fact this savior (as "the anointed one," the "Christ"). Third, the nature of salvation here is the "victory over death" as the natural end of life, that is, the ultimate survival of physical death and attainment of heaven. This is exemplified most perfectly by the sacrificial death on behalf of humankind and subsequent resurrection of Jesus himself, as this story is told and elaborated on in the "New Testament" part of the Christian Bible. Regarding the relationship to fellow humans, Christian thought usually appeals to the divine command to "love your neighbor as yourself" as the basic ethical principle, in conjunction with the evangelistic imperative to convert as many people as possible to the belief that Jesus was the Christ who has redeemed humanity in its troubled relationship with God, and who is again the necessary source of salvation. Like Judaism, further, mainstream Christianity historically has treated the rest of the animate and inanimate natural world as a pool of resources for human use, so that non-human living beings are merely means for human (or divine) ends and have no inherent moral standing that would restrict violence against them.

3. Among Christian theologians there always has been some disagreement about whether the use of violence is consistent with the Christian belief system, but currently there seems to be less agreement than ever regarding what the Christian "truth" really is on this subject. Historical evidence does indicate that the early Christians were mostly pacifist in their attitudes about war, and quite often advocates of nonviolence even in response to the violence regularly perpetrated against them as an identified minority religious group. But as Christianity spread around the Mediterranean and beyond, and was appropriated by more and more political regimes over the centuries, the doctrines were usually interpreted so that warmaking, violent legal punishment, and at least defensive interpersonal violence were seen as consistent with God's will and pious Christian living. This adaptation of the belief system is still especially noticeable today when the distinction between believers and non-believers of the Christian "universal truth" is employed to justify violence against the latter because their very existence is thought to represent a threat to, and potential persecution of, the former.

Islam

1. The religion of Islam developed from the teachings of the Arabian Muhammad in the seventh century, and although it did not emerge directly from

Judaic religion as Christianity did, it too traces its origins back to Abraham and his special relationship with God (or "Allah," in Arabic). The sacred text in Islam is the *Qur'ān*, believed by the faithful to be the words of God revealed to Muhammad by an angel and then written down later by his followers. It includes parts of the Old Testament and the New Testament, treating some of the Hebrew prophets and leaders as earlier messengers of God, including the non-divine Jesus, while Muhammad himself claimed to be the (also non-divine) last messenger of God. So, Islam also incorporated the Hebrew creation story in the book of Genesis, but it has shared with Christianity the relative devaluation of life in the natural world in contrast to the much more important eternal life after death. Heaven is described as a supernatural but sensuous garden paradise the entrance to which can be earned by all those who obey God's will sufficiently during their temporary existence in this profane world, while an eternal hell is for people divinely judged to have lived immoral or unfaithful lives.

2. The direct personal relationship to God is paramount in the Islamic belief system, and is portrayed as properly involving the freely chosen, complete submission to divine will as laid down in the *Qur'ān* and the person's willing acknowledgment of total dependency on God in all aspects of his or her life. There is thus no intermediary "savior" figure in Islam, and "redemption" from humans' naturally imperfect state is achieved by the individual living righteously and in obedience to Qur'ānic authority as much as possible. In addition, since Muslims typically have believed that God wants all humans to submit to "His" will, evangelism historically has been practiced. This was especially the case in Islam's first few centuries when, spreading out from Arabia, a Muslim civilization was created from Spain through North Africa and the rest of the Middle East to India, mostly by means of military conquest. Other things being equal, all human life is valuable as a gift from God, so Muslims are obligated to treat all others with respect and justice, and to care for those in need to the extent they are able whether those others are believers or nonbelievers. And again, Islam remains consistent with the Judaic and Christian assumptions of anthropocentrism in relation to the natural world, seeing humans as a special, superior species set apart from all others and alone possessing intrinsic moral worth.

3. Unlike doctrinal debates in Christianity and more in keeping with doctrinal history in Judaism, there never has been serious controversy within Islam about whether or not it is an essentially nonviolentist belief system. In defense of legitimate individual or community interests and in accordance with the principle of retributive justice, violent means of conflict resolution always

have been seen as acceptable. But although aggressive or predatory violence is disapproved of traditionally, what counts as aggression in the first place has not been without its doctrinal ambiguities. In the contemporary world, when many people think of the moral status of violence in Islam they think of the concept of *jihad*, defined basically as "striving in the cause of God." But there is disagreement among Islamic scholars on how to best interpret this concept and its implications. On the one hand, it has been used commonly to refer to "holy war" waged defensively against perceived enemies of Islam, but others have argued that *jihad* refers to any devout struggle to carry out God's will in the world, including the intellectual or emotional struggle of a person to better understand and fulfill her or his moral duties. Seen in this light, *jihad* is not necessarily inconsistent with what some say is the divine command to work for meaningful peace not only within Muslim society, but between all peoples.

Hinduism

1. As an organized religion Hinduism goes back at least 3500 years, and elements of it are traceable back another thousand years during the time of the pre-Aryan Indus Valley civilization in northern India. It too is a belief system based on written texts viewed as sacred, the oldest of which is the *Rig Veda* (as one of four Vedas, originally compiled from earlier compositions around 1500 BCE, and added to subsequently over a number of centuries). There was no one "founder" of this religion, and its doctrines were created primarily by the priest caste of the Indo-Aryan people who moved into northern India from central Asia between 1700 and 1500 BCE, forcing south the earlier Dravidian inhabitants ("Hindu" is an old Persian word referring to the Indus River region itself, from which comes "India"). As Hinduism evolved it gave rise to many different versions, so that on the one hand it is difficult even to identify a common core of doctrine. But on the other hand, it has been a common view in Hinduism that all spiritual paths can lead to the same goal and thus tolerance of religious diversity in belief and expression has usually been embraced. Concerning the relationship between the natural and supernatural dimensions of reality, Hindu thought has not been as thoroughly dualistic as Christianity and Islam, but the material world is seen as less real than and inessential in comparison with the spiritual essence of all existence. The polytheism that always has been part of Hinduism is qualified typically by the belief that even gods and goddesses are manifestations of Brahman, as the ultimate Supreme Being and impersonal, omnipresent, creative source of all being, and thus over

77

the millennia Hindu cosmology has become as much pantheistic as polytheistic. Most importantly, Brahman expresses itself in the individual immaterial soul (Atman) of every living being which, while existing temporarily in that particular embodied form, retains its essential connection with Brahman and is eternal.

2. Traditionally the doctrines of reincarnation and *karma* are central in Hinduism, so that the consequences of one's thoughts, words, and deeds are believed to cause one's rebirth again and again into one body or another (human or not) until such time as the Atman can achieve spiritual liberation (*moksha*) and no longer be reborn, finally escaping individuated material existence altogether and becoming completely one with Brahman. Since getting off the "wheel of rebirth" is the primary spiritual goal for devout Hindus, the problem then has been how to free oneself from, and "work off," the karmic consequences that keep one tied to the physical, sensory world. This is where the historical acceptance of "many paths to God" becomes very apparent, but there does seem to be a recurrent theme of striving to live in accordance with the principle of "nonattachment," that is, living in this world without ego involvement and selfish concern for what happens. One should also aim to carry out one's moral duties (*dharma*) in the spirit of nonattachment, those duties themselves traditionally being determined by one's place in the caste hierarchy in Hindu society. Since Hindu religion originally was meant for the people of India, there was no duty for evangelism, though in recent times some Hindu teachers have found receptive audiences and made converts in other parts of the world. Regarding the relationship between humans and non-humans, Hinduism is significantly less anthropocentric than the western Abrahamic religions. As all living things are the embodiments of eternal souls, they all deserve some (though not necessarily the same) degree of moral consideration by other moral agents, and of course how we treat any being affects our karma in any case.

3. Since the bodily self is at best only real in a qualified sense compared to the Atman, and the latter survives physical death anyway, physical violence is not in principle prohibited or feared as a great evil in Hindu ethics. Given the emphasis on karma and nonattachment, what is more important is the psychological state of the perpetrator as well as the victim of violence, although it is recognized that most violence results from ego attachments in the first place and in turn tends to reinforce rather than diminish them. So, even though in the traditional Indian caste system the *Kshatriyas* (warriors and political rulers) had an ethical duty to engage in war for a just cause, and violently defending Hindu society against perceived threats from other

peoples has been acceptable and even laudatory for many, there also has been a long history of respect for the principle of *ahimsa* ("nonviolence") as a kind of self-discipline which contributes to a person's spiritual progress.

Buddhism

1. The Buddhist belief system originated with the spiritual enlightenment of the Hindu prince Siddhartha Gautama (born in what is now Nepal, 563 BCE; died, 483 BCE) when he was in his thirties, after which he spent the rest of his life teaching his ideas about how to achieve liberation from the wheel of rebirth. He was called "Buddha" ("Enlightened One") by his followers, and the attainment of Buddhahood became the recommended path to salvation available to everyone, regardless of their caste affiliation. The Buddha's discoveries can be summed up in his Four Noble Truths: (a) Life is suffering/dissatisfaction; and (b) suffering is caused by craving, or selfish desire; (c) the cessation of suffering can be brought about by the cessation of craving (that is, nonattachment); and (d) the cessation of craving can be brought about by following the Noble Eightfold Path: (1) right views; (2) right intentions; (3) right speech; (4) right conduct; (5) right livelihood; (6) right effort; (7) right mindfulness; (8) right contemplation. This eightfold path itself is thought to position a person to achieve "enlightenment" (or "awakening") eventually regarding the true nature of reality: That it is ultimately an undifferentiated Oneness in which all individuated existence, including the individual self, is illusory. On becoming enlightened one can then attain *nirvana* (a Sanskrit term referring to the "extinguishing" of the flame of craving and ego-attachment), and upon death one finally can be freed from future lives and deaths for all eternity. Thus, there is no Supreme Being in Buddhism (personal or impersonal, transcendent or immanent), though in some later versions the Buddha himself and certain other persons thought to have become Buddhas too were divinized and worshipped as individuated celestial beings who had the power to facilitate others' salvation. There is also no continuous eternal soul which is itself reincarnated, strictly speaking, and the person is only a series of transient physical and mental states in keeping with the doctrine of the impermanence of all things.

2. Different orders of monks and nuns emerged early in Buddhist history, focusing either directly on the attainment of enlightenment, or on the worship of deified Buddhas as intermediary figures in the quest for eventual release from recurring mortal existence. Buddhism has a textual tradition as well, though no one "sacred book," and which group of writings are treated as

79

canonical depends on the sect with which one identifies. The most important moral value in all sects and schools of thought is compassion for all living things, given all creatures' vulnerability to suffering in their unenlightened state. It is out of compassion too that efforts to disseminate Buddhist teachings were encouraged over the centuries, so Buddhism does have an evangelistic tradition that partly accounts for its spreading from India through most of Southeast and East Asia.

3. The foundational ethical ideal of compassion has been interpreted often to imply the principle of avoiding harm to all others (again, human and nonhuman), so that even more than in the Hindu tradition, nonviolence in all aspects of life is recommended. Although there have been warriors and military leaders who were Buddhist in Asian history, pacifism and anti-militarism also have played an important role in traditional Buddhist ethics, which to some extent explains the periodic persecution of believers by various political rulers. More consistent with Hindu thought, on the other hand, is the recognition that violence is not only caused in most cases by ego-attachments and craving (for example, the desire for revenge, or for the taste of well-prepared animal flesh), but in turn it usually contributes to further worldly attachments and spiritually enslaving desires. This means that consistently practicing nonviolence, especially as motivated by compassion for all beings, can in its own way condition a person's character so that nonattachment is more achievable.

Jainism

1. Jains follow the teachings of Vardhamana, who became known as the "Victorious One" (*Jina*) for achieving complete nonattachment, spiritual knowledge, and guaranteed release from the wheel of rebirth, after many years of meditation and extreme asceticism. He lived during the sixth to fifth centuries BCE in India, and according to tradition was not the first but the 24th in a line of teachers of Jain principles, elements of which are traceable back to pre-Aryan times. Like Buddhism, Jainism rejects the belief in a Supreme Being and a divinely created universe, though it does not deny the existence of gods as a species of celestial beings, the worship of which is neither mandatory nor even important. Unlike Buddhists, however, and more like many Hindu sects, Jains believe in an eternal individual soul which is trapped inside one material body after another until its final liberation is won. Since there is no Brahman, the soul freed from materiality exists forever in its individuated essence and in a state of omniscience and perfect bliss.

And, much more so than either Buddhism or Hinduism, this belief system is fundamentally dualistic, stressing the real metaphysical distinction between matter and the population of immaterial souls temporarily inhabiting bodies as dictated by karma until their final release.

2. After Vardhamana collections of holy writings eventually appeared, though again, there has been disagreement over the centuries about what should be regarded as canonical. There has been agreement, on the other hand, regarding the monastic life as necessary if one is to have any hope of ever freeing one's soul from embodied existence; hence the central role of monks and nuns in Jainism. Even if adherents choose to remain lay persons in their current lives they recognize that at some point in future lives they will need to start following the severe discipline of physical austerity, renunciation, and meditation required by the monastic orders. Even without the rigors of an asceticism which ideally would include fasting to the point of a heroic death by starvation, Jain laity are expected to respect and avoid harm to all living things, not so much out of compassion as from the recognition that every live being has trapped within it an eternal soul. Concerning the moral obligation to spread these teachings to all peoples, Jain tradition has more in common with Hinduism than Buddhism in not emphasizing "missionary work," although again this spiritual path is open to any sincere seeker regardless of class or ethnic background.

3. More than any other organized religion, Jainism is grounded in the ethical principle of nonviolence (ahimsa) in one's relations to the rest of the living world. Harming any being, whether it is human or nonhuman, animal, plant, or even microbe, is fundamentally wrong, though excusable in varying degrees depending on intentions and on whether one has taken monastic vows or is a layperson. Monks and nuns often wear masks over their mouths to avoid inhaling and killing even the smallest organisms. They often walk with a broom to sweep out of the way insects and other creatures they might step on, and as already implied, they have a very restricted diet. The laity is at least expected to avoid killing animals (and plants too where feasible) for food, and avoid occupations that normally involve the taking of life. Obviously this rules out the military profession, but carpentry too would be an inappropriate occupation insofar as it relies on the killing of trees for wood, as would farming to the extent that it includes harvesting plants and plowing the ground where many small life forms exist. Consequently many Jains have ended up in the merchant class over the centuries (in traditional Hindu society this would be the Vaishya caste), and these days usually pursue careers that do not directly involve either making material things or destroying them.

Daoism

1. Over the last 2500 years Daoism has been one of the major influences in the evolution of Chinese culture, emerging about the same time as and in opposition to Confucianism, and significantly affecting the later development of Chinese Buddhism. The basic ideas of Daoist philosophy are traceable to an older contemporary of Confucius, Laozi (c. sixth century BCE), who tradition identifies as the primary source of the small but foundational text called the *Dao De Jing* (or *Tao Te Ching* in the Wade-Giles spelling), in English *The Classic of the Way and its Virtue*. The central concept for Laozi (or Lao Tzu) was the *Dao* ("the Way") or *Tao*, from which the name of this "philosophy of life" is derived, and in contrast to the Confucian *Dao* that referred more narrowly to the natural moral law for humans, in Laozi's account it was "the Way" of Nature as a whole. That is, the *Dao* is the dynamic rather than static, harmonious rather than chaotic or conflicting, eternal yet natural order of the universe, taken as the primordial flow and rhythm of life itself. It is not created or directed by any transcendent being, but itself is the ultimate creative source and continuing ground of all existing things. Sometime during the first and second centuries BCE various Daoist ideas were incorporated into a religion headed by a priesthood, though the primary concerns of priests were interceding with ancestral spirits on behalf of laypersons, and discerning the mystical elements of Nature to aid such other pursuits as divination, immortality, and the secrets of alchemy.

2. Even though there is no supernatural Supreme Being in Daoism, there is a proper relationship with Nature recommended for anyone who truly wants to live well and be happy, and this is to live in accordance with the *Dao*. The concept of "returning" to this "Way of Life" which is our metaphysical ground is used regularly to imply that most people have deviated from its naturally harmonious flow, making themselves and each other more miserable as a result. They deviate from the *Dao* by acquiring ego-based wants and needs that lead to constant striving for or against this and that, where they wrongly assume separateness and conflict between people, and between humans and the rest of the natural world. Living in harmony with the *Dao* and thus achieving the basic human good of inner peace and tranquility, on the other hand, requires giving up striving and asserting one's interests over and against others. It also requires the reduction of one's desires to a minimum, not in the name of any ascetic ideal but in order to be more easily content. Such a person will have acquired the virtues of humility, simplicity, patience, non-aggressive persistence, and especially *wu wei* ("nonaction") as the habit of allowing things

to happen "naturally" rather than forcing them to happen. This individual naturally tends to be the most beneficial and least offensive to others too, so these virtues together constitute the ideal moral character to develop for life in a community. Further, if a political ruler embodies these virtues and acts in harmony with the *Dao*, peace, prosperity, and security for the whole society will be more likely; the government will function in the most orderly manner possible because there will be a minimum of competition, strife, and coercion, and everything will occur as if it happened on its own. As Laozi said, the sagacious ruler "manages affairs without action (*wu-wei*)," and by "acting without action, all things will be in order" (*Dao De Jing*).

3. Neither as a social philosophy nor as a philosophy of personal transformation has Daoism included any unequivocal moral doctrine of nonviolentism, or pacifism in the face of others' aggression, and in Chinese history adherents of both secular and religious Daoism sometimes were warriors or political leaders directing military strategy. At the same time, since any intentional violence obviously involves striving against others, such behavior is to be avoided whenever possible on both prudential and moral grounds; and again, this was thought to apply especially to rulers in a position to "set the tone" for the whole society. Thus, aggressive violence at the international, inter-group, and inter-personal levels, as well as in human-nonhuman relations, would be generally ruled out from a consistently maintained Daoist standpoint, except in the case of necessary taking of life for food, clothing, and shelter. But even regarding the defense against aggression, Daoist writings include constant imagery of natural things that yield and appear passive but persist and outlast all opposition, such as water that wears down rock, plant sprouts that break through the hardest soil, and the tree that bends but does not break.

Indigenous North American Religions

1. In spite of the diversity of belief systems found among the many native peoples of North America, there are some recurring religious themes that seem to be shared in the traditional teachings of most of these cultural groups. In the view of many Native American and non-native authors, these themes generally are traceable back to pre-Columbian times but continue to inform the worldviews of aboriginal peoples today, depending of course on how much influence European American culture (especially Judeo-Christian thought and imagery) also has had in particular indigenous communities. The metaphysical foundation of these tribal religions typically is a conception of the natural

world as created by a Supreme Being, which is itself most often understood non-anthropomorphically and only referred to as "the Creator" or "Great Spirit." In contrast to much of western metaphysics where a qualitative distinction between the natural and supernatural, and between the physical and spiritual/mental, has been assumed, in indigenous North American thought it has been more common to see a metaphysical continuity in things, so that in a very real sense all natural beings are spiritual beings and vice versa, though varying in degrees of materiality relative to each other. The distinction between life and death is also seen as more fluid and not so fundamentally dichotomous, so that when people die physically it is often believed they live on in a less materialized but still essentially natural dimension of reality. Although in these religions the universe is usually seen as a morally ordered place where causal relations are often explainable in terms of social relations between inescapably interdependent beings, there is no equivalent to the principle of *karma*, and the Creator neither intervenes nor judges, rewards, or punishes people in an afterlife.

2. Since the natural world in native North American religions is not denigrated as "the devil's workshop" or as a "veil of Maya" from which to free oneself, the goal of life is not some better existence after death, but living well, and long, as flesh and blood creatures who are part of this world. A central moral concept thus guiding efforts to live "the good life" is responsibility, where humans are thought to have responsibilities to the Creator, to other humans, and to other nonhuman natural beings. These moral responsibilities are often situational and not always equal; they exclude doctrinal evangelism, and again, they are understood much less anthropocentrically and more ecocentrically than has been the case especially (but not only) in western ethical traditions. For example, in many prayers and ceremonies the phrase "All my relations" is used to acknowledge personal and community interconnection with and respect for all living things and natural forces (in the Lakota language, for example, this is what is meant by the term *Metaku-yeayasi*). Although essential (not merely apparent) species diversity and thus diversity of interests is affirmed, the concept of moral personhood also is often extended beyond membership in *homo sapiens* to include any interested social actor, which practically means any being which can be helped or harmed through its relations with any other beings.

3. In North American tribal religions it is recognized that in the natural order of things all that lives comes into being and eventually passes away again, so in general death is less feared as unnatural, radically other than life, or as an evil to overcome, than is typical in some other religious traditions. On the other hand, other things being equal, life is valued by all natural beings, so

that the taking of life for no good reason is morally wrong. What counts as a "good reason" to kill or inflict any violence of course varies, but even when such conduct is seen as necessary for food, shelter, clothing, medicines, or defending oneself or one's community from attack, indigenous teachings often emphasize an attitude of respect toward the recipient of the violence, whether it is mineral, plant, or animal (human and nonhuman). And, regarding armed conflict between human groups in particular, peace is an important value, but a thoroughgoing pacifism normally has not been a part of religious belief, given the honor traditionally accorded to those who choose to be warriors. These days this valorization of warriors has created a dilemma for some native North Americans, since on the one hand there continues to be a very high rate of participation among their people in the national government's armed forces, but on the other hand (especially in the US, but also in Canada), this same government has perpetrated genocide against them in recent history and has committed its military to wars (not only against them) widely believed to be wrong within many indigenous communities. The way they sometimes resolve this dilemma is by appealing to the principle, "Honor the warrior, not the war."

Indigenous African Religions

1. If anything it is even harder to generalize accurately about the belief systems of indigenous African peoples than is the case with indigenous North Americans, given the larger total population and number of distinct cultural groups in Africa. But since inter-ethnic violence, civil war, and other forms of human-caused suffering affect millions of people on that continent, it is important to identify at least some common native religious beliefs and their possible role in either causing or resolving conflicts. So if we focus on sub-Saharan Africa (that is, the areas not so thoroughly influenced by Islam and Arabic culture), and bracket the effects of Christianity as well as Islam over the last few centuries, it appears in the first place that native religions all affirm the existence of a single creator God who is understood variously as male, female, or genderless. There is also a variety of belief concerning how actively involved in the Creation this God remains, but in addition to this Supreme Being there are usually thought to be other kinds of lesser spirit beings. In some religions these are divided into subordinate deities, evil spirits, and human ancestor spirits; in other traditions there are "nature spirits" inhabiting but not identical with some natural entities (e.g., trees, mountains, rivers, animals), as well as evil spirits and ancestors.

85

Regarding the human person, the distinction between the physical and the spiritual/mental sometimes is conceived dualistically (and quite similar to western dualism), and sometimes more along the lines of the "continuum of being" conception also associated with native North American metaphysics. In any case the relationship between the material and the spiritual is seen as interactive, both in terms of the body-soul relation and with respect to relations between "embodied" persons and the different kinds of non-embodied spirit beings, sometimes including God.

2. In native African religions it is believed that the Supreme Being created a well-organized and basically harmonious natural world within which humans are expected to "fit in" if they hope to maintain any security and prosperity for themselves. The well-being of individuals and communities then depends on following spiritually inspired rules governing many aspects of daily life, and on the consequent aid provided by God and/or good spirits (again, nature spirits, ancestors, or both). On the other hand, harm is caused either by bad spirits (who also can manipulate other people as their proxies) or by the violation of these social norms, in which case God and the good spirits do not usually punish people but simply withdraw their beneficence until some appropriate party has made amends. Further, social relations typically are understood in communitarian and organicist rather than atomistic terms, so self-seeking at the expense of other social members most often is considered wrong. But inter-human ethical obligation is focused primarily on one's own community or people and what is required for that group's well-being, rather than on humanity in general. Still, other things being equal, respect for other peoples and mutual accommodation are seen to bring about the best outcomes. And, for reasons similar to those offered in native North American religions, evangelism is not an expectation in native African religions even though it is not unusual for local religious thinkers to give recommendations, if asked by "outsiders," regarding how the latter might improve their lives by attending more to spiritual matters. With respect to relations between humans and nonhuman natural beings, again there is variety in these religious traditions in how anthropocentric or ecocentric such relations are thought to be; however human dependency and natural vulnerability are commonly recognized, and the obligation to maintain balance in local ecosystems is often (though not always) affirmed as crucial.

3. Since health and long life are basic values in indigenous African societies, obviously violence and death are disvalues, but historically native religions for the most part have not included doctrines of pacifism. Most often in these belief systems interpersonal and inter-group violence is justified

on defensive grounds, though violent retribution is sometimes affirmed too, as is (or was in earlier times) aggressive violence as part of an expansionist political policy. The role of warrior thus has been an honorable one through the ages in native cultures, especially as a protector of community interests against threats posed by other human groups, but also as one who can bring home the "spoils" from successful battle. However, prosperity most often has required peaceful relations with other peoples, and peacemaking is a highly respected skill in most African societies, for both intra- and inter-community conflict resolution.

SECTION 3: RELIGIOUS FUNDAMENTALISM

In recent times "fundamentalist" followers of various religions have been more likely to get involved in violent sectarian conflicts than their non-fundamentalist "coreligionists," so it is worthwhile to identify any distinguishing features of religious fundamentalism that may make it more prone to violence in the first place. Of course this is not to imply that most of the armed conflict between religiously affiliated groups in the contemporary world has been caused by fundamentalist factions, though they more often refer to themselves as "militant" devotees of this or that "revealed truth." For instance, the decades-long Protestant-Catholic conflict in Northern Ireland, and the Bosnian civil war of the 1990s between the Catholic Croats, the Eastern Orthodox Serbs, and the Muslim population, had very little to do with fundamentalist efforts to "defend the faith." Still, fundamentalism regularly is portrayed (not unusually by adherents, and always by critics) as a kind of religious extremism, and since extremist belief systems as a rule more easily justify injury and death for the sake of dogma, its underlying motivations need to be understood and its distinction from the attitudes of other practitioners of the same religion clarified.

In 1920 Curtis Lee Laws, American editor of a Baptist newspaper, coined the term "fundamentalist" to refer to someone who was willing to fight to protect a set of beliefs viewed by some American Protestants as "the fundamentals" of Christianity, against the perceived threat of modern reinterpretation, "updating," and subsequent neutralization. Especially in the second half of the twentieth century, the term was used more and more to designate sub-groups in other religious traditions as well which shared with Christian fundamentalists the commitment to defend what they took to be the "original," divinely inspired and humanly unalterable "truth" of selected religious doctrines from modernist influences. Thus, these days there are also self-identified fundamentalist groups within Judaism, Islam, Hinduism, and by some accounts even in Buddhism.

As a modern social phenomenon religious fundamentalism is not anti-modern in all respects; for example, the comparatively rapid rate and range of technological changes are not opposed but instead appropriated in many cases, as seen in the willing use of the latest information technology along with other consumer products. The "modern" tendencies against which fundamentalists have reacted have more to do with the perceived secularization of the public sphere and the consigning of religious devotion more to the domain of "private life" in the name of civic tolerance. Similarly, they have reacted against the increasing emphasis on rational and naturalistic rather than supernatural explanations of experience, and allegedly too much pluralism, accommodation with nonbelievers, ecumenism, doctrinal relativism, and cultural hybridization. This understanding of "modern life" seems to be grounded in a fear of the loss of personal and social identity, where that identity itself is defined essentially by a relationship to the divine, rather than by any relationship with other mortal persons or in terms of one's own existential self-determination. In this way of thinking the world is divided up into that which allows for the safe, unfettered, and unchallenged expression of this life-defining relationship to the supernatural, on the one hand, and everything (and everyone) else that thereby threatens such expression and is an obstacle to be overcome by any means necessary, on the other hand. So, diversity of opinion in any matter seen as impinging on the "purity" of the relevant core beliefs is regarded as a punishable offense against the Supreme Being, and although converting others to their cause is usually meritorious, generally for fundamentalists if you are not already "with them," you are "against them" and an enemy to that which they hold most dear as the foundation of their very existence.

Most of those who study religious fundamentalism agree that it is not simply the same as either religious "conservatism" or "traditionalism," though these two terms are often appropriated by fundamentalists in their "Us against Them" public presentation of themselves. Throughout much of recorded history there have been organized conservative and traditionalist reactions to social conditions obtaining at the time, but fundamentalism is probably best understood, again, as a peculiarly modern species of this broader and more diverse religious response to social change. Where it typically goes beyond other religious idealizations of some past era is in its additional emphasis on some dramatic, more or less eschatological, divinely directed, victorious resolution in the near future of the perceived crisis that has been generated by alleged incursions against the strict adherence to "the fundamentals." In some fundamentalist sects the leadership recommends a passive approach to this crisis, waiting for God to strike down their enemies and either reward them for their doctrinal fidelity or at least create a social environment free from any diversity that might distract them from the "one and only true path." In other groups this belief that "God's truth" as well as the "true believers" themselves are somehow under attack has led to active defense and retaliation against the supposed attackers, which has taken both nonviolent and violent forms over the last hundred years or so.

There also seems to be agreement among scholars that an essentialist approach to defining fundamentalism is probably untenable, while specifying a list of characteristics that allows for a "family resemblance" identification without treating any one characteristic as necessary (a general approach to classification originally recommended by the twentieth-century Austrian philosopher Ludwig Wittgenstein) will be more productive. So, within the historical context of "modern society" (along with its "postmodern" variants), as indicated above, religious fundamentalism is in the first place an organized defensive reaction against a perceived social threat to a set of religious beliefs seen as crucial to the identity of certain individuals and affiliated groups. Second, again, those "fundamental" beliefs are represented as immutable and not open to adaptation or flexibility in social application without major loss of legitimacy, so coreligionist "moderates" and modernizing reinterpreters are vilified often as much as the infidel/pagan Other. Third, the relevant set of beliefs is traceable to specific written texts taken as sacred, divinely inspired, and thus in principle to be accepted literally in the present regardless of the transient historical conditions in which they originally were composed. This reliance on textual authority also helps to account for the absence of fundamentalist movements, so far, in religions where the central beliefs have been passed on orally over the generations rather than in written form, as in the case of indigenous North American and African traditions. Fourth, it is believed that in addition to the sacred writings' immutability and inerrancy, when "correctly understood" they provide comprehensive normative guidance for all aspects of people's lives. This totalitarian dimension of fundamentalist thinking and practice is usually grounded in the anti-humanist belief that humans are not capable of deciding for themselves how to live, but must instead obey the rules for living set down in this or that sacred text as the expression of some divine will. Not surprisingly, in most fundamentalist groups the "correct understanding" of the relevant writings is dictated by leaders accepted by other group members as having greater knowledge of the nature of this divine guidance, and who thus possess an authority to command as self-proclaimed direct representatives of the Supreme Being itself.

There is nothing in the fundamentalist defense of "true doctrine" that necessarily requires the use of violence, regardless of the religion, but given that fundamentalists interpret their situation in the world as one of crisis and divinely demanded battle against evil, the use of defensive violence as a "last resort" is pretty easy for them to justify when the perceived need arises. For example, when "suicide bombers" blow themselves up in crowded markets to harm as many infidels and presumed apostates as possible, they see themselves not just as fighting "for God" in a holy war where their sacrificial deaths will be supernaturally rewarded, but also always as "fighting back" against forces that somehow threaten "the faith." And similarly, when fundamentalist groups act as the indirect perpetrators of violence (though often unacknowledged) by pressuring a government into military attacks against some other group or state viewed as an enemy obstructing their religious "way of life," they always justify it in part by asserting that there was no other way to remain safe from the threat posed by this alleged aggressor.

When justifying physical violence against others as defense from wrongful attack, fundamentalists regularly appeal to the principle of justice too, though their focus is normally quite different from that of nonviolentist advocates of "social justice" and meaningful peace among peoples. For the most part the discourse of justice in religious fundamentalism is retributive (sometimes with claims of "just compensation" folded in), in the sense that divine authority and/or the "true servants" of this Supreme Will have been wronged, and that the wrongdoers deserve some kind of punishment in return. Such punishment is to be meted out either by divine judgment (in this world or the next) or by fundamentalist devotees themselves acting as "God's instruments." In any case humanly created legal standards of criminality and punishment, as well as international relations, are only seen as legitimate insofar as they are consistent with divine will as expressed, again, in special texts and "correctly read." Thus, fundamentalists not only can criticize particular penal practices or foreign policies of governments as unjust on doctrinal grounds, but also can valorize easily extra-legal violence in the service of a "higher calling" they assume to be exempt from "merely human" rational scrutiny. In this way the logically distinct appeals to retribution and to defense of "the innocent" can be comfortably combined in a religious ideology of open-ended punishment of all "evildoers," without which it is believed there can not be and should not be peace on earth.

SECTION 4: TOLSTOY, GANDHI, AND KING

In the literature on nonviolence Leo Tolstoy, Mohandas Gandhi, and Martin Luther King, Jr. stand out as iconic influences both because of their writings and because of how they conducted their lives as social activists. They also were motivated, each in their own way, by deeply held religious convictions that shaped their understanding of how best to confront physical, psychological, and institutional violence. In this section I will only summarize their ideas that have had such an impact on thinking within the peace and justice movement in recent history, rather than attempt a more thorough exegesis. What these three spiritual leaders advocated as strategies in response to conflict and evil inflicted by others still constitute an especially difficult challenge for those who would be peacemakers these days, and especially for those who have a secular rather than a religious worldview.

Leo Tolstoy (1828-1910)

1. Tolstoy was a Russian novelist, Christian philosopher, and social reformer who was born near Tula into an aristocratic family. After an early period of military service and a later spiritual crisis in the 1870s, he came to reject all social hierarchy, material luxury, government, institutionalized religion, and violence. In Tolstoy's interpretation of Christian doctrine, the life of Jesus exemplifying agapic love and "non-resistance" to violence was the moral model that God had provided as guidance for all people. As he saw it, every person was placed in this mortal world by God with the same basic duty, a job description in effect, summed up in the command to "love one another." So the natural world is only the arena within which we succeed or fail in fulfilling the demands of this life-long "job," and we will be judged accordingly by supernatural rather than worldly standards. Life and death then, as well as the happiness and suffering we experience in this world, are not good or evil in themselves, but only insofar as they are expressions of the divine will which each individual has the responsibility to recognize and choose to follow without coercion.

2. Tolstoy argued that a person's life is not one's own but belongs to God, and this existentially defining relation to the Creator can be illumined by spiritual "tradition" (by which he meant recurrent appeals to the Golden Rule over the centuries rather than ecclesiastical "orthodoxy"), by one's own natural "reason" properly used, and by the deepest aspirations of "the heart." The Christian belief system is to be rationally understood not as laying down rules

to obey out of fear of punishment, but as offering an explanation to humans of their place in the Creation and their potential contribution to the divine plan to bring an end to all conflict and enmity on earth. Tolstoy believed that if we consult our emotional intuitions we also will discover the natural love for our fellow creatures (human and nonhuman) that confirms this rational understanding. Thus, instead of the adherence to ethical conduct principles such as justice, enlightened self-interest, or utility, he emphasized the attitude of indiscriminate love of others as the basis of the moral life, which also invites comparison with Christian situation ethics later in the twentieth century, for example, the version put forward by Joseph Fletcher.

3. Although the divinely willed "law of love" as Tolstoy explained it seems aimed more at a person's own character development than at the specification of obligatory actions, he also treated as its "corollary" the "law of non-resistance," by which he meant the absolute duty to refrain from all violence in our dealings with others. He did believe that this principle of non-resistance can shape our predispositions too, so that an individual can acquire a truly Christian sensibility making it as psychologically impossible for him or her to participate in any violence as it would be (to use Tolstoy's own example) for a normally kind person to kill or torture a baby. Yet first and foremost this "law" was a complete prohibition not only on all aggressive violence but on all defensive acts of violence as well. In fact any use of harm-inflicting force or coercion against anyone seems to be wrong in Tolstoy's account, whether it is in interpersonal, inter-group, or international contexts. As a variation of the definition of non-resistance identified in Chapter 2, however, his use of the term was somewhat less literal, since he acknowledged the morality of interposing one's own body between a murderous attacker and the intended victim as a way to protect the latter, even though such an action would be a *forceful* effort to *resist* evil in its own way. What he argued against mainly was the taken-for-granted traditional maxim to the effect that "sometimes you have to fight fire with fire." This widely accepted falsehood was in part the result of cultural habit going back thousands of years, in Tolstoy's estimation, but also the result of people's misguided embracing of the social and political *status quo* that valorizes violent coercion at all levels of collective life, and that depends on such violence for its continued existence. Finally, he pointed out that most attempts to justify the use of violence for socially worthwhile ends (as in punishment, war, protecting innocents from harm, etc.) appeal to the balance of good over bad consequences to be brought about by such means. But in his view we mortals can never adequately know the consequences of our actions and policies to warrant overriding God's will for us, which on the other

hand we can adequately know, to abide entirely by the "law of love" and the categorical principle of nonviolence, come what may.

Mohandas K. Gandhi (1869-1948)

1. Gandhi was born in Porbandar, India, into a family of the Vaishya caste (the merchant class). His formal education included law school in London, after which he returned to India to practice as an attorney. Soon finding the practice of law unsatisfying, Gandhi went to South Africa in 1893 when it also was under British rule. There he found that the laws of the land were harshly discriminatory in the treatment of Indians as well as other nonwhite peoples, and for the next two decades he fought for Indian civil rights in that country. He returned to India in 1915 and spent the rest of his life working for its political independence from Britain and its establishment as a multiethnic, democratic state. This goal was achieved in 1947 but the partition into two nations, now India and Pakistan, mainly contributed to the already existing strife between Hindus and Muslims. As the recognized moral (though not official) leader of the country, Gandhi now found himself constantly trying to bring about peace between these two groups. At the age of 78, he was assassinated in New Delhi by a high-born Hindu opposed to his advocacy of social inclusiveness and mutual respect among all peoples and religions.

Gandhi always identified with the Hindu religious tradition in which he was raised, though he was quite eclectic in his affirmation and use of ideas from other religions. In his constant references to God then, he usually meant the impersonal yet omniscient Supreme Being, or Brahman, which was both immanent and transcendent in relation to the created universe. The soul (Atman) of every living thing was only superficially individuated in its current bodily incarnation, but essentially one with this all-pervasive God, which of course implied for Gandhi that all souls were essentially one with each other as well. This was the spiritual truth that he claimed was the guiding principle of his life (the subtitle of his autobiography is "The Story of My Experiments with Truth"), so much so that he often literally equated truth with God. Also consistent with a number of traditional schools of thought in Hinduism, he thus saw truth and falsehood not just as epistemological properties of beliefs, statements, judgments, and propositions, but also as metaphysical states of reality and unreality that we can only apprehend imperfectly in our situation as embodied subjects.

2. Gandhi recommended the "pursuit of truth" for both ethical and prudential reasons in our daily activities and interactions with others, especially

when conflicts arose. During his years in South Africa he and others came up with the term "Satyagraha" to denote this idea of bringing truth to light, exposing error in people's treatment of each other, and thereby improving social relations. This term has no exact English equivalent, but he translated it variously as "holding onto Truth," from *graha* ("grasping," "possessing") and *satya* ("truth"), "Truth-force," "Love-force," or "Soul-force." The principle here is that, since all living beings participate in truth even though they don't see it clearly, and since God is "in" everyone and everything, we should listen openly and patiently to the concerns of those who want to use violence and subjugation to get their way with us, but then try to correct their erroneous assumption of separateness and essential antagonism between us by acting toward them in ways that illustrate truth. In light of their metaphysical condition all persons are of equal worth, and thus the practice of Satyagraha emphasizes love, mutual respect, and justice in all interpersonal, inter-group, and international relations, while it is in opposition to all enmity, degradation, and oppression. Gandhi and his comrades became famous especially for their strategy of Satyagraha in response to unjust and demeaning laws in South Africa and India, where their efforts often took the form of nonviolent civil disobedience aimed ultimately at the transformative "change of heart" on the part of legal authorities perpetrating such injustice.

3. Nonviolence (*ahimsa*) is a crucial component of Satyagraha because to use violent means to achieve even good ends, as in the case of struggling against colonialism and other forms of oppression, is to be just as guilty of ignorance and error as are one's oppressors. Further, the choice of means used in liberation struggles actually dictates the nature of ends that will be achieved, so violent opposition to or retaliation against institutional injustice can never bring about a truly peaceful, secure, nonviolent society. In addition, Gandhi argued that consistent nonviolence meant following the principle of *tapasya*, as the willingness to suffer and sacrifice oneself for the truth. His understanding of nonviolentism, while not absolutist, always included this demand to take upon oneself the suffering that might be inflicted in a confrontation with evildoers, rather than inflicting it on them as was urged by the advocates of violent defense against injustice. Responding to criticism in his day that there was no historical evidence that Satyagraha (including *ahimsa* and *tapasya*) has worked in practice, Gandhi pointed out that if we define "history" as the actions of political rulers and the account of the wars in which their states participated, then of course there was little historical record of the successful practice of this Truth-force. But if "history" is simply "what has happened" in the lives of human beings, then nonviolent conflict resolution motivated by mutual respect

and goodwill, aiming at the acquisition of truth and sloughing off of falsehood and ignorance, always has been in fact the norm while violent confrontations have been the aberrations.

Martin Luther King, Jr. (1929-68)

1. King was born in Atlanta, Georgia, and after receiving his undergraduate and graduate degrees as well as becoming an ordained Baptist minister, he served churches in Atlanta and in Montgomery, Alabama during the 1950s and 1960s. At the same time he became involved in political activism, primarily in the southern United States, against the longstanding and widespread official and unofficial racial segregation that kept the black population in a position of second-class citizenship in relation to the white population. As the result of his work he became the most well-known and influential African American leader in the civil rights movement of that era. Because of his efforts to help create a more just society and mutually respectful relations between all racial groups in the US, he too was assassinated, in Memphis, Tennessee on April 4, 1968, at the age of 39.

King's Christian theology drew from a wide range of historical sources, including Thomas Aquinas and Augustine, and he accepted the traditional Christian emphasis on future "heavenly rewards" achievable by human individuals after their lives in this natural world were over. But in his oratory and writings he argued that what is often called the "gospel of personal salvation" had to be supplemented with the "social gospel," by which he meant working for social justice and thereby more truly fulfilling the demands of the New Testament. This theological approach framed his formulation of a version of Christian natural law ethics, with a decidedly more nonconsequentialist than consequentialist orientation, and according to which natural law is "the moral law" and of course also then "the law of God."

2. As was the case with many other modern western Christian humanists, King's understanding of natural law was grounded in the natural equality of all human beings regarding their inherent, inalienable worth in God's eyes. This implied to him the divine expectation that we all live in accordance with natural justice, requiring that we "respect the dignity and worth of human personality." In his 1963 essay "Letter from Birmingham Jail," he also used this principle of natural justice to provide criteria for evaluating positive law in the US enacted by federal, state, or local governments. He asserted that there is a distinction between just and unjust laws, and we not only have a moral duty to

obey just laws but also a moral duty to disobey unjust laws. Just laws are those consistent with "the moral law" and natural human equality, again, and so any law that "uplifts human personality is just." On the other hand, an unjust law is one that is inconsistent with natural law, that is, God's law; it "degrades human personality," enforces unjustified "difference" between people, and also is enacted without the input of all groups affected by it in that particular society. Clearly the racial segregation ordinances in cities like Birmingham were instances of unjust law against which people had an ethical responsibility to act, in his account, in part because "Injustice anywhere is a threat to justice everywhere."

3. By the time he was thoroughly involved in the civil rights struggles in the US King had become familiar with the work of Mohandas Gandhi and the success he and others had by organizing nonviolent direct action campaigns against unjust laws and imperialist oppression in India. Although starting from a different religious standpoint, King too became convinced of the moral superiority of nonviolent direct action and civil disobedience (as described in Chapter 2, Section 2), as well as their strategic efficacy in confronting specific racist and segregationist practices and laws in various cities. To the end of his life he remained a relentless advocate of these nonviolent approaches to confronting social injustice and institutional violence in the face of wide-ranging criticism both within and outside African American communities. More concretely, he identified four steps to be followed in any particular mass protest action: First, the collection of facts to determine if injustices are being perpetrated; second, negotiation with the governmental and/or economic "power-groups," that is, the adversary/oppressor; third, if negotiation fails, then those who would participate in the upcoming confrontation must resolve for themselves the question of whether they can put up with likely physical abuse and injury without violently retaliating, what he called the process of "self-purification" (if a person can't honestly answer "yes" to oneself and to others in the group, then he or she must not participate); fourth, the direct action itself, such as a protest march or a "sit-in" to publicly dramatize the injustices, force public awareness, and appeal to a community's conscience for necessary social change.

SECTION 5: SOME SECULAR VIEWS

There are many different philosophical belief systems that have informed discussion about the moral goals of human life over the millennia, but which have not implied any necessary religious commitment. In this section I focus

96

on a number of these sets of beliefs especially as they continue to influence contemporary understanding of the possibilities, and desirability, of more thoroughly and globally nonviolent social relations. Although many religiously identified people worldwide also embrace versions of one or more of these philosophies, here I will treat them as secular options because they can be explained essentially and then accepted or rejected independently of any religious connections.

Humanism

1. Building on my earlier partial descriptions of humanism, let me first reiterate that generally, it is a view of human life that stresses the universal capability of individuals and whole societies to improve themselves and the natural world in which they exist, without the need for direct supernatural intervention or guidance. In its modern variants, it also typically interprets human history overall as developmental and progressive, whereby this natural ability to solve our own problems is played out by current generations transcending the limitations and correcting the mistakes of earlier generations. In any case, again, humanism emphasizes at both the individual and collective levels what can and should be achieved so that life can be lived well in this world, while de-emphasizing the concern with what happens after one's mortal life is done.

2. Whether we look to the classical Greek idea that "man is the measure of all things," or to the traditional Confucian concept of the Way of Heaven as the objective moral law for humans which when followed leads to a happy life, or to the increasing advocacy in recent times of a universal standard of human rights, we find another recurrent humanistic theme. It is that what matters in this world, and what should matter to us, are exclusively human interests, aspirations, and potentials, and problems of human life and death; all other life only has extrinsic value, as means to human ends. As I have pointed out already this ethical anthropocentrism is logically distinct from the progressive view of human nature and history, but often related anyway, and not inappropriately so, in various approaches to humanist teleology.

3. Historically, humanism has been neutral regarding the moral acceptability of violence as a means of conflict resolution in interpersonal, inter-group, and international situations. Of course, being a recipient of at least physical violence is acknowledged to be a bad thing, and the viability of human physical existence itself is of central concern, but agents' use of violence as a "necessary evil" in the pursuit of some goals is not ruled out generally in humanist thought. On

the one hand, humanists usually affirm as basic social goods peace, prosperity, safety from injury, and self-actualization, but on the other hand, they more often than not have accepted violent means of protecting or promoting those values. For example, many violent forms of legal punishment have been justified as the best way to deal with threats to the security of community members, and a good deal of modern colonialist and imperialist military aggression has been valorized in the name of "advancing human progress" and overcoming the resistance of "backward peoples" still "living in the past."

Liberalism

1. I have also already discussed liberalism to some extent in Chapter 3, but let me point out again that it is a distinctively modern social philosophy which emerged in seventeenth-century Europe, and which has been for quite some time the dominant belief system among western intellectuals. In its typical expressions it has a humanistic foundation, but beyond this it is characterized by its social atomism, or individualism. That is, in the first place, the traditional liberal conception of society is not one of an organic, interconnected whole, but of an aggregate of essentially (though not always actually) rational, self-determining, self-interested human individuals who are only externally related to each other. Second, to this view of the nature of social relations is added the core value judgment of the primacy of liberty in all aspects of a person's own life, and the advocacy of social organization that allows for the maximal liberty of each rational agent that is consistent with the same liberty of all others. In its political dimensions liberalism has provided the philosophical grounding of the democratic constitutions in many modern nation states (both in democratic republics and in constitutional monarchies), and although democratic government as such does not necessarily imply extensive liberties of citizens, it is commonly assumed that personal liberty will most likely not flourish without the legal framework of political democracy.

2. The normative concept of liberty is usually formulated as the negative right to think, say, or do whatever we choose without coercive interference by others, so long as we do not harm others to any significant degree by our choices or deny them their liberty (again, the phrases "negative rights" and "liberty rights" are often used interchangeably by philosophers). If we take this right as morally basic, other things being equal, we all equally possess this right, and thus what we owe each other as a matter of justice is equal respect for another's exercise of liberty whether or not we agree with each

other's choices. So, this fundamental liberal belief in the cognitive ability and moral right of competent human persons to decide for themselves how to live their own lives, consistent with the right of others to do the same, leads to an emphasis on the principle of tolerance as a negative duty requiring acceptance of diversity among people within a larger social whole. It also demands a social environment offering equal opportunity for all individuals to pursue their own interests in their own way, though at the same time liberalism typically has presupposed a general human condition of competition for limited resources, and hence unequal outcomes (since in all competition there are winners and losers) regarding the distribution of goods.

3. Similar to humanism, in the history of liberal thought there has not been any categorical prohibition on the use of intentional violence against fellow humans. However, since the infliction of injury obviously interferes in a coercive way with the recipient's pursuit of self-interest and inhibits one's liberty to act, aggressive violence normally is condemned in liberalism as a violation of the victim's negative rights. The victim of aggression here also is presumed to be "innocent" in the sense that that party has not provoked the attack by prior threats to or incursions against the attacker's own negative rights. On the other hand, in the liberal tradition violence often has been justified if it is in defense against aggression and required for the protection of legitimate interests. As part of this view there has been a strong but highly problematic tendency to treat collective entities such as nation-states, cultural groups, and business corporations as individuals too, and thus strictly analogous to individual human persons in terms of their "self-interests" and right to liberty. Consequently, violence in "self-defense" becomes the operative moral norm at all levels of potential conflict, and is usually extended to the demand that violent means of governmental protection be provided to those who can not sufficiently defend their own interests. So police forces and violent punishment of crime, again, are seen as means of defending citizens' rights, while military forces and war are portrayed both as means by which a state can defend "itself" from aggression by other states or foreign political groups, and as means of aiding some other state or group facing unwanted coercive interference in "its own affairs."

Communism

1. Various versions of what we can call the modern communist belief system started to appear in late eighteenth-century Europe and then really proliferated in the nineteenth century, in response to social problems resulting from

the rapidly evolving capitalist organization of economic life. The labels "communist" and "socialist" have also been used interchangeably often over the last few centuries, and just as often adamantly distinguished by those identifying with one or the other. In any case the common ground has been the rejection of capitalism and the advocacy of an economic system based on the collective, rational control of production and distribution of goods and services aimed at maximizing benefit and minimizing material deprivation for every member of society.

In the Marxist version (see Chapter 3, Section 4) that has had the most influence in shaping communist thought since the latter part of the nineteenth century, capitalism is the most recent dominant form of economy based on hierarchical class relations in recorded history, and since every form of "class society" crumbles eventually (more from internal than external factors), so will capitalism. However, whereas the dissolution of earlier types of class society gave rise to new, more developmentally advanced forms of class society, the outcome of the inherent antagonisms between the dominant capitalist class and the subservient wage labor classes will result not only in the destruction of capitalist social structures themselves, but also in the eventual emergence of a *classless*, egalitarian, cooperative, and truly flourishing society capable of existing without any central government. And historically, those in the international communist movement typically have appealed to this characterization of a radically better, future society as the "communist society" toward which they are working.

2. As a modern belief system, communism clearly is a product of the humanistic tradition, and in many ways builds on liberalism as well. It has a progressive view of human history, more often than not it has been ethically anthropocentric in focusing on making the natural human world a better place, and it presupposes human natural equality and the concomitant moral norm of mutual respect between all individuals. But while it emphasizes personal self-actualization as a primary human good, the communist approach to interpersonal relations is much less atomistic than traditional liberalism and de-emphasizes competition, pointing instead to our social nature, our self-defining interconnectedness with others, and our capacity (and need) for cooperation. In addition, although liberal thinkers usually have argued for democracy as the best form of government for rational, self-determining individuals, communism carries this demand for democratization much further than liberals have been willing to do, to the whole wide realm of economic decision-making regarding what is to be produced/created, how much of it, and who is to have access to it (hence the origin of the idea of "social democracy").

In the typical communist account there is no such thing as an egalitarian class society, nor can there be a one-class society insofar as classes are largely defined relative to each other. Even though economic classes evolve out of historically variable divisions of labor, and thus as social sub-groups are always at least temporarily in relations of forced mutual dependency, they are seen as inevitably arranged in a hierarchy of ownership, control, and power within a specific geographical region. This means that in any kind of class structured social organization there has been a dominant or "ruling" class that maintains its power over the lower classes for as long as it can by political oppression and economic exploitation, whether it is the landed nobility in a feudal society, or the capitalist class as the private owners of technology and resources used to produce commodities for the sole purpose of increasing those owners' private capital, in a capitalist society. This is also why, on the one hand, it is argued that in class society the state (including its police and military forces) is always only the tool of the ruling class; on the other hand, inter-class relations are structurally antagonistic because the objective interests of the oppressor and oppressed classes obviously are in conflict, even if that fact is not always subjectively understood by those affected. The oppression and exploitation of plebeians, serfs, or wage laborers by patricians, feudal aristocrats, or capitalists has been a bad thing over the centuries because it has significantly and unjustifiably diminished the lives of the majority for the benefit of the few. Therefore, the radical transformation of the social world so that it is classless and stateless is necessary if most humans on the planet are ever to have a chance at meaningful freedom, security, and self-actualization.

3. Concerning the causes of violence in human social life, there has been general agreement in the history of communist thought that hierarchically structured group relations, that is, relations of dominance and subordination, are its primary source. The contemporary concept of institutional violence itself is in fact traceable to this longstanding communist critique of economic, cultural, and political stratification reinforced by various oppressive means, especially as such "vertical power" relations have evolved in capitalist society. Along the same lines, all war in recorded history has been caused directly or indirectly by ruling groups (most often dominant classes) interested in maintaining or expanding their own power and wealth, which has required the further exploitation of the labor and lives of the masses populating the subordinate groups/classes.

In contrast to the usual neutrality of liberalism concerning the justification of violence as a means of achieving legitimate ends, there has been an ongoing debate in communist theory and activism about the avoidability of armed insurrection in the effort to transcend capitalism and reorganize society to achieve true communism. For most of the last two hundred years Marxist and non-Marxist communists, socialists, and social democrats have argued about the possibilities for nonviolent social revolution, the effectiveness of armed force versus moral suasion, and whether revolution itself rather than evolutionary change within the existing capitalist order was the best path to follow. Again, what almost all positions have had in common is the belief that physical, psychological, and institutional violence, whether in interpersonal, inter-group, or international situations is largely eliminable in human life, but only with the communist transformation of society. In this view nonviolent, truly peaceful and just, mutually supportive relations between all people are in fact more in keeping with basic human values and aspirations. But, how to get from this alienated, dysfunctional present to that better, "truly human" future continues to be the main problem.

Fascism

1. The term "fascism" is derived from the Latin word "fasces," which were bundles of rods or sticks containing an ax with the blade protruding, carried by "lictors" (attendants) of public officials in ancient Rome as signs of the latter's authority and punitive power. Benito Mussolini (1883-1945), founder of the Fascist Party in Italy and that country's dictator from 1922 until 1943, first coined this term to designate a political doctrine and "whole way of conceiving life," which among other things rejected the humanism, liberalism, and communism/socialism of the eighteenth and nineteenth centuries. As a clearly anti-modernist reaction against those belief systems and against political and social democracy, Mussolini believed that fascism better expressed the destiny of the Italian people in particular, as well as other "superior" European peoples in the twentieth century. As he put it in his 1932 essay "The Doctrine of Fascism": "It is to be expected that this century may be that of authority, a century of the 'Right,' a Fascist century."

In many ways fascism developed as a uniquely twentieth-century belief system which nonetheless still exerts influence today around the world (even if it is not as often called "fascism" anymore), though some of the ideas and values associated with it, taken separately, can be traced to earlier eras. It is also more amorphous and less constrained by standards of rational coherence than the other belief systems discussed in this chapter (except religious fundamentalism, with which it shares a great deal), and in fact is often openly anti-intellectual and opposed to critical thought, so that it has many variations found among different authors, political leaders, and parties. And of course, fascist thought and politics during Mussolini's time was not limited to Italy; most notably, Hitler and his National Socialists in Germany, and Franco and his Falangists in Spain, are commonly identified as fascists too.

2. Fascism generally romanticizes the collective identity of an ethnic group and its allegedly distinctive cultural traditions (including its majority religion), so that the "spirit of a people," or "the national spirit," is treated literally as a greater metaphysical reality determining the essence of all its individual members. The fascist view of social relations is thus organicist (holistic) rather than atomistic, but this organicism is understood politically in the sense that the modern nation state is the highest manifestation of a "national spirit" and deserving of complete obedience by its citizens/subjects. The central government is also then the "higher reality" of the individual, whose own ethical mission in life is to submerge personal interests in the interests of the state, and be willing to sacrifice even one's life to help fulfill the destiny of the nation as interpreted by a visionary dictator or ruling elite.

Fascist thought tends to reject the belief in moral or social progress in human history and denies that there is any overarching goal for humanity as such, though fascists usually haven't been opposed to technological advances. What is affirmed instead is the idea of human life as an eternal struggle of wills, where conquest, domination, and control of the weaker by the stronger are glorified for their own sake, as is competition between individuals, groups, and nation states, and being a "winner" rather than a "loser." This is associated with the rejection of natural human equality and the anti-egalitarian valorization of traditional social hierarchies of privilege and power, making fascism normally racist, ethnocentric, sexist, and classist as well. Since there really is no human destiny, only a national destiny romantically portrayed as being played out on a world stage of conflict with other nations, and since power over others is embraced as an intrinsic and not only an extrinsic good, from a fascist viewpoint patriotism, chauvinist aggressiveness, and contempt for those who are culturally different are virtues, while dissent against authority, independent thinking, and concern for the well-being of all people are vices.

3. Following from the basic belief that meaningful human existence requires struggle between individual wills, and more importantly between the collective wills of peoples, fascism sees situations of physical and psychological violence as welcome opportunities for testing personal and national character, while at the same time viewing nonviolentists and pacifists as cowardly and weak-willed. This

also has translated often into the advocacy of totalitarianism carried out through terrorism and nationalist fear-mongering by the state against its own people, on the one hand, and militarily reinforced imperialism abroad, on the other hand. Further, fascist thinking generates a cult of heroism, where anybody can aspire to the status of hero through any action that can be interpreted dramatically as evincing "the spirit of the nation." This includes both violently reacting to the threat of violence and engaging in aggressive violence as an expression of strength of will, as long as the actors appeal to something like "national pride" or "preserving our way of life." Consequently, in interpersonal, inter-group, and international relations bullying is highly esteemed unless it is perceived to be directed at "Us" by an alien "Them," in which case "our honor" must be defended even to the death, and any death is glorified as heroic if it can be associated with the national struggle against external and internal enemies. Because they involve mutual respect, internationalism, cosmopolitanism, and peacemaking are rejected in principle then, while warmaking and patriotic enthusiasm for all things military are affirmed by fascism as signs of a healthy and vital people. As Mussolini put it: "War alone brings up to their highest tension all human energies and puts the stamp of nobility upon the peoples who have the courage to meet it." Related sentiment was expressed in the 1930s by the Spanish Falangists's motto *Viva la Muerte* ("Long Live Death!"). And, in a similarly romantic vein, a favorite saying among members of the US Marine Corps brings the same basic idea down to a more personal level: "Live fast, die young, and make a good-looking corpse."

Feminism

1. Ideas associated with the affirmation of women's perspectives on life and the feminist critique of patriarchal (male-dominant) society can be found in ancient times in a variety of cultural contexts, but as a more systematized body of thought and as a progressive political movement feminism became more influential in western culture within the last two centuries. Whether manifested in earlier campaigns for women's suffrage, or in arguments for women's civil and moral rights generally (where, again, Wollstonecraft is seen as a groundbreaking thinker in this area), or as seen in more recent theory and activism, there has been great diversity in feminist agendas and orientation to the issues. And yet, there also has been a common thread running through it all which the contemporary philosopher Rosemary Tong has summed up simply as the refusal "... to identify the human experience with the male experience."

As part of this modern (and now postmodern) challenge to patriarchal power and conventional authority, and to the dominant androcentric (male-centered) definitions of human reality, the feminist belief system focuses in the first place on the nature of and the causal factors underlying the male-dominant/female-subordinate organization of most social relations. Second, feminists have tried to illuminate the ways in which this sort of structural hierarchy between the sexes has been damaging to women and to men, as have been the typical ideological denials of this debilitating state of affairs. Third, feminists have formulated many alternative visions of and strategies for achieving a post-patriarchal, truly just, sexually egalitarian society where all persons can live freer and more self-actualized lives.

2. Feminist social philosophy generally and feminist ethics particularly often takes a synthesizing approach to the atomism/organicism distinction regarding the nature of human relations, though the many variations of this appear on a continuum from a strict liberal individualism to a more completely holistic or communitarian view of social entities. The emphasis here is on the centrality of personal relationships (possibly with supernatural as well as natural beings) for individual self-definition and for group identity. In addition, this points to the responsibilities flesh and blood moral agents have for the well-being of others with whom they are in relation and for maintaining the integrity of those relationships themselves. As I indicated in Chapter 1 (Section 4), the "ethics of care" have been developed on this feminist foundation, and in explicit contrast (though not necessarily opposition) to what is often called the "ethics of justice" as the specification of moral rules for exchanges between formal subjects possessing equal, mostly negative, rights.

The focus on the existentially grounding interconnections between nonetheless unique individuals, and thus on real life relationships, responsibilities, and the care principle, rather than on abstract rights, rules, and a version of justice that demands equality though not often equity, usually has been formulated anthropocentrically in feminist theory and practice. But in recent decades alternatives have been offered, sometimes drawing on other more ancient traditions, which expand the range of moral subjects for whom we might take responsibility. On the one hand there are "extensionist" accounts, which extend moral status to various groups of individual living beings beyond *homo sapiens* (for example, all sentient creatures, or all animals sentient or not, or all animals and plants). On the other hand, ecofeminism is an approach that unites the ecological understanding of biological relationships collectively constituting "the web of life," with the feminist critique of patriarchal power and androcentric assumptions about whose interests are more important in human relations. This viewpoint then generates more ecocentric rather than narrowly anthropocentric conclusions about our moral responsibilities as actors with choices, and also stresses that in the same way the socially structured, historically predominant oppression and exploitation of women by men is morally wrong, so also are human efforts to dominate and control the natural world for exclusively human ends. Ecofeminists especially point to traditional western culture in this regard, where the common gendering of this alleged "struggle" between "Man" and "Nature" (as female), and the usually violent imagery of "Man's triumphs over Nature" in forcing "Her" to submit to "His" will, clearly highlight this analogy of destructive power and control.

3. Similar to the debate in modern communist history regarding the utility of violence in radical social transformation, in feminist thought and activism there has been much controversy regarding the causes as well as the legitimacy of violence in the pursuit of egalitarian and emancipatory goals. Part of this debate has involved the question of "essentialism" in gender identity, that is, whether or not there is an essential femininity and an essential masculinity that, among other characteristics, naturally incline girls and women toward nonviolence, and boys and men toward violence. Many feminists, though certainly not all, are critical of gender essentialism insofar as they view gender (as distinct from biological sex itself) as socially constructed and thus changeable, as well as being most often in recorded history the product of patriarchal ideology used to reinforce the exclusion of women from social power and authority. At the same time, it is recognized that in the vast majority of politically organized societies the men have been in control of the available weapons technology used for either hunting or battle, and have done most of the killing. Women on the other hand, along with female and male children, have been in the majority of instances the direct and indirect unarmed victims of physical violence, particularly in times of war. These facts have led to both essentialist and nonessentialist speculation (though no consensus) about the likelihood of a dramatic decrease if not complete permanent cessation of warmaking and most other violent group conflict around the world once patriarchy is finally outgrown.

It is not surprising that the objective differences in the historical situations of women and men in matters of war and peace would lead to culturally conditioned differences of "sensibility" in response to violence over the generations. But, does this imply that women in general are better peacemakers than men have been in interpersonal, inter-group, and international contexts, or would be if they had much greater opportunity to contribute to conflict resolution in these domains? Again, feminists disagree on this, though they would mostly agree that a categorical "Yes" or "No" is unjustified, in light of the complexity of variables involved in attempting such an assessment. For example, some have argued that the very nature of mothering as a practice of nurturing children and protecting them from harm, though culturally scripted, naturally sets up women more than men to be concerned about the impact especially of physical violence on the bodies, personalities, and biographies of specific persons to whom they are somehow related. From this experiential standpoint desensitizing abstractions like "collateral damage," "national honor," "show of strength," "measured retaliation," and so on, are largely irrelevant if not insidiously evil in their use, when what really matters is the actual pain and damage inflicted on sons and daughters, husbands and wives, fathers and mothers, other relatives, friends, and acquaintances. Such a concretized orientation to the suffering and death caused by violence thus can dampen the enthusiasm for it as a means of conflict resolution, and inform anti-war political activism as well as nonviolent strategies in more localized disputes. However, apart from the fact that not all women become mothers and not all men avoid nurturing activities, some feminists also have pointed out that maternal tendencies toward protecting, caring for, and keeping included all related persons, do not always exclude "Us against Them" interpretations of social reality, nor do they exclude the acceptance of violence to negate the threat posed to "Us" by some presumably hostile Other. Still, thinking concretely, realistically, and thus more honestly about what violence actually does to human and nonhuman living beings can help us avoid being seduced by sanitizing abstractions and ideological rationalizations legitimizing suffering and carnage. To the extent then that female experience has generated this way of thinking more often than has male experience (so far anyway), it has a crucial role to play both in intra- and inter-cultural movements to transcend the habits of violence which, after all, have been exploited most often in the attempt to preserve or expand the power and social control of this or that group of men.

FURTHER READING

Section 2

Lawrence S. Apsey, James Bristol, Karen Eppler, *Transforming Power for Peace* (Philadelphia, PA: Religious Education Committee of Friends General Conference, 1986).

Wing-Tsit Chan, translator and editor, *A Sourcebook in Chinese Philosophy, op. cit.*

Vine Deloria, Jr., *God is Red: A Native View of Religion* (Golden, CO: Fulcrum Publishing, 1973, 1992, 2003).

Kwame Gyekye, *An Essay on African Philosophical Thought: The Akan Conceptual Scheme* (Cambridge: Cambridge UP, 1987).

Thich Nhat Hanh, *Being Peace* (Berkeley, CA: Parallax Press, 1987).

Riffat Hassan, "Peace Education: A Muslim Perspective," in *Education for Peace*, edited by Haim Gordon and Leonard Grob (Maryknoll, NY: Orbis Books, 1987); 96-106.

John S. Mbiti, *African Religions and Philosophy* (New York: Praeger, 1969, 1990).

Thomas W. Overholt and J. Baird Callicott, *Clothed-In-Fur and Other Tales: An Introduction to an Ojibwa World View* (Lanham, MD: UP of America, 1982).

Gail M. Presbey, "Contemporary African Sages and Queen Mothers: Their Leadership Roles in Conflict Resolutions," in *Peacemaking: Lessons from the Past, Visions for the Future*, edited by Judith Presler and Sally J. Scholz (Amsterdam: Rodopi, 2000); 231-45.

Sarvepalli Radhakrishnan and Charles Moore, editors, *A Sourcebook in Indian Philosophy* (Princeton, NJ: Princeton UP, 1988).

Allan Solomonow, editor, *Roots of Jewish Nonviolence* (Nyack, NY: Jewish Peace Fellowship, 1985).

Donald A. Wells, "Ambiguous Roles of Religions in War and Peace," in *Peacemaking: Lessons from the Past, Visions for the Future*, edited by Judith Presler and Sally J. Scholz, *op. cit.* 75-90.

Section 3

Chris Hedges, *American Fascists: The Christian Right and the War on America* (New York: Free Press, 2006).

Bruce Lawrence, *Defenders of God: The Fundamentalist Revolt Against the Modern Age* (San Francisco, CA: Harper and Row, 1989).

Martin E. Marty and R. Scott Appleby, *Fundamentalisms Observed*, Volume I of *The Fundamentalism Project* (Chicago, IL: The U of Chicago P, 1991).

Section 4

Joseph Fletcher, *Situation Ethics: The New Morality* (Philadelphia, PA: Westminster Books, 1966).

Mohandas K. Gandhi, *Nonviolent Resistance* (New York: Schocken Books, 1961).

Martin Luther King, Jr., *Why We Can't Wait* (New York: Harper and Row, 1964); see especially "The Sword That Heals," 15-38, and "Letter from Birmingham Jail," 77-100.

Leo Tolstoy, *Tolstoy's Writings on Civil Disobedience and Non-Violence* (New York: Bergman Publishers, 1967).

Section 5

Richard H. Hudelson, *The Rise and Fall of Communism* (Boulder, CO: Westview Press, 1993).

Immanuel Kant, *Perpetual Peace and Other Essays*, translated by Ted Humphrey (Indianapolis, IN: Hackett Publishing Co., 1983).

V.I. Lenin, *State and Revolution* (New York: International Publishers, English edition, 1932); originally published, 1917.

H.B. McCullough, editor, *Political Ideologies and Political Philosophies* (Toronto, ON: Wall and Thompson, 1989).

John Stuart Mill, *On Liberty* (Indianapolis, IN: Hackett Publishing Co., 1978); originally published 1859.

Benito Mussolini, "The Doctrine of Fascism," reprinted in *Communism, Fascism, and Democracy*, edited by Carl Cohen (New York: Random House, 1962); 349-64.

Robert O. Paxton, *The Anatomy of Fascism* (New York: Alfred A. Knopf, 2004).

Sara Ruddick, *Maternal Thinking: Toward a Politics of Peace* (Boston, MA: Beacon Press, 1989).

Rosemary Tong, *Feminist Thought: A Comprehensive Introduction* (Boulder, CO: Westview Press, 1989).

CHAPTER 5

War and Peace

SECTION 1: WAR AND REALISM

Certainly in modern times the kind of violence that has most captured the public imagination is war, if for no other reason than the sheer number of dead victims it tends to create in a short time, compared to other violent conduct. As weapon technologies have advanced, making possible more and more destructive wars at the same time that all human societies are more and more interconnected, the moral complexities to be confronted seem to have multiplied as well. Thus, it is not surprising that many advocates of nonviolent conflict resolution, peace, and social justice spend much of their time and energy pointing out the causes, harmful consequences, and overall immorality of warmaking. But of course to defend the position that war is wrong, or that war instead might be justified in certain limited circumstances, we have to do a little preliminary meta-ethical work once again, to clarify what war *is* in the first place, and what it is not. So in this section I will do this briefly, and then show that war is the kind of activity that at the very least *can* be assessed morally, in contrast to the time-honored and unfortunately still common view often called realism, which treats war as an amoral phenomenon not susceptible to such evaluation.

To start with then, war is an activity of organized group violence for political and/or economic ends, where there are at least two collective parties (or "sides") engaged in a contest of mutual physical injury, and where the immediate internal aim of each party is to out-injure the opposing party/parties. The publicly professed goals of war ("national destiny," "defending national interests," "carrying out God's will," "making the world safe for democracy," "liberation from oppression," etc.), as external to the fighting itself, are used as the rationale for this intentional violence even if they are never achieved, but the war itself usually continues until one of the contestants reaches the point of perceived intolerability of further injury to its own side. At that point it chooses to drop out of the contest by ceasing its efforts to injure the "other side" and to otherwise oppose the latter's actions. The party that quits the carnage first then either surrenders to another party still willing to participate in the injury contest, with the hope of getting it to stop also, or tries to negotiate some kind of truce or other all-sided cessation of "hostilities," conceding to the "will" or agenda of the other group(s). Political commentators subsequently designate the party that quits injuring first in this context the "loser," while the party forcing the other to quit in this way typically is seen as the "winner."

This characterization of war excludes as merely metaphorical or hyperbolic uses of the term such as "the war on drugs," "the war on poverty," or "a war of words," and limits it to human group conduct (at least among species on earth). It includes war between political states in the conventional sense, various kinds of civil war and armed insurrection, wars between organized gangs not affiliated with or vying for control of governments, and war between a government's military forces and armed non-governmental groups based outside its national borders. For purposes of basic definition the distinctions made between "declared" and "undeclared" war, and the uses of "conventional" versus "unconventional" weapons, are thus irrelevant, though as will be seen, they become relevant in determining the justifiability of this or that war.

I am using here a more formal definition of war as a contest of out-injuring, but if we are intellectually honest we can never overlook or deny the fact that all this injuring is first and foremost aimed at living human bodies and their material possessions (in the "boot camp" experience of many US military recruits, one of the first things they are told is that they are being trained primarily "to kill people and wreck their stuff"). That is, weapons wielded by individual persons (working singly or in teams) are directed at other flesh and blood persons in order to kill, maim, and disable as many of those biologically and biographically unique beings as possible, as well as destroy the maximum amount of their injuring equipment and relevant resources such as food, medical supplies, and housing. Even if we can't avoid using some abstractions like "armed forces," "civilian population," "captured territory," "kill ratio," and so forth, in discussing warmaking and its strategies, we must remember that it all comes down to organized, premeditated, concrete efforts to make living individuals suffer pain and death, and make it impossible for them to continue functioning normally as sentient organisms. On the other hand, there is a whole discourse for describing and legitimizing military violence that has evolved historically, which includes a wide range of intentionally distorting abstractions and euphemisms regularly used by those who hope to gain from the carnage, in order to gloss over this central fact about war and make it more socially palatable. These distortions should be challenged and deconstructed if we are to understand accurately what really is at stake when anybody advocates or glorifies war; they should not be treated merely as benign linguistic conventions of neutral political import. Referring to civilian casualties as "collateral damage," the slaughter of local inhabitants potentially sympathetic to an enemy as a "pacification of the area," massive bombing attacks as "surgical strikes," and the use of phrases such as "police action," "theaters of battle," "the road to victory," and especially the abstraction "the enemy" itself, all serve to reinforce the uncritical acceptance of the gruesome physical injuring of men, women, and children of all ages that actually takes place.

The so-called "realist" position on war maintains that questions of ethical obligation are irrelevant in assessing war activities, that the unquestionable sole aim is to win in any way possible rather than lose the war, and that if political or military authorities are unwilling to accept the costs of entering into or continuing a war they must submit to the demands of an opponent still willing to fight. Those who embrace this kind of realism (not to be confused with the usual metaphysical and epistemological varieties of realism also familiar to philosophers) tend to appeal to the old cliché: "All's fair in love and war." They portray war as one of those forces of nature that just *happens to* people periodically like bad weather, or as a situation where all that matters are prudential concerns with getting what one wants and protecting oneself from others, or as a confused conflation of both. At most realism allows for the quasi-moral principle that "might makes right" in the assessment of inter-group and international conflict, putting it more in line with the anti-modern fascist ethic described in the last chapter. In this general rejection of ethical rules as restraints on warmaking or war preparation, self-proclaimed "realists" usually present themselves as being merely "pragmatic" in describing "how things really are in the world," without illusion and sentimentality regarding geopolitical power relations and human nature, and what rational, exclusively self-interested agents can do about it. However, this professed amoral and "hard-headed" view of war and peace also typically valorizes militarism, understood here both as a policy of privileging military solutions to conflict and military "priorities" in economic activity, and as a culturally diffused attitude toward political life, as evidenced in the special status attributed to "our men and women in uniform" because of their regimentation, perceived discipline, and "sacrifice."

As indicated by the realist's tendency at least in the contemporary world to applaud all things military, one of the main problems with an amoral position on war is that it always has been difficult to maintain consistently. In the first place, realists generally have agreed with the strong emphasis on duty, obedience, and loyalty for military personnel within a rigidly stratified command structure, and not only in the sense that one also would approve of keeping a car well-maintained so it runs better. They are after all referring to individual persons "in uniform" and what they should or should not do within their assigned roles; clearly such judgments are not essentially prudential regarding those actors, but ethical in nature. And of course, realists seem to be just as inclined to romanticize "military virtues," "the code of the warrior," and so on, as anyone else attracted to group violence as a way to feel involved in something having a decisive impact on one's world. Secondly, the realist position is used as a justification (more often, as a rationalization) for war, usually in terms of it being in the best interests of the state in a particular case, and where the state itself is treated as the self-interested though amoral actor. But if we break down the idea of the state into the actual relationships constituting it, we see that questions concerning the duties a government has to its people, and vice versa, are inescapable if we want to make any sense out of "the state's interests." Throughout the ages it has been in fact a very common belief that any government has primary ethical obligations to maximize security and prosperity for its own people, even if until recent times the predominant view also was that governments had no such duties to any other peoples. Consequently war has been treated as a potentially effective means by which governments can fulfill these foundational duties, and both realists and non-realists (or "moralists," in this context) historically have either presupposed or explicitly argued for war as a justified option on this basis.

Another major problem with realism (or "war realism," as some label it) once again has to do with the nature of an ethical judgment about voluntary human conduct. Most realists do not advocate a general amoral approach to human interaction, but try to limit it to these "special cases" like war, or business practices in a competitive economic environment, or if they really take seriously the old cliché, romantic relations. But such cases really aren't special insofar as they too essentially involve actors (individual persons or collective entities) who are making choices that significantly affect the well-being of others. In any scenario like this we can always plausibly ask not only what those actors might owe themselves prudentially, or what is best for them, but also what they owe others who might experience the consequences of their actions. Obviously, reasonable people can disagree about what actors actually do owe others in different kinds of situations, including situations of actual or potential war, but such disagreement is by its very nature ethical because to ask what people owe each other is always to ask how they are obliged to treat each other, in other words, what their ethical obligations are to each other given the circumstances. So, choices whether or not to participate in war, as well as choices regarding practices, strategies, and other conscious behavior internal to this grotesque and bloody group contest of out-injuring, all are susceptible to moral evaluation, and the realist position itself appears in the end to be the most unrealistic and self-deceptive about the reality of meaningful human action.

SECTION 2: JUST WAR THEORY

In the western intellectual tradition, the most commonly advocated alternative to the so-called "realist" approach to the legitimacy of warmaking has been the set of interlocking principles referred to as "just war theory." Although versions of these principles can be found in other traditions, including that of Islam, this theory of a "just war" is generally recognized as the original product of medieval Christian theologians who developed it over many years, with some of its ideas being traceable back to Augustine in the early fifth century. During the European Middle Ages, Christianized states were regularly making war on other Christianized states (not to mention all the Crusades against non-Christians in the Mediterranean), with no apparent end of the bloodshed in sight, and many writers saw that merely realist rationalizations of these occurrences didn't really square with Christian ethics at the time. Christian thought during that long era allowed for and often defended socio-economic and political inequality among human beings, but there was wide agreement that all individual souls were equally vulnerable to God's moral judgment, whether one was a serf, merchant, priest, or monarch, and that this was especially important regarding possible punishments and rewards in an eternal afterlife. Thus, a war ethic was needed that met the doctrinal demand for moral accountability on the part of every professed Christian (military personnel too), and which also acknowledged the assumption that God sees our true intentions as well as our actions even if no other mortal can. Of course, we might argue that these theologians should have spent their time developing and disseminating a pacifist ethic more in keeping with Gospel values and the actual practices of early Christians in the first few centuries after the execution of Jesus. But from the standpoint of most medieval intellectuals such a project most likely would have seemed politically unfeasible, and highly imprudent for anyone to seriously recommend to some local sovereign.

As a formulation of rationally consistent criteria for the ethical acceptability of war, this theory is still widely utilized today by both religious and secular thinkers who agree that reasonable people should be able to determine when warmaking activities and policies are morally right or wrong. Where ethicists and other social analysts appealing to just war principles usually disagree is in particular cases where it isn't clear whether the justifying criteria have been met, and also when problems of weighing these criteria relative to each other have to be addressed. Traditionally then, according to this theory the requirements for morally justified war are to be divided initially into those dealing with the choice to go to war in the first place, and those focusing on how the combatants in a war conduct themselves. In Latin this distinction is that between *jus ad bellum* (basically, as "justified going to war") and *jus in bello* (as "justified conduct in war"), which in English is often rendered simply as "just cause" and "just conduct" (or more precisely, "justified cause" and "justified conduct," so as not to confuse the discussion immediately with what justice itself may demand). In the last decade or so some scholars have argued for the need to address a third set of moral requirements as well, focusing on the termination of war. This has been called *jus post bellum*, unsurprisingly, and deals with justified "exit strategies" and the transition to a "just peace." As will be seen, most of the ethical concerns raised in this dimension of warmaking can be folded into questions about *jus ad bellum*, *jus in bello*, and the achievement of both "negative" and "positive" peace, so for present purposes I won't treat *jus post bellum* considerations separately.

Just war theorists identify six distinct conditions, each of which usually is taken to be necessary, that together can fulfill the *jus ad bellum* demand and provide sufficient reason for some collective actor to go to war. Most often this collective actor is assumed to be a state in legal control of military forces, but in recent times the concept has been extended to non-governmental groups that might be engaged in civil wars, revolutionary insurgencies, or other kinds of organized group violence. In addition, states and other collective entities in this approach typically are treated as functioning in a way loosely analogous to how individual persons are presumed to function as rationally self-interested agents who also possess certain moral rights and duties. So for an individual nation state, say, to go to war justifiably against another state, the following requirements have to be met to an adequate degree.

1. *Just Cause*: This demand is seen often as the most important of the *jus ad bellum* considerations, and not unusually is used as a kind of abbreviation for the whole category of right reasons for engaging in war, as indicated above. For most but not all of the theory's proponents, this principle stipulates that war is *only* justified in defense against aggression. In other words, in order to defend innocent parties from attack by an aggressor the use of military violence by a

state is morally permissible; otherwise it is wrong. This has been understood primarily as justifying a state's defense of itself against aggression by other states, in the same way a person who kills in self-defense is thought to be justified. But, many agree that it also includes one state coming to the defense of another state (or social group) under attack, or under threat of imminent attack, by a violently aggressive third party.

2. *Right Authority*: The idea here is that morally permissible warmaking can only be initiated by legitimate political authorities, which means in most cases the legally and/or internationally recognized rulers of a state. Vigilante groups, mercenary adventurers, or independently acting military personnel thus cannot justifiably make that decision for a state or its military forces, or on behalf of a civilian population even in its defense.

3. *Right Intention*: Treated as distinct from "just cause" though closely connected to it, this principle demands more precisely that the intentions for going to war are to be focused exclusively on stopping the aggression being wrongly imposed on the state or some other innocent party, and on bringing about peace. War is to be a time-limited, defensive means for achieving peaceful ends and for "making right" the wrong done in this sense, but not in the sense of punishment, revenge, or regaining the (usually deluded and always artificial) sense of "national honor." Even more clearly, right intentions exclude empire building and other kinds of political expansionism, or "protecting" the predatory business practices of private enterprises whose profits contribute to the "national economy" (or at least to the coffers of various political parties).

4. *Last Resort*: This condition specifies that all nonviolent alternatives in the attempt to resolve the conflict be pursued first, and only when these have been exhausted after serious effort can the resort to war be morally justified. Negotiation, diplomacy, appealing to international tribunals, economic boycotts, and so on, are all more or less nonviolent strategies that must be tried before the obviously violent use of military force is used, as the only way left to protect the legitimate interests under attack in the situation.

5. *Probability of Success*: If a state has vastly less carnage capability than an aggressor, so that there can be no viable deterrent presented, nor significant losses to be inflicted on the stronger party resulting from its aggression, and so that armed defense against attack is only an impotent gesture of defiance unless it provokes other states to come to its rescue, then the morality of such defense is seriously undermined. On the other hand, if the stronger party might otherwise have defensible reasons for going to war against a much weaker party, but it is unlikely to be decisively victorious or capable of bringing about a meaningful peace, or it lacks a viable "exit strategy,"

then the moral defense of its warmaking also is significantly weakened. Put more strongly, going to war even for a good cause with no reasonable chance of winning or forcing peace militarily is immoral, other things being equal (even if it makes for entertaining reading, television, and cinema for some). And again, the essential criterion of "success" here is the achievement of a state of peace that is much more than just a temporary break from the state of war.

6. *Proportionality*: Since all wars cause terrible suffering and death for many people, with damaging consequences even for survivors that go well into the future, it is ethically required that aspiring warmakers answer the question in every particular case, "Is it worth it?" In other words, does the alleged good end to be achieved by war clearly outweigh the total evil (understood in terms of injury and suffering) likely to be incurred, taking into account the impact on all parties involved and not just "our side"? If an honest and empirically adequate assessment indicates that the answer is even a probable "No," then going to war is not justified. Keeping in mind that injury is a disvalue to be avoided whenever possible, and also allowing for the ethical relevance of differential degrees of harm, the "burden of proof" always should be on those who would advocate the extreme kinds of injuring involved in warmaking, rather than on those who argue against it.

Depending on how they are interpreted, there are either two or three sub-principles under the *jus in bello* heading, and they too have been treated as individually necessary and jointly sufficient for justifying the actual injuring behavior of combatants involved in a war, apart from the issue of whether their side was justified in going to war in the first place. Although different military forces in modern times have employed different "rules of engagement" by which they were guided, at a more basic level these official codes of conduct in battle haven't often strayed too far, at least in spirit, from the following "just war" requirements.

7. *Discrimination*: This principle specifies that only combatants on the opposing side and their equipment are legitimate targets of violence and destruction; violence to noncombatants (in most cases, "civilians") must be avoided whenever possible. For example, bombing cities with no significant military installations, slaughtering unarmed villagers who might have ethnic ties to some other combatant group, as well as firing on the military forces of a neutral third party, all violate this moral rule and again would undermine the justifiability of continuing that particular war. And of course, a very straightforward basis for morally condemning all terrorist attacks (whether carried out by government agents or nongovernmental groups) is that they are intentionally unpredictable

and *indiscriminate*, aimed at terrorizing a civilian population into some sort of change in behavior.

8. *Proportionality*: For this requirement to be fulfilled, no more violence can be used than is necessary to "achieve victory," or to achieve the more specific military objective at hand. Allowing for some latitude in determining how much death and destruction is really enough but not too much in bringing about desired outcomes, it would be disproportionate and thus wrong then to kill all prisoners of war after the other side surrendered, for example, as it also would be wrong to launch a nuclear missile attack against a terrorist hideout. In contrast to the *jus ad bellum* proportionality principle in (6) above, this *jus in bello* demand does *not* focus on whether the *goals* themselves *are good enough* to justify the likely carnage that will result, but focuses instead on *how much violence is warranted in order to win* the contest of out-injuring (including how long it takes to "win"), with respect to either particular combat operations or the war overall.

9. *Double Effect*: This requirement is often folded into the principle of discrimination as a way of more fully fleshing out the latter, but it also can be used to make more precise the evaluation of unintended excesses of violence addressed by the proportionality criterion, as well as being treated as a distinct ethical rule. Basically, the principle of double effect demands that intentional violence in war always be directed only at legitimate military targets, but that some unintentional violence suffered by noncombatants, or "innocents" (usually, civilians not significantly involved in the war effort), is morally excusable. It distinguishes between intended results which would be worthwhile, and unintended bad results which are unavoidable even if foreseeable in the situation, if those "good" results are to be achieved. As a way of handling the problem of so-called "collateral damage," this principle excuses the actions causing such bad results (where ethical excusability is even weaker than permissibility and of course much weaker than mandatoriness) as long as they truly are unintended and thus also are not treated as means to otherwise legitimate ends.

Even proponents of just war theory recognize that there are both conceptual and practical problems associated with all of its principles, but they also point out that whatever problems are not entirely solvable are still not enough to negate the value of the just war approach in evaluating particular cases of organized group violence. If the alternatives are realism or pacifism, just war theorists argue that the different justified cause and justified conduct criteria offer the most workable combination of rationally consistent ethical decision-making and situational flexibility, in making sense of the real-life complexities surrounding this fundamentally destructive activity of war. Still, these problems can't be ignored, so I will identify a number of them here without providing either a complete list or the various solutions attempted over the years within the just war literature. In any case, the debate continues on all of these issues.

With respect to the justification for going to war, an initial problem is the longstanding tendency to treat nation states, societies, and other organized groups as collective actors, each with its own collective and presumably rational selfish interests which would be harmed by violence inflicted by some other such actor. As indicated above, in this way of thinking relations between these social entities are analogous to relations between individual human persons, so that whatever a person is justified doing to protect or further her or his interests, a state or society is also justified doing for the sake of its own interests. This sort of conceptual reductionism, however, glosses over the obvious fact that there is almost always a diversity of interests among the many persons making up a larger social whole, and the larger the population in any organized social entity the more diversity of individual and subgroup interests there probably will be. Further, in hierarchical societies stratified by power, authority, and access to resources, the interests of the dominant or ruling groups are often contrary to the interests of the subordinate groups whether or not this fact is recognized by those affected (and which is thus a major factor in the perpetuation of institutional violence, as discussed in Chapter 2). Appealing to something like the "common interests" of a society then, or the "national interest" allegedly shaped by a citizenry, is much more empirically implausible than is often portrayed by mass media commentators and political leaders, and has particularly harmful consequences when it comes to warmaking. In modern times governments usually have employed their military forces to "defend" and/or expand the economic power and control exercised by the small percentage of people at the top of their respective social hierarchies, and have done so at the expense of the less privileged social majorities (from which subordinate populations also come almost all combat personnel). Subsequently, the question of whose "legitimate" interests really are being defended here presents a very serious challenge to any attempt at morally justifying a state's going to war.

Another problem with *jus ad bellum* considerations is the concept of defensive war and how clearly it can be distinguished from aggressive war. Given the typical "just cause" moral prohibition against wars of aggression, we have to be able to determine in actual cases when resorting to war is for sufficiently defensive reasons, but it is not always so easy to tell. Apart from the problem of whose interests within a nation state are to be violently defended by its own military in the first place, when there are two "sides" in a war we have to figure out "Who started it?" and whether, for example, a "preemptive strike" by one side is, or was, truly a defensive tactic or just a propaganda cover for aggression. In addition, if we allow for instances where one state's forces are used to defend another state against an aggressive third party, the complications increase and the lines between defense and aggression, and between legitimate and illegitimate interests, become even more easily blurred. It has been a common tactic after all, for a state intending to extend its geopolitical influence to take sides in a conflict between other states, and pretend that defense of its ally against the aggression of the other side(s) is its moral justification. Also, military intervention by outside forces in a state's internal conflict (often, a civil war) has been disingenuously argued for both as a defense of a government against some of its own people, and as a defense of people against their own government; in either case the international moral and legal principle of state sovereignty is being overridden for a claimed greater good.

A third general problem area in applying the justified cause criteria has to do with the reliability and believability of government officials in their war-related decision-making, including their efforts to increase public support for particular war campaigns. The greater the possibility that these civilian or military officials are incompetent, mistaken, or dishonest (with others and maybe with themselves) in their assessments of the need for war, the less likely it is that these moral criteria actually will be met, and the more reason there is for mistrusting a government's war plans. Now, there is obviously no shortage in the historical record of incompetence, bad judgment, and deceit (not to mention power addiction, delusional thinking, narcissism, and amoral cynicism) amply demonstrated by political rulers and military commanders. There is also no good reason to believe that warmakers in the contemporary world are any better in this respect, and thus more reliable or believable, the advances in political democratization and technological capability notwithstanding.

A fourth problem comes up when we focus on the fifth and sixth *jus ad bellum* criteria, the probability of success and the proportionality of evil means to an overall good end. To put it simply, can we ever know ahead of time that *any* war will be "successful" (as defined above) enough to justify the carnage that we do know will occur? Historians have a hard time even agreeing on the good and bad outcomes of past wars after most of "the facts are in," but the presumed value of these moral principles is in their use ahead of time to decide for or against war, when all of the outcomes are still in the uncertain future. And, even if we do rely on information about past wars to help us understand the possible trajectories of present and future armed conflicts (as we should if we are to avoid the myopic trap of thinking "But this war is different!"), we will find that most wars have not brought about meaningful, sustainable peace after their conclusion, and rather often were instead major causal factors contributing to the start of other wars. So on the one hand, based on the historical evidence, the chances seem very slim that any warmaking in the present and foreseeable future will bring about enough success to be morally worth it. But on the other hand, in light of the inability to determine adequately beforehand what effects the advocated killing and destruction will lead to in fact, and given the untrustworthy nature of the cost/benefit/risk accounts typically offered by political and military warmakers, it also seems that these two justified cause principles become practically useless as moral constraints in particular cases, because they require knowledge of possible states of affairs beyond the combat itself at a level which is most likely unachievable.

Turning to the ethical requirements for justified conduct in a war, in recent times the most often cited problem is the difficulty of distinguishing between combatants and noncombatants as demanded specifically by the principle of discrimination, but also implied by the principle of tactical proportionality. In medieval times when these principles originally were formulated, it was usually quite a bit easier for combat personnel to identify and target only opposing combatants, given the logistics of the average battle and the available weapons technologies (which is not to say that cities weren't sacked and atrocities against civilians weren't committed anyway). It is widely acknowledged that in "modern war," however, the range of who and what may be a legitimate military target has been expanded significantly, to the point where the question arises whether discrimination these days imposes an impossible and thereby nonbinding demand in practice (remembering the moral maxim that "ought implies can").

In the first place, not all combatants wear identifiable uniforms in many ongoing and recent wars, nor do they all separate themselves in daily activities from civilians not directly involved in the fighting. Second, military installations are regularly located in or very near nonmilitary population centers, and in spite of advances in weapons precision and the dissembling of military public relations professionals touting the infallibility of their "smart" arsenals, bombardment of these otherwise legitimate targets usually is not very precise at all (hence the need for repeated attacks), and causes massive noncombatant injury and death. Third, the amount of destructive capability generally is valued over precision of targeting anyway in weapons research, marketing, and deployment, and as weapons continue to become more powerful in this respect the ability to discriminate effectively between classes of victims is lessened, even putting aside the problematic distinction between "conventional weapons" and "weapons of mass destruction." Fourth, many social analysts have pointed out that for well over a century now we have been living in an international environment of "total war," where in effect everyone and everything has become a potential target of military violence. Some have characterized "total war" simply in contrast to "limited war," so that the latter is seen as confined to the intentional targeting of military personnel and equipment on the opposing side even though allowing for some unintended "collateral damage," while the former is unlimited insofar as it also includes intentional attacks against civilian populations identified with "the enemy." Others have used the concept of total war to account not only for this deliberate blurring of the combatant/noncombatant distinction by military strategists, but also to highlight the fact that whole societies in modern times often have become mobilized for warmaking. Under such conditions economic production, cultural creation, educational training, and governmental legislation all turn into domestic "war fronts," and are reorganized accordingly for the sake of "the war effort." World Wars I and II provide the best examples of how industrially advanced societies especially became organized for total war. Yet world history since 1945 also shows us not only the relentless pursuit of ever more powerful weapons which can totally destroy human societies, if not all life on earth, but the creation of a permanent war economy in many of the more powerful nation states, most notably in the US, and this too is an integral part of the current total war phenomenon.

A related problem for the *jus in bello* criteria explicitly having to do with "weapons of mass destruction" is the implausibility of believing that the actual use of nuclear, biological, or chemical weapons could ever meet the requirements of either proportionality or discrimination. The very nature of these kinds of weapons is such that the extent of the destruction they would cause would be so uncontrollable, that as means to achieve specific military objectives (or more generally, to achieve "victory") their use would always be disproportionate and indiscriminate in any realistic scenario. Of course, we could conclude then from the just war standpoint that any use of "WMDs" is immoral and to be opposed always, and that these principles themselves are what justifies taking this stand. But it is not unusual for contemporary just war theorists to be against the actual use of such weapons, on the one hand, and in support of their possession as a deterrent aimed at forcing restraint on potential enemies, on the other hand. A major problem here however is that, given the possibility of accident, theft, inadequate security, bad judgment, and the widely acknowledged tendency on the part of governments to use new weapons once they are acquired, the very existence of functional WMDs still may pose a disproportionate risk of harm to millions if not billions of people, which the ostensibly defensive grounds for such weapons possession by a state would not morally counterbalance.

One more problem worth mentioning in the assessment of these justified conduct constraints has to do with the status of human rights and the degree of their inviolability in times of war. That is, if bombing noncombatants, or using "special forces" to violently terrorize a citizenry, or torturing prisoners, is deemed necessary to achieve victory and thereby is proportionate and at least not excessively indiscriminate, then such tactics are morally acceptable by just war standards even though they clearly violate basic human rights spelled out in international agreements such as the Geneva Conventions and the UN *Universal Declaration of Human Rights*. For those who view the moral rights of persons as more easily overridden by other moral considerations, especially in the extreme situations created by war, admittedly this may not be much of a problem apart from the obvious misfortune of the victims. But for both consequentialists and nonconsequentialists who believe that it is very important to draw a line at internationally recognized negative human rights at least, which no amount of political or military expediency can warrant crossing, a viable criticism could be that the *jus in bello* requirements (including the rationalizations allowed by "double effect") still permit too much in the way of foreseeable abuse, suffering, and death imposed on human persons, and are therefore morally inadequate in the end as guides for the use of military violence.

SECTION 3: PACIFISM

As stated in Chapter 2 (Section 2), pacifism is first and foremost a nonviolent strategy of conflict resolution adopted by a government or some other politically organized group, whereby military violence against another collective entity is not employed or threatened. As an ethical position we might take then, pacifism is fundamentally the opposition (or "conscientious objection") to war and the affirmation of nonviolent alternatives as more justified, well beyond what most versions of just war theory have recommended. What pacifism and the just war tradition do have in common, in contrast to realism, is the initial premise that warmaking can and should be evaluated morally. In addition, some contemporary theorists of pacifism, such as the American philosopher Duane Cady, argue that the relationship between these two positions is better understood along the lines of a "moral continuum" of permissibility, with coherent overlapping occurring at some points, rather than as a distinction of mutual exclusivity. Even accepting a non-categorical approach to the matter, however, we can still see a significant difference at least in theory even if in particular applications of principles we reach the same conclusions. In just war ethical evaluation, war in general is neither right nor wrong as such; if the *jus ad bellum* and *jus in bello* requirements are sufficiently met particular instances of warmaking are justified, and if they fail to meet those requirements they are unjustified. On the other hand, the pacifist position is that war *is* immoral activity, but in most accounts under certain conditions there might be justified exceptions to the general rule.

Pacifists also have often emphasized that there is no single, homogeneous pacifist position regarding war or other kinds of violence, but instead a wide range of argumentation and moral criteria offered from both religious and secular standpoints, so that actually there has been quite a bit of disagreement among pacifists in both theory and practice. In summarizing here the main variations advocated in recent years, I will rely to some extent on Cady's descriptions in his book, *From Warism to Pacifism.*

1. *Absolute Pacifism*: As traditionally understood, this position rejects the legitimacy of any interpersonal, inter-group, or international violence. In other words, it asserts that not only war violence but all violence in human affairs is always morally wrong, with no exceptions (hence its "absolutist" character). This means that violently defending oneself or some other person from a would-be murderer or rapist would be unjustified for the same reasons that both defensive and aggressive war would be so judged, although normally absolutists allow for the defensive use of nonviolent force in the form of non-injurious restraint or coercion. As shown earlier, this position can be found in the principles of Jainism most unambiguously, as well as in the religiously based writings of Tolstoy and King. Again, most people identifying themselves as pacifists have not in fact embraced this absolute moral prohibition on all violence, nor have they accepted moral analogies between the actions of an individual person and the actions of a state, which also often are used to criticize all pacifism as inconsistent. The other commonly defended versions of pacifism all focus on the peculiarities of war itself as the reason why that kind of organized collective violence is wrong, and so are more properly "anti-war" positions (as well as being variants of what Cady calls "collectivist pacifism").

2. *Fallibility Pacifism*: Also sometimes called "epistemological pacifism," this approach stresses the chronic lack of sufficient knowledge possessed by humans when it comes to making decisions about something as complex as war, beyond the inevitable fact that destruction, suffering, and death will occur for many if warmaking takes place. Regarding the causal factors of the conflict to which war is considered a possible response, or the conditions under which the

mutual injury contest would happen, or the likely "body counts," or the other short- and long-term consequences of war, the fallibilist argues that the relevant decision-makers never can know enough to warrant the carnage; therefore in effect, they should follow the maxim "better safe than sorry" as a principle of maximal restraint. Logically, this position would exempt from condemnation a case where enough relevant knowledge was acquired ahead of time to justify warmaking for a good enough cause. But the historical evidence and current global realities speak very strongly against this ever happening in fact, so for this kind of pacifism there simply is no empirically adequate guarantee that any war will be worth all the injury. We also should notice here the practical similarity to, and logical compatibility with, the *jus ad bellum* proportionality principle, although again, there is an important difference: The fallibility pacifist asserts, "War is wrong *because we can never know* if it will be worth it," while the just war proponent can claim, "*If it can be known* that a war will be worth it, then (given all the other just war conditions) that war is morally right."

3. *Technological Pacifism*: Pacifists who identify themselves this way focus on the radically increased destructive capabilities of the weapons of war in modern times, compared to the weapons used in earlier eras (although it is not completely clear where one should draw the historical line between "modern" and "pre-modern" warfare). That is, they will allow for the possibility that some warmaking in pre-modern times was ethically defensible in light of (though not solely because of) the limited nature of the weapons used, but modern technology has created means of such massive destruction of both the "conventional" and "unconventional" variety, that all wars using such weaponry have been and will be into the foreseeable future immoral. Obviously the main concern here is with the practical impossibility of controlling the amount of damage caused by many modern weapons, which again, in just war terms implies the impossibility of ever fulfilling the discrimination and proportionality requirements in the conduct of war. Among the technological pacifists distinct sub-groups have emerged, one of which uses the label "nuclear pacifism" to designate the opposition not only to any actual use of nuclear weapons, but also to all war preparation and readiness that includes possession of nuclear arsenals, given the risk of catastrophic consequences. The development of chemical and biological "weapons of mass destruction" has created an exponentially greater global threat as well in recent times, and thus is rejected typically along with nuclear capabilities for similar reasons. Another sub-group here are the "ecological pacifists," who point out that the technological advances in warmaking have also led to extensive damage to the natural environment in most regions of the world, and so for the sake of the sustainability of ecosystems on which we all

depend, all war must be opposed. We can argue for this kind of pacifism either on anthropocentric grounds (only looking at environmental effects on past, present, and future human interests), or by taking into moral consideration other living beings too in their own right. The critical focus in either approach is both on the destructiveness of war itself and on the research, testing, natural resource consumption, and manufacturing of war products within a system we have gotten used to calling the "military-industrial complex."

4. *Pragmatic Pacifism*: This version of pacifism is sometimes portrayed as imposing the least stringent moral prohibitions on warmaking, by emphasizing only the questionable viability of specific military policies regarding actual achievement of goals. From a pragmatist perspective, our beliefs are justified if they lead us to have expectations which are subsequently fulfilled to a sufficient degree in practice, and beliefs are unjustified if they lead us to have expectations about situations and outcomes subsequently disappointed in practice. This would apply to both moral and prudential beliefs as well, including the reasons given for and against going to war. Pacifists taking this approach can apply it to war in general or to specific wars they oppose, and their argument basically is that war as a means usually does not bring about whatever ethically legitimate ends might be intended, and is therefore unjustified. Put another way, these pacifists are very pessimistic mainly about the probability of success in a given war (that is, the fifth just war criterion), especially if "success" is defined again in terms of establishing meaningful, sustainable peace. They too can point to historical evidence and extensive information available about conflict in the contemporary world, to show that war just does not work as a way to enhance truly peaceful and secure social living for humans, and that the means used really do affect the nature of the end to be achieved.

As mentioned earlier, in past and present societies pacifists often have been viewed with suspicion and hostility, as unreliable and/or subversive members of political communities because of their unwillingness to support military violence as a means of furthering those communities' interests. For example, one of the reasons for the persecution of early Christians in the Roman empire prior to the reign of Constantine was their constant refusal to fight in the Roman armed forces, so that their loyalty and usefulness to the state were questionable. In modern times conscientious objection to warmaking by one's government also has been treated regularly as traitorous and a way of giving aid to "the enemy." Even where exemption from combat duty because of personal moral convictions is legally allowed (depending as well on whether military service for citizens is mandatory or voluntary), those choosing that option are considered to be somehow deviant both officially and at the level of unofficial "public opinion." Further, in civil wars, revolutionary wars, and other kinds of inter-group violence apart from war between nation states, those physically capable of fighting typically are pressured to do so and to take sides; if they instead take a pacifist stand against such participation they quite often are treated very badly.

The opponents of pacifism have used a variety of arguments to discredit it as a viable ethical position, from charges that it cannot be adhered to consistently, to contractarian appeals (see Chapter 1, Section 4) to one's duty to the state, to concerns about it contributing in practice to the perpetuation of social injustice that realistically can only be overcome by armed resistance. Most of the time, however, critics are operating with the prior assumption that the burden of proof here is on the pacifist to show why war should be avoided, rather than on the advocates of war. This seems clearly perverse, in light of the extensive injury and death we know war *always* causes, and about which there is widespread agreement even among war supporters these days (excluding sadists, traditional fascists, and those who believe they can get to heaven more expeditiously thereby) that such effects are bad although sometimes a "necessary evil." Rationally, the burden of proof must always be on those who think such massive harms might be warranted, if they also do acknowledge that harm is bad for those on whom it is imposed and that, other things being equal, we thus should not harm others. Looking at it this way, both just war theorists and war realists have a harder case to make than does the pacifist, at least to start with, and even if social mores over the centuries have conditioned most people to assume otherwise, majority opinion here is not sufficient grounds for privileging any war valorization over pacifism.

Regarding the charge of inconsistency, most often this involves characterizing all pacifism as absolutist, and then discounting non-absolutist positions simply for failing to fit the absolutist mold created by the critics. In the study of logic, this is a good example of what we call a "straw man fallacy," where you intentionally or unintentionally misconstrue an opponent's position, and then go about refuting that inaccurate version while claiming to refute the actual position held (hence the old, and unfortunately violent, imagery of knocking down a straw man facsimile rather than correctly knocking down the real man one is attacking). For critics who avoid this mistake but still want to focus on absolute pacifism, they can argue that it would be impossible in fact to follow consistently a total prohibition against all violence in all conceivable conflict situations. Or, they can argue that even if internally coherent, such absolutism always depends in the end on particular interpretations of religious doctrines which do not compel agreement from other followers of the same religion, nor more obviously from "nonbelievers." Of course, non-absolutist pacifists often accept these criticisms of absolutism in varying degrees themselves, the point being that they can do so without inconsistency.

In response to the criticism by some contractarians that if we enjoy the benefits of citizenship in a nation state, we are obliged (by a tacit "social contract") to pay the accompanying costs including the active support of warmaking for the sake of "national interest," a couple of related points can be made. First, few if any nation states have ever even come close to equally distributing the benefits of citizenship, and to the extent that some groups in a society have less access to these benefits due to the continuing racism, sexism, classism, heterosexism, and religious supremacism which reinforce the social stratification of power, privilege, and the vulnerability to violence, contractarian justice would seem to require what is not usually the case, that these groups bear fewer of the costs. Second, especially if we look at socio-economic class and ethnicity, members of the less privileged, lower status, more materially vulnerable groups are more likely to fight and die in the military defense of the state's purported interests, and so here the burden of defending one's society from threats also is quite unequally shared: people in these groups receive fewer benefits of citizenship while at the same time paying a *higher* price for it than others. Third, the contractarian belief in the moral duty to go to war for the state, or at least not oppose warmaking because one presumably benefits from the increased security one experiences as a result, once again relies heavily on the empirical assumption of a "common interest" which actually does not seem to exist in any heterogeneous, economically and politically stratified nation state.

Finally, a more difficult problem for pacifists is what to do about cases of revolutionary war, civil war, or armed liberation movements initiated by oppressed groups within a society who have been victimized by physical and psychological violence perpetrated by the dominant power groups and institutionally reinforced by legal, extra-legal, and ideological means. In such cases, the aggressors would be these dominant groups in *de facto* control of the society, and/or the governments that do their bidding, and members of the subordinate groups would have finally organized armed resistance in defense against this relentless and violent aggression as a desperate last resort. For people living with this kind of systematic abuse and deprivation, if the evidence indicates that nonviolent resistance and appeals for justice will most likely just encourage their oppressors to impose more of the same, that the future appears to hold only the promise of their ongoing terrorization by the state's military and paramilitary forces, or even the threat of genocide, and that there is no reasonable hope of international intervention, then it becomes much more difficult to conclude that violent struggle to stop these evils would be wrong. Since improving the chances for social justice to flourish is usually a very high priority for pacifists, and is essentially linked with the activity of peacemaking itself for most of them, the possibility that a pacifist approach to oppression in a particular case could lead to worse consequences and more injustice for the oppressed would pose a serious dilemma for an advocate of this strategy. Pacifists rightly point out the need for skepticism regarding the efforts to legitimize military action by states, since such legally protected violence either perpetuates or worsens the existing conditions of injustice in the vast majority of cases. But for an abused sub-group that has very little left to lose within a social hierarchy, organized violent defense against violent oppressors, especially in conjunction with other nonviolent strategies of confrontation, reasonably might be a worthwhile risk. Naturally, the absolutist pacifist would disagree with this assessment, but the other more qualified anti-war positions could treat a scenario like this as involving an excusable exception to the general moral rule.

SECTION 4: NEGATIVE AND POSTITIVE PEACE

Both in theory and practice we can agree that the suffering and destruction of war are evils to be avoided whenever possible, whether we use realist, just war, or pacifist reasoning to justify that belief. As can be seen from the preceding discussion, this "whenever possible" clause also is often the major point of disagreement between these three approaches to evaluating war, while peace is pointed to usually as the goal in any case. But the nature of the peace to be achieved in inter-group and international conflict needs more clarification here, as does the recurring problem of the best means to arrive at that end. For many decades now these issues have been addressed in the peacemaking literature by distinguishing initially between negative peace and positive peace (though there is no unanimity within the peace and justice movement that this is always a useful distinction). Negative peace usually is defined as the simple absence of war, though Martin Luther King also used the phrase more disapprovingly to characterize the avoidance of any confrontation (including nonviolent direct action) and open conflict between oppressor and oppressed groups in the context of the US civil rights struggles during the 1950s and '60s. Either way, negative peace has been viewed as only temporary and as insufficient in itself for bringing about social justice, even if the actual cessation of combat in a war is the necessary prerequisite for establishing long-lasting peaceful relations. "Positive peace," on the other hand, refers to a social environment (local, regional, or global) organized in a sustainably peaceful manner and permeated by practices of nonviolent, mutually respectful, and equitable interaction and conflict resolution. Physical and psychological violence are radically reduced in social conditions of positive peace, but institutional violence too must be undone if this peace is to remain viable and so that real social justice can flourish. Positive peace and justice thus mutually imply each other, and where they do not exist in human life even negative peace remains tenuous at best, and is quite often merely a lull in the fighting (hence the slogan of many peacemakers, "No justice, no peace").

This distinction between negative and positive peace also has been correlated with a difference between anti-war (or "critical") pacifism and positive pacifism, by Cady and others, where the latter approach to peacemaking demands working not only *against* war but *for* social change in the direction of positive peace. Helping to avoid war or trying to stop the armed hostilities quickly once they have started are necessary steps to take, but from this perspective pacifists need to go further with a commitment to the social justice without which the causal conditions for future violent conflict will remain dangerously vital. As indicated above, however, a problem for pacifists is that their vision of a truly just and peaceful social order might be embraced by proponents of just war principles and even by realists, who simply argue that sometimes organized violence is necessary to achieve those goals. The usual pacifist response to this is to re-emphasize the essential inseparability of means and ends in conflict resolution, pointing out that violent means can never bring about sustainable nonviolent ends, nor will even righteous war bring about positive peace. Strategies of large-scale social problem-solving that rely on violence or threats of violence inevitably become (and for centuries in most societies have been in fact) cultural habits that, once acquired, cannot be immediately erased merely by a particular act of will. Although we humans are capable of voluntarily changing our ways, individually and collectively, there is a kind of cognitive and behavioral inertia resulting from habit formation that keeps people trying the same old approaches to new situations perceived to be similar, often long after those methods have shown themselves objectively to be counter-productive. This is why pacifists are generally pessimistic about the chances in a putatively "new and improved" (that is, more just and peaceful) society for successfully "kicking the habit" of reliance on military and law enforcement violence in dealing with new instances of conflict and wrongdoing, if such violent means also were used to dismantle the "old order."

One more reason for being skeptical of realist and just war appeals to the goal of sustainable peace is the likelihood of equivocation in the conceptions of peace they are using in the first place. Using either prudential or moral reasoning,

respectively, to justify protection of a state's interest, realists and just war proponents both move back and forth easily from affirmations of the ideal of a "just
peace" within and between existing societies, on the one hand, to arguments for
"keeping the peace" understood in terms of maintaining the social *status quo,*
on the other hand. Given the economic power hierarchies determining relations both within and between states in the world today, and thus the realities of
institutional violence locally and internationally, calls to ensure the "national interest" or "defend" those interests against "attack" usually amount to ideological
covers for reinforcing the dominance of the already dominant groups as well as
sustaining the relative vulnerability and powerlessness of the subordinate groups.
This way of thinking also has helped to legitimize violent "police actions" initiated by affluent and more militarily powerful states in modern times, in the
name of "international peace and security" but essentially presupposing the
continued global dominance of those same states, in the same way that violent
police action within a particular state is often valorized while primarily serving
the purpose of protecting the existing stratification of power and control. So in
this sense, peacemaking aimed at actually bringing about real positive peace is
undermined and more easily marginalized by confusing it with policies to merely
"keep the peace." As a result, the power of privileged groups remains protected
from serious challenge; those who live in fear and material insecurity continue
to prefer even the deprivation they already know to significant structural change
that has no perceived guarantee of improvement for themselves; and social activists working for radical positive change who, for whatever reasons, go along with
this equivocating portrayal of peacemaking as only "peacekeeping" may well
reject it as conservative obstructionism.

FURTHER READING

Section 1

Carl von Clausewitz, *On War,* translated by Michael Howard and Peter Paret (Princeton,
NJ: Princeton UP, 1976); originally published 1832-34 (3 volumes).

Jean Bethke Elshtain and Sheila Tobias, editors, *Women, Militarism, and War: Essays
in History, Politics, and Social Theory* (Savage, MD: Rowman and Littlefield,
1990).

Robert Holmes, *On War and Morality* (Princeton, NJ: Princeton UP, 1989).

Elaine Scarry, *The Body in Pain: The Making and Unmaking of the World* (Oxford:
Oxford UP, 1985).

Dan Smith and Ane Braein, *The Atlas of War and Peace*, 4th edition (London: Earthscan, 2003).

Mark Twain, *The War Prayer* (New York: The Mark Twain Company / Harper and Row, 1923, 1951).

Section 2

Andrew Fiala, *The Just War Myth: The Moral Illusions of War* (Lanham, MD: Rowman and Littlefield, 2008).

James Turner Johnson, *Can Modern Wars Be Just?* (New Haven, CT: Yale UP, 1984).

John Kelsey and James Turner Johnson, editors, *Just War and Jihad: Historical and Theoretical Perspectives on War and Peace in Western and Islamic Traditions* (Westport, CT: Greenwood Press, 1991).

Douglas Lackey, *The Ethics of War and Peace* (Upper Saddle River, NJ: Prentice Hall, 1997).

Herbert Marcuse, "Ethics and Revolution," in Richard T. DeGeorge, editor, *Ethics and Society* (New York: Doubleday, Macmillan, 1966).

Michael Walzer, *Just and Unjust Wars: A Moral Argument with Historical Illustrations* (New York: Basic Books, 1977).

Section 3

Peter Brock, *Varieties of Pacifism: A Survey from Antiquity to the Outset of the Twentieth Century* (Syracuse, NY: Syracuse UP, 1998).

Duane L. Cady, *From Warism to Pacifism: A Moral Continuum* (Philadelphia, PA: Temple UP, 1989).

Ward Churchill, *Pacifism As Pathology: Reflections on the Role of Armed Struggle in North America* (Oakland, CA: AK Press, 1998, 2007).

E.E. Cummings, "i sing of Olaf glad and big," no. xxx in *VIVA* (New York: Liveright Publishers, 1959).

Robert Phillips and Duane L. Cady, *Humanitarian Intervention: Just War Vs. Pacifism* (Lanham, MD: Rowman and Littlefield, 1996).

Section 4

Marge Piercy, *Gone To Soldiers* (New York: Ballantine Books, 1987).

CHAPTER 6

The Shaping of Public Opinion

SECTION 1: IDEOLOGY, PROPAGANDA, AND TRUTH

In offering brief interpretations and analyses of different belief systems, philo-sophical positions, and moral principles in the previous chapters, I have oper-ated with the assumption that it really does matter what we believe in many aspects of our daily lives, because our beliefs do guide our actions and our actions do affect others in our world. Consequently, when philosophers have tried to make themselves socially useful down through the ages, most often they have focused on how we can choose what to believe based on good rea-sons, and why we should avoid embracing beliefs that depend on bad reasons. Without getting into the long-standing debates regarding the criteria for truth, what counts as sufficient justification of belief, and the variety of "ways of know-ing," let me just point out what also is often taken for granted because it is so obvious upon reflection: Having accurate/true beliefs about ourselves and our world is a good thing rather than a bad thing, because normally it is productive for us in further deciding what short- and long-range goals are worth pursuing and how best to achieve them. But the natural processes of acquiring as well as changing beliefs over time never take place in a social vacuum for problem-solving creatures like us, and clearly we are all influenced in what we believe by other people, past and present. So, if we are interested in social change in the direction of widespread positive peace, it is important to determine how our approval or condemnation of violence, war, and injustice can be shaped by social forces operating often beyond our immediate awareness.

One very powerful, and many would say pervasive, influence on people's understanding of their social world is the ideological conditioning to which they are subject. As indicated in Chapter 4 (Section 1) the relatively modern concept of "ideology" has been employed variously by social theorists, but

I have always found most useful its characterization as an essentially politicized account of social relations put forward on behalf of one group to justify its interests over against some other group(s), especially regarding access to resources and life opportunities. Originally developed in the Marxist analysis of the economic class relations structuring a society and how people are conditioned to interpret or ignore the conflicts and tensions therein, this version of the "ideological" subsequently has been applied to the study of other antagonistic group relations (for example, those of race, ethnicity, or sex), both internationally and within specific nation-states. Where the "political" refers to "vertical power relations" between groups, that is, the acknowledged or unacknowledged degree of *power over* others possessed by some group and the extent to which the others contest that power, the political function of ideology becomes clear, as does its conceptual distinction from worldviews and belief systems as such.

Thus, an ideology provides a description, explanation, or interpretation of some aspect of social reality; it implies (explicitly or implicitly) an appropriate response to that alleged reality; and again, it is always biased (whether or not admitted) in favor of a particular group's interests and against the interests of others co-existing in an environment structured by inter-group antagonism and struggle for power. So, justifying the exclusion of women from the exercise of governmental power and authority on the grounds that they are "naturally" weaker, more "soft-hearted," and more averse to violence in the protection of the community, is an example of patriarchal ideology that goes back thousands of years and is still widely utilized today in rationalizing the male-dominant organization of society. Similarly, the portrayal of human nature as fundamentally greedy and selfish becomes part of capitalist ideology when it is used to justify capitalism itself as a competitive system of production and distribution. Such an account helps legitimize thereby the continued control over and exploitation of the various classes of paid laborers by the capitalist class (i.e., the class of private owners of the means of capital-increasing production) on which this economic system is based. In both examples, the more widely accepted as "just the way life is" these interpretations of human relations become, the more they reinforce the power and status of the dominant group (by sex or economic class, respectively) in the existing social hierarchy, and the more easily marginalized and discounted as "unrealistic" are all efforts to radically critique and transform the social *status quo*.

In the late nineteenth- and early twentieth-century development of communist ideology, as one product of the international workers' movement against the depredations of an increasingly monopolistic and globally dominant capitalist class, ideological doctrines and explanations of social phenomena sometimes also have been openly and self-consciously partisan, even while aiming for as much accuracy of information and understanding as possible. But although ideologies can provide more or less distorted (or to use traditional terminology, "mystified") accounts of social life, and are more or less deceptive as they influence people in one direction or another, most often the extent of their social acceptance has depended on the relative power of the groups whose interests they serve to have them more widely and relentlessly disseminated over a longer period of time. At a certain point then, ideological ideas can turn into habits of thought for enough people that they become socially normative, uncritically incorporated (though not always coherently) into a larger cultural worldview, and transmitted to subsequent generations for a longer or shorter period of a society's history.

Now, it is widely recognized that the dominant ideologies in any stratified society tend to be those that reinforce the position of the dominant groups (again, as differentiated by class, sex, race/ethnicity, age, and so on), because those groups have the most access to and control of the means by which ideas are disseminated and alternative views are suppressed. Second, it has been common for representatives of the dominant groups to deny, often sincerely, that these self-serving characterizations of social relations are ideological in the first place, thereby further reinforcing as well as demonstrating to critics the distorted thinking (or "false consciousness," as some have called it in this context) of dominant group members themselves. Third, inter-group antagonisms born of the domination/subordination relations in a hierarchical society are usually asymmetrical in terms of the institutionally protected power available to the groups in conflict, although in times of significant social instability and rapid change the traditional means of maintaining group dominance can become ineffective and the power differentials can become more closely equalized. On the one hand, this means that without organized countervailing education members of subordinate groups tend to take on and internalize the ideological reality interpretations, including the definitions of themselves and their "proper place" in society, imposed on them by the dominant groups, just as an outcome of the processes of socialization all functional humans undergo from infancy to adulthood. This phenomenon is sometimes referred to critically as the internalization of oppression, and it has had harmful consequences historically for many people, because it results in their conditioned acquiescence to their own seriously diminished life opportunities for the benefit of some dominant, more privileged group. On the other hand, this is why those who have identified with various liberation movements in recent times have emphasized the need for "ideological struggle" as essential to the broader struggle against oppression, exploitation, and violence suffered by many to enhance the material position of the few, in other words, the necessity to "speak truth to power" in spite of the great disadvantages often faced by such dissenters. And fourth, ideological rationalizations for the acceptability of the existing power hierarchy in society also help legitimize all of the institutional violence to be found therein. This can happen either by means of "blame the victim" explanations of people's disproportionate vulnerability to violence, or by romanticizing people's hardship as the expression of their patient, loyal willingness to sacrifice for the good of their community, more accurately recognized of course as the good of the dominant group defined as what is good for all.

The usually unequal contest between these different biased versions of social reality subsequently provides the backdrop for more focused, intentional efforts at persuading large numbers of people to go along with some particular sub-group's agenda. In such situations propaganda is often used to shape public opinion and increase people's support regarding policies and collective actions toward which they might not otherwise be inclined. "Propaganda" is derived from a Latin verb (*propagare*) meaning "to propagate," and refers both to the effort to spread information across a targeted population and to that information itself. As such, there can be both true and false propaganda, and it can be used for either morally good or bad ends. Over the course of the last century the term has in fact taken on largely negative connotations of deceit and "duping the public," in part because its purposes are never value-neutral, so that in inter-group and international conflict one side will dismiss the public pronouncements of the other side as "mere propaganda" in contrast to its own declarations of "the truth." But if a local law enforcement agency initiates a campaign to inform its community of the dangers of methamphetamine, that too is "propagandizing" strictly speaking, even though the information disseminated is accurate and for a good cause. On the other hand, if we want to accuse national government officials of wrongly spreading propaganda about the military intentions of some other state in order to legitimize their intended aggression against that state as "defense of our country," this accusation probably would have packed into it our presumably warranted suspicions that this propaganda is intentionally false, in part or altogether, that it is being used for an immoral end, and that our fellow citizens should be wary of being tricked.

So, when those in positions of power try to gain public support for their policies of violent conflict resolution, what kinds of propaganda strategies work best? Whether we are talking about war-mongering, punishment practices, or the continued suppression of some economically or culturally subordinate group, in general there seem to be three primary approaches to garnering widespread acceptance if not also aggressive enthusiasm that have been regularly employed throughout recorded history, and that are unfortunately still often successful today: (1) the appeal to fear; (2) the creation of enemies (i.e., the "enmification" of some Other); and (3) the appeal to collective identity. These strategies can be used together in mutually reinforcing ways although again, there is no requirement for rational consistency for their conjoined effectiveness, given humans' capacity for responding to what psychologists call "cognitive dissonance" with "doublethink" (as described by Orwell in the novel 1984). Also, other common propagandistic appeals basically have been variations of one or more of these three, such as the appeal to divine will as grounds for violence. Provoking fear of going against this divine will, or portraying the intended targets of violence as enemies of the relevant divinity, or appealing to a divinely ordained duty incumbent upon a community of "believers" against "outsiders," or a combination of all of these tactics, have been regularly employed to manipulate credulous populations. Similarly, dehumanizing characterizations of the Others to be treated violently usually play on people's fears of subhuman "monsters" or "vermin," and they reinforce the "Us versus Them" interpretation of the conflict that strengthens the identification of "Us" as good in stark contrast to "Them" as an evil opponent undeserving of "our" respect or civility.

As indicated above, not only philosophers but almost all people in all cultures assume that truth is more valuable than falsehood in their own decision-making activities, even though in some philosophical systems (for example, in some of the Asian traditions) this "value pair" has been *defined* more metaphysically in terms of the "real" and the "unreal," while in other philosophies (more often in western history) truth and falsehood have been *defined* as more exclusively epistemological properties of beliefs, statements, propositions, and judgments *about* reality. Most people thus would find it much more strange for someone to claim that he/she actually prefers falsehood to truth, than the more common situation where someone asserts something to be true which just about everybody else believes to be false, but where everyone involved presumes that truth is a value and falsehood a disvalue in any case. The value distinction itself is not really problematic here, and the problems (both theoretical and practical) that typically arise instead have to do with whether specific beliefs and descriptions of "the facts" are most likely true or false, and how we can most justifiably decide that. Of course in addition, we again have to recognize the power of emotional need in our *wanting* to believe some things to be true or false even without good reasons, as well as the quite sophisticated human abilities in rationalization and deception of both self and others. Here too the nature of our social relations has an essential and not merely accidental role in influencing what we are willing to believe about our world and ourselves, and is at least presupposed in all philosophical discussion of honesty and dishonesty, trustworthiness, moral integrity, and the "ethics of belief."

As we try to assess situations where violence occurs or is threatened, as well as possible nonviolent responses, we are deciding both what *is* happening or *will* happen in those situations as a matter of *fact*, and what relevant actors *ought to do* in light of relevant moral values and the choices available to them. And, since all of us are located within particular social and historical circumstances that guarantee only a more or less partial perspective on human affairs and exclude the possibility of omniscience, we all have to depend to some extent on what others tell us about how things are and how they should be. This leads to the problem of who counts as an "authority," who is to be believed because of her or his presumed special position regarding the truth of the matter at hand, and the more the lives, deaths, and suffering of sentient beings are at stake, the more important it is that authorities be reliable. If we just take the examples of war, crime and punishment, and the oppression of a particular ethnic group within a larger heterogeneous society, we can see how much most people have to rely on information and assessments provided by others perceived to be more knowledgeable about these kinds of often interrelated, injury-producing social situations, and whose recommendations for action are thereby thought to be worth following. To decide whether another political entity (foreign or domestic) really is a threat to one's own nation-state and thus whether war is justified, or whether someone really did commit a violent crime and whether violent punishment should be used against that person in return, or whether members of an ethnic group are in fact being directly or indirectly suppressed, subordinated, and made targets for abuse by more powerful groups, and whether anything should be done about it, requires in each case input from others who have more access to relevant information and insight than we usually do ourselves, if we are to arrive at rationally adequate answers. None of this is to imply that autonomous thought is not also an important value, and although in past and present societies around the world "independent thinking" has not been a universally recognized good, some version of it is often assumed at least by many scholars these days to be basic to the virtue of intellectual integrity itself. Yet realistically, for conscientious rational inquiry into human-caused injury and its avoidance the issue is not *whether* we appeal to some others as authorities, but *which* possible authorities are legitimate and which are not in different kinds of cases.

The matter is further complicated here by the fact that there are two distinct types of "authority," which are neither mutually exclusive nor mutually implied necessarily, but which are often wrongly and even disastrously conflated by people who have been ideologically conditioned to accept the stratified power relations structuring their society. On the one hand, there is the "authority" that amounts to the socially sanctioned power to coerce others and command obedience, as in the case of government and ecclesiastical "authorities," or the head of a household who wields "authority" over other family members. On the other hand, there is the "authority" of expertise in a certain area of knowledge or skill, which is sought out by others who desire to benefit from that expertise but which does not entail coercive power over any others. These latter authorities again can be more or less reliable, and their expertise more or less extensive or beneficial, but clearly, if you need help understanding a concept in mathematics you consult a mathematician; if you want to know how to cook a certain dish you consult an expert cook; if you want to learn how to electrically wire a house you consult an electrician; if you need therapy you consult a therapist, and so on.

This second type of authority has been crucial to the functioning of any society with a division of labor (no matter how changeable over time), and although almost any kind of expertise can be used for evil ends in individual instances, generally special knowledge or skills become the most potentially dangerous when they are appropriated by the first type of authority in its enacting of policies imposed on the collective whole. Science used to create more destructive weapons for war, religious literacy used to threaten the illiterate with damnation for disobedience, and information technology used to spy on people and manipulate them, would all be obvious cases of this danger. The threat is significantly increased, however, when people confuse these two types of authority and believe that those with coercive authority "know what's best" just because they occupy those positions of vertical power in the first place. This confusion has done a lot to reinforce uncritical obedience to authority in organized society, and the problem is that these same authorities have been, and continue to be, the instigators of the vast majority of violence in human affairs.

If we want to increase substantially the levels of nonviolent interaction, peace, and justice both globally and locally, then we must also always be skeptical of the claims to knowledge and understanding about these topics made by those with coercive social power, and never simply assume without sufficient evidence that they "know what they are talking about" or that they are being honest with us, just because they have that power. It is in this light that we can best understand not only the ancient warning that "truth is the first casualty of war," but also how all social valorizations of interpersonal, inter-group, and international violence have their origins in the interests of those who want to protect or enhance the power they possess over others. Vertical power can become an addiction it seems, so that any injury inflicted on other living beings can be easily rationalized for the sake of this power, and like many other addictions the predisposition for it gets passed on from one generation to the next. Organized peace and justice advocacy thus can provide a kind of "intervention" in response to this especially destructive social sickness, but it requires challenging coercive authority, whether in the governmental, economic, or cultural spheres, and "holding up the mirror" to those who would intentionally or unintentionally cause suffering to others in order to maintain their own power and privilege. And again, this challenge inescapably includes exposing and refuting mystifying ideologies, deceptive propaganda campaigns, and other distortions of the truth used to make socially acceptable the injury and death of "Them" so that "We" allegedly can be secure and prosper.

SECTION 2: ENTERTAINMENT AND VIOLENCE

The anthropological evidence shows that some level of fascination with violence can be found in all identifiable cultures, though naturally most humans have not wanted to be victims of it themselves, nor have they personally intended to inflict it on other humans (the treatment of non-humans is another, and even more complex, story). This fascination is quite understandable as an evolutionary by-product of the highly developed human faculty of imagination, which itself has had essential survival value in part by allowing us to visualize, be fearful of, and make plans to avoid potential injuries before they happen to us or to those we care about. Many sacrificial rituals, for example, and many stories told of legendary heroes, involve imaginative portrayals of violence that would have in common with gladiator contests and public executions a targeted audience interested in vicariously experiencing this violence from a relatively safe vantage point. Of course, often these presentations of giving and receiving injury are supposed to have educational and even "transformative" effects for audience members, but almost as often it seems that their purpose is primarily to entertain people, and it is this latter social goal that I will emphasize here for reasons that will become apparent.

The relevant sense of the verb "to entertain" in this context is to hold someone's attention by offering an experience of something pleasantly interesting, that is, to provide amusement as a temporary *diversion* from other practical concerns. The person who is to be entertained is in a position of passive receptivity compared to the party who provides the entertainment, so that not much is demanded of the former other than to focus on the stimuli presented by the latter (though one can entertain oneself too, and in effect play both parts of this entertainer-entertainee dyad). Hence the traditional associations with "escapism," putting aside for a time one's "daily burdens," temporary freedom from responsibility, and ethical insignificance, all of which make entertainment so attractive as a domain of superficial and presumably harmless pleasure. Certainly entertaining and educational content can also be mixed together, more or less successfully, in particular creations such as a children's television show, a story, an athletic contest, or a billboard advertisement, and most individuals probably come to such an experience with more but not exclusive interest in one dimension rather than the other. But basically the aim of entertainment is to divert attention from the responsibilities of "real life," while the aim of education is to increase knowledge and understanding in ways somehow useful for functioning in that "real world," so they really are fundamentally different in intent.

Even allowing for extensive variety in the cultural scripting of entertainment throughout history and around the world, I think that the underlying motivations of those who seek to be entertained have remained roughly the same, as already indicated: To be temporarily and pleasurably distracted from attending to the tasks of practical life, where one enters into an experiential situation perceived to be disconnected from "the everyday," less "serious" because it lacks consequences that carry over into other areas of meaningful activity, and more a matter of just having fun for its own sake. On the other hand, the motivations of those who provide entertainment have been more diverse historically, depending in large part on what kind of social hierarchy existed and where they themselves were located within it. For example, many political rulers have encouraged street entertainers, circuses, and the like, as a way to distract the lower strata of society from the political oppression and material scarcity they confronted in their daily lives, supposedly making it easier for them to put up with more of the same. Similarly, during the heyday of state-supported violent "sport" at the Roman Coliseum, some of Rome's political elite apparently thought that by viewing bloody chaos and carnage confined to the arena, the citizenry would have a socially safe outlet for its bloodlust and thereby be less inclined to support violent rebellion against the government itself. The actual performers in these different environments rarely if ever had a social control agenda of their own, not surprisingly, but were interested in "giving the people what they want" (within parameters dictated by "the authorities") most often out of a need for income, or maybe as a way to buy someone's freedom from slavery (in the case of some gladiators), and sometimes even out of a passion for performance.

In industrialized societies these days, entertainment options are much more widely commercialized than they were in earlier times, in the sense that the providers either receive payment for the experience itself (say, charging admission to a movie), or they create a product which people buy in order to entertain themselves (for example, a deck of cards). We can still amuse ourselves without spending money, but the commodification of entertainment (which includes the treatment of performers as commodities too) has evolved into one of the most essential and lucrative dimensions of contemporary global capitalism. This is partially due to changes in the nature of the workday for many paid laborers in more affluent capitalist societies, and the resulting contrasts between "work time" and "free time." It is also in part because for over a century now entertainment has been bought and sold both as an end in itself, and as a means to sell other goods and services, most notably in commercial advertising. Keeping in mind that a commodity is anything created in order to be exchanged on "the market" (usually, in order to be sold for money) rather than to be used directly by the creators themselves, and that the goal of such exchange is to increase the wealth of those who already own the means of producing these commodities, we can see clearly how the quest for continuous capital accumulation in a competitive economic environment has fueled the innovations in communication technology during the capitalist era, and subsequently many of the changes in the forms as well as the content of entertainment. We should also not be surprised if, in an economic system completely dependent on constant consumption of commodities (and in light of the discussion in Section 1), what amusement producers are often doing when they "give the people what they want" is to *sell* people what they have been socially conditioned to *believe* they want.

Modern technological advances have led to the creation of thoroughly passive types of entertainment such as television shows and movies, as well as more active/interactive forms such as video games, Internet role-playing games, and paintball contests. But regardless of the degree of physical or intellectual activity required of the "consumer," the old cliché that "violence sells" continues to hold true. The fascination with violence has been an irresistible resource to exploit in the entertainment market, so that whether the imagery presented is explicitly fictional as in a horror movie, or factual as in broadcast news programs on commercial stations (called "infotainment" shows by many critics), titillating audiences with the suffering and death of others is still considered an indispensable strategy if financial gain is the overall goal. Further, like other capitalists, violence marketers try to make their products available to as many potential customers as possible, and want as many repeat purchases as possible with minimal consumer satiation, and these motivations too are important forces driving constant technological innovation. And, if we add to this mix the intertwined though basically conflicting values of novelty and trendiness that have been so much a part of modern western consumer culture, the following scenario appears: Sellers of amusement violence relentlessly expand their reach around the world, always at the same time looking for new media variations and trying to create new imagery (especially more brutal, grotesque, intense images, with more "shock value"), with the net effect being that more people, in more societies, have more opportunities to experience vicariously a greater range of injury, both in kind and degree, as a diversion and *for fun*.

As the rhetorical question goes, "What is wrong with this picture?" Of course, for some the question would be, "So what?" implying the judgment that there isn't a problem here, and no need for alarm. For others, however, the past and present success of the peddlers of violent entertainment implies something symptomatic of deeper dysfunctions in human society, or a cause of major harm in social life, or maybe of significance as both cause and effect of other problematic social and psychological phenomena. Many important factual questions arise here which require adequate evidence to be answered in a rationally justified manner, but I will mainly try to clarify the issue of whether and to what extent violent imagery in entertainment amounts to a form of social conditioning that causes violent behavior in other areas of everyday life.

One position to take is that entertainment violence does not cause people to be more violent in their actual relations with others, and if there is a causal connection it is the other way around, that is, violence in the "real world" stimulates the creation of violent imagery for amusement as a reflection of that world. It is often argued here, first, that commercial entertainment providers are only mirroring public perceptions, common prejudices, and the concerns, fears, and desires of consumers, and thus again are simply "giving people what they want." Second, it is also argued that the experiential disconnection between the virtual violence encountered in novels, movies, video games, music lyrics, etc., and the actual world is marked enough in any case that the former does not bleed into (so to speak) the latter because "people know the difference." A contrary position then would be that heavy exposure to violence in entertainment does make it more likely that someone will resort to violent means of conflict resolution in their own lives, or at least that it contributes to people's increasing acceptance of (or resignation to) violence as a normal part of life in general, which is still to encourage it indirectly. On this side it can be argued, on the one hand, that even just mirroring consumers' perceptions more often reinforces rather than changes them, so that if enough people feel somehow that their fears can be allayed, real or imagined enemies neutralized, and collective identity in opposition to others enhanced by violent means (to recall the three themes favored by propagandists identified earlier), and such scenarios are constantly portrayed for entertainment, the outcome is that the resort to these means in turn will be even more likely in real life. On the other hand, many will argue that even if people typically can make the distinction intellectually between "fact and fiction," or between actual and virtual injury, their feelings and emotional needs can be conditioned to tell them otherwise, and this distinction can break down psychologically in varying degrees. In addition, there is growing consensus among professionals in pediatric care, based on extensive research over many years, that children especially do not easily distinguish between "real" and "pretend" violence, that there is in fact a causal link between entertainment violence (factual and fictional) and aggressive behavior in significant numbers of children, and that children's exposure to a lot of media violence can emotionally desensitize them to real world violence later in life.

In making sense out of this issue I think it is important to keep in mind what kinds of violence are presented in different media for profit-making amusement. What seem like endless variations (again, the more novelty the better) of interpersonal, inter-group, and international violence are offered to consumers, but the violence portrayed here also can be psychological and institutional as well as physical, and it can be treated in particular cases in ways that glorify it more, or trivialize it, or even condemn it. Accounting for all these differences certainly makes analysis more complex, but it can also shed light on a dimension of this causality question not often enough addressed directly: If the concern with entertainment violence is that it contributes to more actual violence in social life, then who are the most likely victims of this causal tendency? To narrow it down somewhat, if we were to focus just on how commercial entertainment presents war, crime and punishment, pornography, and poverty, and recognize that they all involve varying combinations of physical, psychological, and institutional violence, which groups in society will probably suffer the most harm from the dissemination of imagery associated with these subjects for purposes of voyeuristic diversion rather than honest education?

First, as was discussed in Chapter 5 those most obviously victimized by any kind of war are civilians in "combat zones," whether they are killed, maimed, or forced to become refugees, and any valorization of war in entertainment legitimizes that victimization, at least by making it appear inevitable and thus normal. Additionally, in recent history young men and women in the middle and lower classes have been more attracted to military service as a means of greater economic security and increased social status, and because of these needs they also have been more easily seduced by glorifications of state war-making in entertainment as a way of vindicating their choice to make themselves vulnerable to injury and death. Also, whether or not military service in a particular nation-state is by law mandatory, those in the upper classes have not been similarly compelled to choose it and in fact have been able to avoid it much more easily, so that in turn war as amusement would not have nearly as many harmful consequences in their lives, and may well profit them if they are in the right business.

Second, the treatment of crime and punishment themes in various entertainment media usually has relied, once again, on fear, enmification of an Other, and the audience's desire to identify with an "Us" in opposition to some encroaching "Them," often in order to provide the context for portrayals of deserved and undeserved punishment. So, to whatever extent this kind of amusement violence does provoke more "real life" violence, those most likely to be harmed in the first place would be those identified as "Them" within a specific society, whose differences and outsider status in contrast to "Us" make them automatically suspect as potential criminals, stereotyped as less likely innocent of evil, and thus felt to be more deserving of harsher penalties, independent of what a rational assessment of justice would require. Another type of victimization occurs when individuals mimic crimes they are first presented with as entertainment, and act as "copycat" perpetrators of injury to innocent others. Additionally, some harm is more directly psychological, whereby extensive exposure to the amusement violence of crime and punishment stories can cause people to be generally more fearful in their daily lives. To be always afraid is to suffer emotionally, and obviously this does damage to us psychically, as well as affecting negatively all of our social relations.

Third, pornographic entertainment has been included for decades now in the debates about entertainment violence, because the sexual imagery offered to consumers often has involved the objectification, degradation, and physical as well as psychological abuse of some of the participants. Although the dictionary definition of "pornography" has been simply the presentation of explicit sexuality for purposes of audience sexual arousal rather than aesthetic contemplation, another definition originally inspired by feminist criticism distinguishes between "pornography" and "erotica," where both categories of imagery are still intended for audience arousal but the latter portrays the sexual activities of equally autonomous and consenting adults, while the former emphasizes relations of unequal autonomy and the often violent, often nonconsensual domination by some "characters" (usually adult males) of other "characters" (usually women or children). If we assume that this distinction is still useful today and focus on who can be harmed by pornography, the most obvious victims are those who are forced into pornographic performances against their will. Young children are not able to give informed consent for such activity in any case (hence the illegality of child pornography internationally), but many researchers agree that in the case of adult women, most who participate in pornography are coerced to a significant degree, whether the performances are commercially produced by organized crime groups as part of the international sex slavery business, or by exhibitionist amateurs at home for Internet file-sharing.

Returning to the causal question of whether heavy exposure to the physical and psychological violence of pornography makes it more likely that a person (keeping in mind that most pornography consumers worldwide, by far, are men) will inflict sexual violence on others, the evidence generated by many studies has been somewhat mixed but strong enough to indicate a substantial danger here for potential recipients (most often, women and girls) of such "acting-out." Further, the psychic damage that has been shown to occur in children who encounter lots of entertainment violence would generally also result, with its own dysfunctional variations, from exposure to pornographic violence. But adults also are vulnerable to similar damage, even though it would be more clearly self-imposed and they should be held more responsible for their own entertainment choices. On the one hand, pornography becomes an addiction for some people, exhibiting all of the usual symptoms of self-destructiveness and loss of self-control associated with other addictions. On the other hand, since the fantasy/reality distinction doesn't hold equally well for everyone, and the expectations sexual partners have of each other and themselves are shaped in part by that distinction, being a consumer of this kind of amusement violence runs the risk of blurring other important distinctions in the domain of intimate relations, that is, between what is injurious and non-injurious, abusive and affirming, unhealthy and healthy, and violent rather than nonviolent.

Fourth, the treatment of poverty for entertainment purposes regularly mixes in the themes of war (including gang war), crime and punishment, and the "sex trade," and as with the presentation of these other topics also can be compatible with, though still distinguishable from, educational or "consciousness raising" goals. But the voyeuristic amusement derived from stories and imagery of poor people generally does not motivate consumers to attempt changing the socio-economic *status quo*, or even to critically question it. Thus, the institutional violence to which people are subject because of their poverty might be more or less accurately mirrored but hardly ever seriously challenged in the commercial world of entertainment media, partly because it may not be sufficiently entertaining to do so, and partly because it would be to challenge the whole commercial system itself which has generated such debilitating outcomes for so many worldwide. The range of responses elicited by these entertaining portrayals can be anything from "Isn't it a shame" to "It serves them right for being so lazy and irresponsible," and regardless of their own economic status audiences will both cheer on individual characters who "pull themselves out of poverty" to become wealthy, and jeer characters who use their wealth for evil. But the basic power hierarchy of the rich, the poor, and all those in between who live in fear of joining the latter and being ruined by the former, normally is presented as in itself ineliminable and again, "just the way life is." Though the good and bad social effects of this kind of "violent content" in entertainment seem to be mostly indirect and unintentional, I think it is fair to generalize then, that the wealthier people are, the more they benefit materially from the contemporary business of entertainment because it does tend to reinforce this social hierarchy, while the poorer people are the more their vulnerability to harm is enhanced by these same conservative tendencies in commercial mass media.

Even if we acknowledge that violence in entertainment has been a product of human society for a very long time, and that the causal connections between violent imagery used for amusement and actual violent conduct in everyday life are somewhat unclear at least in the case of adults, it is still reasonable to ask how contemporary nonviolentists should respond to all this. If entertainment violence is only a symptom of deeper social dysfunction, then working directly to decrease the level of violent interaction in society would be necessary before that symptom could disappear or at least be significantly altered. On the other hand, if exposure to violent content in entertainment desensitizes adults or children to "real life" violence inflicted on others, or encourages either their personal resort to it or their fearful acquiescence to others' use of it, then trying to diminish those harmful effects by somehow acting against that cause would be worthwhile.

A common strategy historically for limiting the perceived undesirable effects of entertainment has been censorship, and it is still employed today in many societies to a greater or lesser extent. Philosophical discussions of whether censorship is justified in this cultural domain also have been going on for millennia, although often the focus has been on the arts generally and not just forms of entertainment. Leaving aside here the issues surrounding the similarities and differences between art and entertainment, and whether all art is pressured to become "mere entertainment" in a commodity-based economy, the question of censorship is essentially about the appropriateness of social control exercised over created imagery, sensations, ideas, and information that might be made publicly available. The argument in favor of censoring violent content in stories, music, games, and other current forms of amusement usually assumes that some institutional authority (political, religious, or educational) will act as censor, and concludes that by having this coercive authority restrict access to or suppress such content, enough bad social consequences will be avoided and good consequences brought about to warrant this intervention in cultural production. In contrast, the argument against censorship of entertainment violence by the authorities typically asserts that more social harm than good will come from it, because it wrongfully infringes on people's rights to choose their own forms of amusement, or because it paves the way for even more suppression of the personal liberty required for a satisfying life, or because it wastes limited social resources on an effort which mostly fails anyway to achieve its stated goals.

In societies where there is more totalitarian control over personal lives, normally backed up by various religious or political doctrines (see Chapter 4, Sections 2, 3, and 5), censoring of entertainment content would be a consistent, predictable, and probably less contested institutional strategy, even if it was not morally defensible. But in societies with liberal democratic traditions (again, see Section 5 of Chapter 4) any kind of censorship by the authorities will be problematic both in principle and in practice as long as those traditions remain vital, even though commercial entertainment providers in such societies do engage in a kind of self-imposed censorship themselves, based on what they think will be most profitable to produce. And, this leads us back to the unfortunate fact that violent imagery is very profitable in a market economy, though of course violence is not the only thing that "sells" in this context. Sex sells, patriotism sells, and fear sells too; and sexualized violence by patriots protecting the fearful from alien "evildoers" sells really well.

Government censorship of amusement products incorporating these profit-generating themes is pretty minimal in affluent capitalist societies, focusing mostly on token restrictions of access for children, because such content not only poses no threat to the existing political and economic order, but often in fact romanticizes many aspects of state violence (especially in military and law enforcement settings) employed in the protection of "our way of life" and "our great nation," in other words, the economic *status quo*. Even in the case of children, apart from the riches to be gained by marketing violence to them in the form of toys, games, and so on, some might argue that their regular exposure to entertainment violence better serves the government's militaristic interests. After all, if no little girls or boys wanted to grow up to be in the military or the police force because they hadn't been conditioned to see violence as a normal part of conflict resolution and the exercise of social control, what would happen to national policies? So, assuming that living in a liberal democracy (though not necessarily a capitalist one) is better in the long run than living in a totalitarian state, at least insofar as we are part of a large, heterogeneous, and inescapably interconnected population, we cannot rely primarily on efforts at state-imposed censorship to reduce effectively our own and others' exposure to violent imagery in entertainment. Legal challenges to particular products with extremely violent content can and should continue however, at the local level as well as nationally and internationally, and this can be done by appealing to the standard moral limit on the liberty of autonomous actors—*avoiding significant harm to others*—if it *can* be shown empirically that such harm to real persons (or other living beings) does happen as result of the production or distribution of these titillating diversions from everyday responsibility.

Beyond legal activism, nonviolentists can persist in their roles as social "gadflies" and community educators, encouraging open, honest, widespread, *critical* discussion of the causes, effects, and social significance of violence in entertainment. Rejecting the responsibility-avoidant rationalizations that "It's just a movie," "It's just a book," "It's just a game," etc., allegedly having no impact or relevance beyond the immediate amusement experience of the audience, nonviolentists on the contrary can find many opportunities to call attention to the connections between these products and how people function in the "real world." This would require some ability to critically deconstruct entertainment materials and performances, identifying their ideological influences, the accuracy or inaccuracy of their social representations, and even their propaganda potential. But of course many people do this regularly anyway, for fun and for increased understanding (for example, while they are arguing with their friends about the qualities of a movie, or when parents talk with their children about what they have just watched on television). I don't believe that those who are committed to radically reducing violence in human affairs are obligated either to avoid all violent content in entertainment themselves or to condemn it categorically for other consumers, especially given the deeply rooted fascination with violence most people acquire as a result of living in our social world as it has evolved thus far. But I do think we can maintain an

actively critical stance toward the business of entertainment, exercising rational and healthy choice for ourselves and our children, giving priority always
to the educational rather than the escapist value of violent imagery, and refusing to accept amusement violence as an ultimately meaningless product to be
enjoyed by the audience in a temporary moral vacuum.

SECTION 3: REVENGE, RETRIBUTION, AND RECONCILIATION

When nonviolentists publicly advocate alternatives to violence in interpersonal,
inter-group, or international conflict, one of the biggest obstacles in the way
of their being more widely persuasive is the strong human tendency toward
revenge. The impulse to retaliate or to approve of others' retaliation, when
some individual or group is seen as being wrongfully harmed by another party,
has been pointed to for millennia as basic enough in human nature to make
consistent nonviolentism untenable for most if not all members of the species.
Contemporary neuroscience seems to reinforce this ancient understanding as
well, in research showing that brain activity (specifically, in the dorsal striatum)
associated with feelings of satisfaction is stimulated by anticipating opportunities for revenge. Of course, given the injury continuum (roughly, from the
life-threatening to the trivial) that I have been assuming throughout this book,
we should be much less concerned with the desire to retaliate within the rules
against an opponent in a game of chess than, for example, the desire to have
one's government launch a military attack against another state for the sake of
"restoring national honor." But if these are only different manifestations of the
same basic "instinct," how much success is realistically possible for us either
in sustaining negative peace or in creating positive peace in our social world,
when violent "payback" in response to harm inflicted by others just "feels so
right" to so many people? Unless we can effectively transform social conditions
first, so that the intentional initiation of injury itself becomes such a rarity that
most people no longer imagine anything to retaliate violently against, we have
to figure out how to neutralize the emotional attraction of revenge as a *reaction
to* that injury, if we are to bring about reconciliation in conflict situations and
avoid cycles of attack and counterattack which can go on for years.

In this section I will once again focus more on clarifying what I take to
be relevant problems for peacemakers than on providing thoroughly developed
solutions, and I will make more apparent why the desire for revenge, the related
demand for legal retribution, and the benefits of reconciliation are all themes
regularly addressed by those involved in the shaping of public opinion regarding

the acceptability or unacceptability of any kind of violence. Referring back to the previous section, the entertainment value of these three themes is huge in the contemporary world, especially with the visual media now available for presenting stories in many different formats and languages, although they were often the subject matter of the arts in earlier times too. And again, given the problematic nature of the fantasy/reality distinction here, the question has to be raised concerning the degree of good or bad impact on our attitudes toward real-life conflict, resulting from our exposure to movies, television shows, video games, novels, paintings, epic poems, classical tragedies, etc., that portray scenarios of retaliation and punishment as well as the overcoming of enmity between moral actors. Building on the discussion in Section 1, on the other hand, those trying to sway public sentiment as part of an ideological or propaganda campaign often do so by vilifying particular individuals, groups, or whole nations as "evildoers" whose actions must be avenged, and sometimes instead by celebrating the "normalization of relations" between former antagonists.

Whether the aim is to amuse an audience or to put a "spin" on events and policies for political purposes, and whether these agendas are carried out more sincerely or more cynically, the human attraction to revenge particularly as a consequence of moral outrage is almost universally recognized as a reliable force to be exploited in motivating people in one direction or another. But the complex interplay between reason and emotion that generates the demand for revenge makes the evaluation of it as ethically justified or not more difficult than we might at first think. Humans have regularly demonstrated a willingness to "get back" at someone who has harmed them or those they care about way beyond what they know rationally is in their best interests, and in fact even when they know they will suffer much more harm as a result of their efforts. Contrarily, the reasonable fear that they will experience further harm if they *do not* retaliate in some situations often has led to plausible calculations that vengeance must be sought at least for its hoped-for deterrent effect. Both the judgment that revenge is automatically appropriate as a rational strategy of self-protection, and its dismissal as a merely irrational impulse indulged in by the emotionally immature, are probably too simplistic here, even though the values of self-protection and self-control cannot be overlooked by those working for nonviolent conflict resolution in various social situations.

A realistic appraisal of how moral values might be affirmed or undermined by vengeful actions has to take into account the diversity of cultural contexts in which such conduct occurs, and in very general terms I think an initial division can be made between two kinds of cultural environment in this respect. On the one hand, there have been cultures throughout history and around the world where taking revenge has been an ethical duty imposed on all those with sufficient social responsibilities and resources to carry it out, and where failure to do so to an adequate degree has constituted a major ethical violation, though not usually a legally punishable one. Loss of social position, loss of honor, shame and humiliation, and sometimes even loss of life, have been outcomes of failing to avenge culturally defined wrongdoing perpetrated against oneself, one's family and friends, one's nation, or one's religion, and so the motivation for being successful in revenge could easily overwhelm other desires in spite of the toll it would also often take on one's life. The norms guiding the Samurai class in feudal Japan, the ancient warrior culture described by Homer in the *Iliad*, medieval Viking society as described in the Icelandic *Sagas*, and traditional Arab culture in its medieval and contemporary forms where living in shame as the result of failure to avenge wrongs done to self and community is worse than death in the view of many, are all cases where the natural impulse to retaliate has been culturally transformed over time into a widely recognized ethical imperative. This duty became more or less binding on individuals or whole families depending on their social ranking, so that slaves and peasants, for example, weren't usually expected to seek revenge at least for themselves, while it would be demanded of their masters and overlords in similar circumstances.

On the other hand, there are cultures today and in the past where revenge generally does not have the status of moral obligation, even if it is acknowledged (more or less begrudgingly) as an understandable emotional response in situations where somebody really has been treated badly. But even when people in this kind of society have some sympathy for the righteously indignant seeking to inflict "payback," vengeance has been often interpreted as a basically irrational, counterproductive, and socially dangerous reaction which should be strictly contained and discouraged, in large part because it can so easily spin out of control and cause much more harm than was originally expected. In the contemporary world many societies, which during medieval and ancient eras did include duties of revenge as part of their general *ethos*, have successfully made the transition to ethical norms which now devalue it as a sort of "submoral" though still sometimes excusable response, and the difference between the Viking culture of a thousand years ago and Scandinavian cultures of today provides an instructive example in this regard. And, the argument that there has been at least some moral progress in human history (with the implication that more progress is possible of course) is bolstered to some extent by the fact that, overall, there are more societies in the world now where the status of revenge has been lowered from social duty to merely personal emotional response, than was the case in pre-modern times.

Having said that, however, it is not the case that this revenge-as-moral-obligation *versus* revenge-as-personal-desire distinction correlates simply with the loose distinction between pre-modern and modern societies. The ancient Greek tragedian Aeschylus (525-456 BCE), for example, was responding to a recognized social concern in his own time with his trilogy *The Oresteia*, in which he illustrated an evolution from vengeance killing by individuals (first by Clytemnestra and then by Orestes) to a legal trial (Orestes' own) for murder presided over by an impartial judge (Athena in this case). The prosecution here was presented by the three goddesses of revenge, the Furies (who are in the third play eventually called instead the Eumenides, the "kindly ones"), the defense was argued by Apollo, and it was all before a jury of Athenian citizens. Moving up to medieval Iceland, for centuries there was no central state as such, or ruler, but at least once a year all the farmer-warriors in the country (if they weren't off "viking" somewhere) would gather together along with family members and supporters, acting collectively as a law-based parliament (the *Althing*) which had as one of its primary tasks the mediation of conflicts which had arisen that year among the Assembly members. The right and duty to seek revenge for wrongs suffered was legally recognized, but extensive efforts usually were made to employ nonviolent means of restitution in order to minimize the social disruption and hardship caused by violent retaliation and the cycles of inter-family feuding it often generated. In both of these pre-modern instances (one fictional, one actual) the strategy at work is the institutionalization of vengeance so that it becomes codifiable as legal retribution and thus more socially controllable, increasing the chances that public order can be maintained, while still making allowances for the satiation of retaliatory desires without which presumably there would be no real peace either.

In contemporary moral and legal philosophy there has been some debate about how similar or different revenge and retribution really are, and whether the latter especially is only a conceptually or legally rationalized version of the former. As mentioned in Chapter 1 (Section 4), the principle of retributive justice requires that one who has wrongfully harmed others be harmed in return, and that this deserved punishment be proportionate if not exactly equal to the offense. Thus, punishment is justified as "payback" here, as the proper way to "right wrongs" against innocent parties, and to this extent is of the same basic nature as revenge. In arguments advocating either, there is also already the assumption made that if no harm comes to the offending moral agent as a consequence of the wrong done, a bad state of affairs results in that particular social context which must be avoided if at all possible. Further, most of the time in practice *both* revenge and retribution are mediated rather than immediate responses to perceived wrongful harm, involving a varying amount of lag time between the original offense and the actual "payback" actions, as strategies are devised or mandated procedures followed. This fact also then invalidates the argument sometimes made that revenge is only barely susceptible to ethical scrutiny because it is simply a reflex response stemming from animal instinct, and not conduct about which the human individual can truly exercise rational choice.

Apart from these commonalities however, there are some differences between revenge and retribution that are important to keep in mind for nonviolentists, as they try to counter emotionally inflammatory calls for violent retaliation against some individual or collective "evildoer" in the name of "justice." Maybe most obviously, retribution usually has been the province of the state in its impartial, magisterial function, while revenge always comes down to the desires of individuals who respond singly or in groups. Even though we know that as flesh and blood human beings themselves state officials can be motivated by prejudice and partiality too, the legally defined role of judge in criminal and tort cases in principle demands an impartial standpoint assumed by someone not personally affected by the conflict to be resolved or the guilt to be decided, whereas revenge is always at bottom "personal." In addition, as social contract theorists have pointed out for centuries, individual members of a politically organized society retain a basic right to self-protection, but a functional government is much better able to protect reliably and uniformly those individuals from the predations of others. A universally applied system of retributive punishments then is viewed as part of that state protection insofar as it deters future transgressions, even though of course it cannot undo past wrongful harm. Actually, what state-enforced retributive justice aims at reinforcing is the equitable, balanced, and fair treatment of persons within relevant jurisdictions. Thus, the state also should be protecting individuals from unfairness, and when people "take the law into their own hands" it is often because they believe (rightly or wrongly) that the state is incapable of fulfilling this responsibility. Finally, since the primary focus in matters of retribution always is on what wrongdoers rationally deserve and only secondarily on the prevention of future harm, the proportionality of the punishment in relation to the severity of the offense is a crucial guiding principle that does not, however, similarly limit revenge strategies. In fact, depending on what the avenging party can "get away with," disproportionately more severe "paybacks" in retaliation are widely accepted as appropriate (as long as the "good guys" are doing it to the "bad guys"). In part this is because of the assumed superior deterrent value that results, again, and in a related way partly because successful disproportion of this sort has been linked in many different cultural contexts to the regaining of social status and the appearance of competence in self-protection, which were compromised by one's perceived victimization.

By discussing some of the problems of revenge and retribution in the context of efforts to influence people's beliefs about violence, I want to emphasize that such efforts themselves can be for either good or bad ends, and can be carried out either dishonestly to disguise more nefarious agendas, or honestly and openly to improve social relations at all levels. Not all attempts to shape public opinion about "villains" and "victims" amount to merely "duping the masses" more or less successfully (though there has been plenty of that too throughout history), and if we look beyond the demands for "payback" to the possibilities for meaningful reconciliation and the lasting resolution of injurious conflict, the need for widespread public understanding and support, honorably achieved, is especially apparent. Reconciliation involves re-establishing connection and relations of mutual respect between two or more parties who have become estranged or divided from each other in hostility, and it occurs in different ways and to different degrees in interpersonal, inter-group, and international situations. When an individual has stolen from other people in his or her community, for example, the practices of restorative justice aim at getting the perpetrator to accept responsibility for the fact that he or she has harmed real persons rather than "the law," and must take action to overcome the estrangement caused by the crime. This is so that the victims can be compensated materially or emotionally as the way to reaffirm their own value, and also so that ultimately the wrongdoer can be reintegrated back into that community and live "at peace" with the others. For reasons of fairness already indicated, legal retribution is also often part of the process of forcing the individual to take responsibility and make amends, but the goal of *restorative* justice here is interpersonal reconciliation (even if complete forgiveness is not forthcoming) as well as the offender's own *rehabilitation*.

In the aftermath of violent inter-group conflict within one nation state, peacemakers always have to educate the affected population and create as much support as possible for the reconciliation strategies attempted, if they are to avoid having the social pressures to seek vengeance for all of the suffering already experienced build up to the point of causing a resumption of combat. In the case of a civil war, the movement from truce, to negotiated settlement, to disarmament, to investigation and possible redress of grievances, to reconciliation and truly peaceful coexistence or even more thorough social integration, takes a long time and never has a guaranteed successful outcome, with the criteria of success themselves being subject to debate by the different interested parties. And yet the alternative of continuing the violence until one side "finally wins" is almost always contrary to the interests of the large majority of combatants and noncombatants involved (the financial interests of weapons manufacturers and dealers notwithstanding), and people can recognize that fact when they are honestly provided with accurate information about what has been going on, beyond what they have seen already in their immediate experience.

Whatever can be said about the difficulties and benefits of somehow reconciling two or more violently opposed groups within one society applies to an even greater extent when the enemies have been whole nation states. Also, as has been implied in much of the previous discussion, in recent history when government leaders try to mobilize their populations either for war or for *their* version of peace with foreign governments, the likelihood of systematic dissembling and hidden agendas detrimental to the well-being of their citizenry seems to increase, so skepticism regarding the sincerity of official proclamations about international reconciliation, "new partnerships," and "putting the past behind us" remains rationally warranted. Stopping the overt armed conflict between states is of course a good thing, but even after peace has been declared sometimes the violence continues in ways covertly encouraged by the governments (including the military leadership) involved. Further, the official end of hostilities may leave formerly warring parties in a highly asymmetrical power relationship, so that treaties and peace agreements might only be legitimizing the forced unilateral dependency, increased vulnerability to new violence, and *de facto* colonization of the weaker state. Another not so unusual situation historically occurs when states remain in relations characterized more by mutual fear than mutual respect in spite of truces and other efforts at peaceful coexistence (the continuing tensions between Pakistan and India, both of which have nuclear weapons, is a worrisome case here). Still, while we should not normally take government statements about war and peace at face value, and even though the contemporary cliché that "fear sells" is a true one in most societies whether the fear-mongers are "infotainment" marketers or political officials trying to stay in power, and given that a sufficient level of fear *requires* enemies, we don't have to approve of all the relevant actors' *intentions* before we can applaud the actual *outcome* of reduced death and destruction when it occurs, in the case of stopping a war between states. Meaningful reconciliation still may be a long way off, but those first steps of establishing negative peace have to be taken before positive peace has a realistic chance of being created, as former habits of retaliation and mutual finger-pointing are eventually outgrown. And in any case, if we take our civic responsibilities seriously we should not simply accept the historical observation that "truth is the first casualty of war" as if it were a dictate of human destiny. In all matters of war and peace the often acknowledged duty to be informed (national and global) citizens requires that we be willing to assess critically our own and others' beliefs, prejudices, and fears, and the forces of social conditioning that can shape them for better or worse. I think that in this sense, if it is true that there is ultimately no peace without justice, it is also true that there is no peace or justice without understanding.

FURTHER READING

Section 1

Alison Bailey, "Race-Making as the Process of Enmification," 259-72 in *Peacemaking: Lessons from the Past, Visions for the Future, op. cit.*

Harry G. Frankfurt, *On Bullshit* (Princeton, NJ: Princeton UP, 2005).

Nancy C.M. Hartsock, *Money, Sex, and Power: Toward a Feminist Historical Materialism* (Boston, MA: Northeastern UP, 1985).

Edward S. Herman and Noam Chomsky, *Manufacturing Consent: The Political Economy of the Mass Media* (New York: Pantheon Books, 1988).

Sam Keen, *Faces of the Enemy: Reflections of the Hostile Imagination* (San Francisco, CA: Harper and Row, 1986).

Naomi Klein, *The Shock Doctrine: The Rise of Disaster Capitalism* (Toronto, ON: Vintage Canada, 2007).

Kai Nielsen, *Marxism and the Moral Point of View* (Boulder, CO: Westview Press, 1989).

Friedrich Nietzsche, *On the Genealogy of Morals*, translated by Walter Kaufmann and R.J. Hollingdale (New York: Vintage Books, 1969).

——, "On Truth and Lie in an Extra-Moral Sense," in *The Portable Nietzsche*, translated and edited by Walter Kaufmann (New York: The Viking Press, 1954, 1968), 42-47.

Martha Nussbaum et al., *For Love of Country?* (Boston, MA: Beacon Press, 1996, 2002).

Charles Sanders Peirce, "The Fixation of Belief," in *Collected Papers of Charles Sanders Peirce*, Volume V, Charles Hartshorne and Paul Weiss, editors (Cambridge, MA: Harvard UP, 1934), 223-47.

Robert W. Rieber, editor, *The Psychology of War and Peace: Images of the Enemy* (New York: Plenum, 1991).

Donald W. Shriver, *An Ethic for Enemies* (Oxford: Oxford UP, 1995).

Section 2

American Academy of Pediatrics, "Joint Statement on the Impact of Entertainment Violence on Children: Congressional Public Health Summit, July 26, 2000" (Elk Grove Village, IL: American Academy of Pediatrics, 2000); <http://www.aap.org/advocacy/releases/jstmtevc.htm>.

Sissela Bok, *Mayhem: Violence as Public Entertainment* (Reading, MA: Addison-Wesley, 1998).

Noam Chomsky, *Pirates and Emperors: International Terrorism in the Real World* (Brattleboro, VT: Amana Books, 1990).

Andrea Dworkin and Catherine MacKinnon, editors, *In Harm's Way: The Pornography Civil Rights Hearings* (Cambridge, MA: Harvard UP, 1997).

Harold Schecter, *Savage Pastimes: A Cultural History of Violent Entertainment* (New York: St. Martin's Press, 2005).

Robert Weiss, M.D. Schneider, Jennifer Schneider, *Untangling the Web: Sex, Porn, and Fantasy Obsession in the Internet Age* (New York: Alyson Publications, 2006).

Section 3

Aeschylus, *Oresteia*, translated by Robert Fagles (New York: Viking Press, 1975); see especially the third part of this trilogy, *The Eumenides.*

Peter French, *Cowboy Metaphysics: Ethics and Death in Westerns* (Lanham, MD: Rowman and Littlefield, 1997).

——, *The Virtues of Vengeance* (Lawrence, KS: UP of Kansas, 2001).

Homer, *Iliad*, translated by Stanley Lombardo (Indianapolis, IN: Hackett Publishing Co., 1997).

John Locke, *Second Treatise of Government*, C.B. Macpherson, editor (Indianapolis, IN: Hackett Publishing Co., 1980); originally published 1690.

William Ian Miller, *Bloodtaking and Peacemaking: Feud, Law, and Society in Saga Iceland* (Chicago, IL: U of Chicago P, 1990).

Martha Minow, *Between Vengeance and Forgiveness: Facing History after Genocide and Mass Violence* (Boston, MA: Beacon Press, 1998).

——, *Breaking the Cycles of Hatred: Memory, Law, and Repair* (Princeton, NJ: Princeton UP, 2002).

Jeffrie G. Murphy and Jean Hampton, *Forgiveness and Mercy* (Cambridge: Cambridge UP, 1988).

Njal's Saga, translated by Magnus Magnusson and Hermann Palsson (Baltimore, MD: Penguin Books, 1960).

Adam Smith, *The Theory of Moral Sentiments* (Amherst, NY: Prometheus Books, 2000); originally published 1759.

Nicholas Tavuchis, *Mea Culpa: A Sociology of Apology and Reconciliation* (Stanford, CA: Stanford UP, 1991).

CHAPTER 7

Concluding Hopes, Fears, and Dilemmas

SECTION 1: OUR GLOBAL COMMUNITY

In trying to make sense of the human choices of violence or nonviolence, war or peace, and justice or injustice from a philosophical standpoint in this book, I have dealt with metaphysical and epistemological as well as political and moral questions, as they have been addressed in past and present times in many different intellectual traditions around the world. I have emphasized also the inescapable connections between the subjective concerns of the individual person, the goals of more localized groups to which he or she might belong, and the objective interests of vast human populations in various regions of the planet. My general aim has been to provide greater understanding of the concepts, arguments, and real life outcomes associated with the issues identified, but in this concluding chapter I would like to focus on the reasons we might have for being more or less hopeful about the future. In this context of course hopefulness would be directed toward the chances of radically reducing the physical, psychological, and institutional violence in human relations (and secondarily in relations between humans and nonhumans), thereby creating the conditions where positive peace and real social justice could flourish for most if not all people. So really, what are the chances that any of this will happen, or alternatively, to what extent are such things happening already in various parts of our world on the basis of which further substantial progress can be achieved? In circumstances where it seems that progressive social change could occur but it is not in fact, what obstacles stand in its way? And, what can we do about any of this?

Since it is impossible for me here to provide any kind of in-depth assessment of "the state of the world," and there is an already voluminous literature on this broad topic which is being added to daily, let me just point out what I take to be the most important factors to consider before deciding whether optimism or pessimism is more justified. Consistent with the practical principle followed by many peace activists, to "think globally, act locally," we should start with what is going on currently in international and intercontinental relations. This means first and foremost that we must recognize the fact of what is called "globalization," and understand its nature and consequences. This label has been applied in recent decades both to an existing state of affairs actually originating back in the era of European invasion and colonization of most of the rest of the world (though falsely viewed by some only as a post-World War II phenomenon), and to the continuing worldwide dissolution of geographical limits to communication and commerce. Going back to the nineteenth century anyway, globalization has resulted from the expansion and evolution of capitalism, especially with respect to capitalists' desires to acquire natural resources, to create markets for their commodities, and to exploit cheap labor wherever they could find it. For those who celebrate this historical development beyond merely acknowledging its inevitability, globalized capitalism is seen as dramatically increasing the interconnectedness of all humans across cultures and great distances, with the presumed outcome being increased familiarity and thus increased cooperation, mutual tolerance, and mutual benefit for people who otherwise would have remained ignorant about and indifferent to each other. This is judged to be a good thing on balance, as indicated by the positive references to "our global village," "the human family," and so on, even though it has not been equally comfortable for everybody. And, it is admitted that countless new conflicts, big and small, also have been generated through forced interaction between peoples who could have simply avoided each other in the past.

On the other hand, this global interconnectedness and the greater potential for moral common ground it fosters also has evolved during an era when the modern nation-state has achieved exclusive status as the basic unit of political and legal organization in global human relations, with its characteristic features of centralized government, standing armed forces, and penal institutions for dealing with illegality within its (always artificial) borders. Since this kind of state came into being as a means of protecting the economic interests of those with the most wealth in particular societies, as those interests expand over time beyond existing national borders, efforts to expand state power similarly increase, now in the name of "defending national interests." Military adventurism, war between states, and economic imperialism have been predictable results. Even though capital itself has no national or ethnic identity, the largest percentage of it created globally continues to accumulate as the private property of an extremely small percentage of the world's population which does identify with, and seek the protection of, this or that government and its coercive capabilities. The wealthy elites whose home bases are in the most affluent nation-states with the most military might are especially able to wield significant influence around the entire globe, in pursuit of their own financial interests. Apart from simply being able to buy more of the earth and more human labor-time than most other people, they have been able to assert their economic and political power through control of organizations such as the World Bank, the International Monetary Fund, the so-called G-8, and even the United Nations, as well as by pressuring the governments who serve them to threaten with violence other governments or targeted peoples deemed insufficiently compliant. Further, this ongoing agenda of global economic domination gains support from a substantial portion of the population in the "home country" by means of propaganda campaigns glorifying nationalism and stimulating patriotic fervor, coupled with fear-mongering regarding the harmful material deprivation allegedly to be experienced with any loss of "our great nation's" status (that is, privilege) in the world.

Finally, no account of the current international state of affairs should leave out the global weapons market and its major contribution to the initiation and continuation of violent conflict worldwide. "Globalization" here just means, on the one hand, many more chances for arms manufacturers and dealers to advertise and sell their wares to anyone with the money to pay; on the other hand, it means greater opportunities for trained intellectuals from many countries to participate in the research, development, and testing of ever more destructive and mobile weapons. In a capitalist global economy it is difficult to see how this particular type of commodity production and distribution can be stopped, especially given the huge profits to be made within the different facets of the arms business (research and development, production, sale, and resale) and the consequent legal protection capitalists in that economic sector typically enjoy. But as long as the market in tools for inflicting suffering and death continues to be at all lucrative, even with international efforts to impose restrictions, the chances for ending war and creating widespread sustainable peace don't appear to be very good. With no more war there would be many fewer buyers of "the product," "business would suffer," and this would be unacceptable to those who benefit financially by maintaining the violent *status quo*.

If we focus next on more localized inter-group relations, mostly within particular nation-states but also across national boundaries, I believe that the three most important social variables to account for are economic class, sex, and ethnicity. As obviously interwoven as they are in actuality, these three types of social identification are also distinct in their causal influences, and together they go a long way in explaining what changes would be needed in this or that society if the hopes for positive peace and social justice are to be warranted. First then, as indicated above, the relations between the capitalist classes and the working classes (urban and rural) determine the levels of relative affluence and poverty, and consequently the levels of violence and injustice in local circumstances, even while those relations themselves have become more globalized as capital continues to chase cheap labor across great distances. Many intellectuals who support (and who often benefit from) the practices of international capitalism deny that this basic relation between private owners of the means of production and paid laborers is important for predicting the violence and nonviolence people experience, or they deny instead that class differences even exist beyond simple quantitative variations in annual income. But I would argue that class status essentially involves both the degree and kind of relative control over material resources possessed by groups of people within large-scale social divisions of labor, and thus also the extent of the power some of these groups generally have over other groups as well as over their own lives. Less economic power, less access to resources, and less material autonomy naturally mean more dependency on the preferences of others, and more vulnerability to the suffering caused by material deprivation and other aspects of institutional violence. And, in both affluent and impoverished regions of the contemporary world, who isn't and who is subject to these harms is decided largely by who owns capital and who doesn't.

Second, the patriarchal, male-dominant organization of social life continues to be the norm almost everywhere around the world, maintained in most environments by centuries (if not millennia) of cultural reinforcement, and especially debilitating for women in societies where poverty is widespread. Certainly the various strands of the modern feminist movement have had significant impact internationally by pushing gender relations in more egalitarian directions, with respect to both legal and cultural institutions. There also has been a correlation (which many say is causally relevant as well) between growing affluence in particular societies and an expanded range of life choices for the female portion of those populations compared to earlier times, often in conjunction with the equalization of educational opportunities. But compared to men, women worldwide are still much more likely to be raped, forced into sexual slavery, victimized by domestic violence, abandoned with children, kept illiterate, paid less for the same work, coerced into economic dependency, and denied political participation in their communities.

Third, ethnic identification is still a volatile source of enmity between groups both in close proximity and more geographically removed from each other, even though there have been many efforts (not entirely unsuccessful) in recent times to educate people about the benefits of tolerance, respect for cultural diversity, and peaceful co-existence. In this characterization of ethnicity I also include race and organized religion: The former is a politicized conceptual category often used in social relations of domination and subordination, rather than a specific biological trait; the latter has its primary social function in the embellishment of localized worldviews with a supernatural dimension as part of their interpretation of collective *ethos* and place in this natural world (there is, after all, no such thing as a one-person religion). Insofar as ethnicity is socially constructed then, racial and religious identity also are social creations historically integrated into ethnic identity, whether or not an individual is fully aware of that fact in her/his own case. Although the "Us versus Them" thinking underlying violent conflict can be articulated in terms of doctrinal difference ("our true religion" against "their false belief," or "their heresy"), the typical claim that others must submit to "our" religion before conflict can cease is just one version of the ethnocentric belief that "those others" *must be like us* before "they" are no longer a threat or a target for conquest; and if "they" remain different than "us" there is something wrong with "them," so that "they" deserve less moral consideration when it comes to the infliction or avoidance of injury. Sometimes called "tribalism" too, this usually fear-based distinction between "people like us" and "those people" is at the heart of ethnicity, and so deeply connects with many people's emotional coloring of their worlds that it can be easily exploited by those who seek to benefit economically and politically from inter-group antagonism.

Moving from inter-group relations to interpersonal relations, of course we have to recognize that the latter are always lived out within the context of the former, but at the same time the former are really only experienced concretely by individual persons in interaction with other individual persons. And, individual persons respond to inter-group as well as international phenomena in different ways, depending in large part on their beliefs about how they themselves are being treated by some others and how they are justified treating those others in return. The likelihood of a more nonviolent, peaceful, and just future for more people then also depends on the human potential for personally responding to others (both familiar and unfamiliar to the individual) in ways more conducive to the normalization of these values than has been the case so far in most regions of the world. Objective social forces are real and have causal power, but they are not separate "things" in themselves acting on humans as much as they consist of the repeated and often habitual actions of individuals in concert with each other, who can be more or less unconscious of this ultimately intersubjective fact. The human tendency for reification as a way of accounting for the experience of something greater than oneself explains why people treat institutions, social structures, nations, and so on as entities with a life and agency of their own. But fundamentally, these are all just relationships between persons involving more voluntariness or more coercion. As such they are all in principle changeable in the same way any habits are changeable, even though challenging the coercive power of others often does include the risk of physical or psychological violence to oneself as well. Many peace and justice activists for years have acknowledged that subjective thought and desire alone won't overcome violent and oppressive social conditions, in other words, that "wanting it so won't make it so." But on the other hand, objective social change usually happens only because enough human subjects translate their thoughts and feelings into actions leading to consequences, intended or not, which are different from what obtained before.

As discussed in Chapter 3, our understanding of what individuals are capable of doing to improve their social world is also informed by our views on human nature, and my own conclusions on this subject are in line with those who say that humans are inherently neither good nor evil, but educable and malleable within the limits of our genetic code. As a species of social animal, we have the potential to develop both undesirable traits (for example, egoism, cruelty, cowardice, vindictiveness) and desirable traits (for example, sympathy, kindness, courage, generosity). We also have basic physical and psychological needs that seem to be transcultural and transhistorical, with the degree of their fulfillment determining to quite an extent whether we actualize these other potentialities. The needs for basic health, adequate nutrition and hydration, shelter, safety, affirmation and respect from others, positive self-image, as well as the sense of belonging or being "at home" in some social environment, and some experience of pleasure along with the minimization of pain, are all pretty much universal for biologically functional members of our species, though there always has been great diversity in how these needs are culturally scripted, interpreted, and acted on. When people feel threatened in their efforts to provide for these needs, they usually become fearful, and fear can easily lead to hostility directed at actual or imagined others associated with the threat. A great deal of interpersonal conflict as well as "Us versus Them" thinking thus has resulted from the failure, and the fear of failure, in the meeting of these basic human needs, and has been exacerbated by fears of personal inadequacy, humiliation, and powerlessness. Obviously, the less fearful individuals are, the less likely they are to become hostile and hateful to others, and the less likely they are to resort to violence themselves or feel compelled to accept its use by those who claim to provide protection against alleged enemies.

If this overview of how things are in the world at present is accurate, and if the moral goal is to maximize nonviolence, positive peace, and social justice in human affairs, and if we also keep in mind the dictum that "ought implies can," then we can focus next on what moral agents can do realistically to make progress toward that goal from this time forward. Given the rich and multi-faceted history of peace activism in modern times (not to mention the various traditions of peacemaking going back millennia), agendas for progressive social change will for the most part amount to a continuation and expansion of previous efforts, both by building on past achievements and learning from past failures. There are already countless organizations devoted to these ends in most parts of the contemporary world, and a wide range of resources available to individuals who want to contribute to the transformation of social relations locally and globally by the radical reduction of physical, psychological, and institutional violence. The recognition that not only personal change, but also national and international systemic change is needed naturally will lead some people to see the problems involved as so overwhelming and complex that they give up hope. But we should never underestimate the value of what true peacemakers have actually accomplished thus far around the world using a variety of official and unofficial, and legal as well as illegal means, even though the tasks have not been completed and obviously much more needs to be done. As bad as things are for hundreds of millions of people today, without past and present organized movements against slavery, "sweatshop labor," war, the production and deployment of "weapons of mass destruction," and colonial occupation, and for gender equity, civil rights, and environmental protection (just to mention a few), things would be even worse now for more people, as they also would be without the late twentieth-century establishment of the various international conventions on human rights. Partial successes in these areas of moral concern seem clearly preferable to no success at all, and similarly, although no one person can "do everything" and significant social change rarely happens immediately, almost everyone can "do something" productive if they have adequate information about their own and others' circumstances.

In thinking about moral agents taking responsibility for social change, since a good deal of the discussion and action will be unavoidably political in nature, it is always crucial for citizens to be willing to pressure their government officials and those with the most economic power in their country, by all means possible, to either change their ways or get out of the way so that those committed to the creation of positive peace can exercise more influence. At the same time, it is irrational to criticize or praise what we do not understand, so educating ourselves and supporting the education of others regarding the relevant issues is essential, with respect to both factual information and value choices. Unfortunately, but inevitably, this means we will have to wade into the ideological morass of what passes for public political discourse these days, where "spin" is often more highly valued than truth, self-deception can parade as forthrightness, rationalization easily replaces good reasoning, half-truths are manufactured to distract us from pursuing accurate understanding, and the addiction to power over others (directly or vicariously experienced) as well as the fearfulness which is its source masquerade as "realism" and "political savvy." But as discouraging as it can be to confront constantly the shameless dissembling and relentless distortions of social reality aimed at legitimizing the violence- and injustice-dependent *status quo*, giving in to the temptation to simply respond in kind in the name of superior moral aims is counter-productive, if we really want to increase our knowledge of how to go about actually improving our world. Even though these truly are life and death matters for many people, so that patience in our analyses of problems and their possible solutions may seem like a luxury, there really is no substitute for careful empirical investigation and honest rational reflection regarding *what is, what can be,* and *what ought to be.*

As indicated above, governmental and especially nongovernmental organizations (NGOs) focusing on education (for example) and motivated by a peace and justice agenda already exist in many countries, and often among poorer populations an educational priority has been promoting basic literacy, widely acknowledged as one of the single most socially empowering changes a person can make in her or his life. As some of these organizations disband new ones are formed, some operating at a more "grass roots" level among the urban and rural working classes, while others are affiliated with academic or other public institutions as research or training centers for peacemaking and nonviolent conflict resolution. And of course, in a growing number of colleges and universities at least in affluent countries regular programs in Peace Studies also are now offered. Although classroom learning doesn't necessarily lead to social change, it can provide the impetus for taking significant action, and to this extent an increasing interest in formal academic as well as more directly experiential peace education is a hopeful sign.

In any case, wherever education campaigns are successfully carried out, one important outcome is that people learn to see that they have choices of what to believe on many topics of concern, that there are better and worse reasons for making the choices they do, and that they are thus able to choose to believe that which is most rationally warranted in comparison with the alternatives. This may put individuals at odds with the prevailing norms of their community or with their own upbringing, but if progressive social change is the goal and thought is what guides conduct, existing habits of thought may have to be given up and new ways of understanding one's world embraced. Again, humans *are capable* of doing this, and even though they are social animals and need some kind of social reinforcement for changing their beliefs, that same need which helps conserve old assumptions independent of their actual truth or falsehood also can motivate people to seek out other people similarly open to thinking beyond what is customary, until the point is reached where they can act together on these consciously chosen beliefs to bring about objective social improvement.

On the basis of relevant education, concerned individuals can direct their energies to any of a number of complex social problems, none of them new, having local and global implications for the amount of violence to which people might be subjected. For instance, one obvious goal of peace activists for a long time has been the demilitarization of human relations, which includes getting rid of all weapons of war as rapidly as possible ("conventional" weapons as well as "WMDs"), and getting governments to dispense with other military expenditures (for personnel, bureaucracy, research and development, and so on). This should also include changing the culture to de-romanticize and de-valorize contemporary "military service" and the anachronistic cult of the warrior. Another obvious obstacle in the way of widespread peace and social justice is the maldistribution of material wealth in most parts of the world, resulting from a competitive economic system over the last few centuries whereby one party (the winner) typically only gains at the expense of another party (the loser). Even though the concepts of poverty and wealth are not always as clear and uncontestable as we might assume, we must also resist the temptation to hide behind some kind of relativistic filter allowing us to ignore the realities of malnutrition, disease, unsafe housing, and the other aspects of institutional violence to which the poor are chronically vulnerable. Continuing efforts by anyone who *can* help thus are needed to maximize local and regional economic self-sufficiency (though *not* isolation), relying on environmentally sustainable practices of resource and technology utilization, and especially aimed at impoverished populations which have ended up existing from one generation to the next in conditions of economic dependency on the desires of the affluent, lacking functional life opportunities, meaningful autonomy, and all reason to hope for anything better in this mortal domain.

Such efforts can work hand in hand with all other efforts to transform economic relations in both (currently) rich and poor countries, from systematized competition, antagonism, and hierarchies of power, to systems of cooperation and true social democracy. Success in this area can in turn contribute to agendas of disarmament and demilitarization, since again, economic competition leads to competition between states (and sometimes between political groups within states), which leads to military conflict, which causes large-scale death and destruction.

Instead of acquiescing to the nationalistic interpretation of domestic and foreign affairs, and bowing to the social pressures to appear patriotic, those who want international peace and justice should promote internationalism whenever they can, and condition themselves to think in cosmopolitan terms, identifying themselves as "citizens of the world" rather than having emotional ties to any one nation-state. But, until enough people get over the unjustified belief that sovereign nation-states should remain the basic units of global political organization, it is reasonable to support as best we can international policymaking organizations such as the United Nations itself, and the World Court, insofar as they operate on the principles of equal protection of positive and negative human rights, and honorable cooperation among states for the benefit of all, rather than to simply reinforce domination by an elite few. Along with this would go anything to help strengthen international law and its consistent, equitable application in relevant conflict situations, including the pressure on governments to respect it in the first place and to commit to abiding by international legal rulings.

Finally, the connections between war and social injustice on the one hand, and environmental destruction on the other hand, have been pointed out for years, and since the causality often has been reciprocal, programs to stop or even reverse damage to the natural environment (again, locally and globally) can contribute to peacemaking and the overcoming of poverty, and vice-versa. However, it is my impression that until recently many people's hopes for substantial reductions in interpersonal, inter-group, and international violence have not really accounted for the impact of future natural disasters on fundamental social change. Of course, history is full of documented examples of how volcanic eruptions, earthquakes, droughts, hurricanes, and so on, have destroyed cities and even whole civilizations, forced migrations, and rearranged political relationships. And, the movie business has cranked out endless, more or less apocalyptic "disaster films" (which really would include the majority of alien invasion films too), many of which show humans putting all their differences aside as they unite across cultural, national, and class boundaries to deal with a common threat from some nonhuman source. But more serious analysis of whether the potentials for nonviolence in human affairs would be diminished or enhanced by extremely disruptive, socially destabilizing natural events is needed, apart from questions about the human role in the causes of some of these phenomena.

Such a focus is especially crucial as people learn more and more about the dangerous consequences of worldwide climate change caused by global warming. No matter how hopeful we are about human nature and our natural abilities to function peacefully and avoid violent conflict, once the effects of global warming as currently projected do come into play, significant social change will be inevitable along with a great deal of conflict. Whether this conflict will be managed more violently or nonviolently is hard to predict at this point, but it is clearly within the range of human choice in either direction. So, as yet one more reason for demanding an internationalist rather than a nationalist approach to solving complex social problems, likely global disasters require coordinated global responses, and thus all possible support should be given to international *cooperative* rather than *competitive* efforts to prepare for such eventualities, if we care about minimizing harm to all those who will be affected and maximizing the future chances for positive peace.

SECTION 2: DILEMMAS IN THE STRUGGLE FOR SOCIAL JUSTICE

To complete these brief reflections on the causes and effects of physical, psychological, and institutional/structural violence in interpersonal, inter-group, and international relations, and the possibility of changing all this for the better, I will identify two practical problems that must be confronted by everyone seriously interested in creating socially just environments of lasting peace. First, as discussed in earlier chapters difficult decisions have to be made regarding the connections between means and ends, especially, whether violent means can ever be used justifiably in order to achieve peace and justice. Gandhi and King always warned against the temptation to use violence to end violence, as have many other nonviolentists in modern times, primarily on the grounds that the very nature of the means used substantially affects the nature of the outcome, so that only nonviolent strategies can lead to truly peaceful results. But the majority of those identifying themselves as nonviolentists and/or pacifists have not taken an absolutist position on this issue anyway (including Gandhi himself), so from their standpoint, the problem remains of determining when responding to violence with violence would be defensible, at least as an exception to the rule.

When an individual is confronted by a violent attacker, we might easily conclude that as a last resort (that is, if fleeing to avoid the situation is not possible), violent self-defense would be appropriate. But is violent punishment of violent crime, or the threat of violence as a deterrent to future crime, the best approach to minimizing interpersonal violence? If the goal is the significant reduction of crimes against persons and property, and the causes of most such crimes are traceable to various socio-economic conditions rather than simply to an insufficient personal fear of punishment, and the evidence shows that threatened violence does not make people more nonviolent in the long run, then dealing effectively with those underlying conditions deserves much more emphasis than merely reacting to their violent symptoms (the image of putting a bandaid on a cancer comes to mind here).

Further, within a particular heterogeneous society where some groups have been victimized by systematic oppression, exploitation, and deprivation by some politically dominant group (usually with direct or indirect aid from governmental forces), the question regarding legitimate means of defense against such abuse also must be addressed. To use the example again of the treatment of African Americans by white Americans and white-controlled local, state, and national governments throughout US history, there were those like Martin Luther King, on the one hand, who argued for nonviolent active resistance to and confrontation with the oppressors. On the other hand, others during the same era like Malcolm X, and different representatives of the Black Panther Party, argued that armed defense against legally protected and extra-legal white racist violence was morally justified when necessary. On both sides of this debate there was acknowledgment that the ends to be achieved had to do with both the security of black citizens constantly at risk in the face of hostile political and cultural forces in US society, and the need for radical social change so that all citizens eventually could co-exist in peaceful, respectful, and just relations regardless of racial affiliations. Thus, the problem often came down to which set of strategies was going to lead to more success in accomplishing these worthwhile goals, and yet even from our present vantage point decades after the assassination of progressive leaders like Malcolm X and King, this means-ends debate has not been clearly resolved by pointing to what has happened since, and we are often left speculating about "What would have happened, if ...?" And, even though every group conflict situation is unique in some ways, this issue of violent *versus* nonviolent organized defense against oppression comes up in all political liberation and empowerment movements anywhere in the contemporary world, and is especially difficult for nonviolentists to decide the more desperate things are for the oppressed, where massive suffering is likely to continue if no collective action is taken.

In international relations these days, an ongoing dilemma for those opposed to the use of military violence to resolve conflicts has to do with the practice of "humanitarian intervention," and whether such action can ever be a justified exception to a generally antiwar ethical position. As the phrase implies, the idea here is to intervene coercively and usually with military force in the internal affairs of some nation-state for humanitarian reasons, normally understood in terms of the protection of innocent populations within that state from extensive harm. The intruders in this case are other states or international organizations such as the United Nations or the African Union, and the conflict to be stopped within the targeted state can be a civil war, a revolutionary war, programs of genocide, or forced dislocation from homelands. More often than not this kind of large-scale intrusion is carried out against the wishes of the state's governing officials, and in fact overrides the internationally recognized negative right of sovereignty possessed by every state. But sometimes when a national government requests "outside help" to end an internal violent conflict, or to put down an insurgency and protect itself, it is also called (somewhat more suspiciously in my estimation) "humanitarian intervention."

As indicated in Chapter 5, both just war theory and some variations of non-absolutist pacifism could support particular military campaigns of humanitarian intervention construed as "police actions," if the proper ethical criteria were met. But if we accept the pacifist presumption against military invasions of other people's lands, we at least must remain skeptical of all claims of moral legitimacy on behalf of this or that violent intervention allegedly because it is a "unique situation." As I have tried to show, ethical *rationalization* of unethical government policies is a time-honored ideological and propaganda strategy, and given the history of military interventions officially driven by altruism but pervaded by ulterior motives, the chances are slim that successfully protecting large groups of innocents from further harm is really what is either intended in the first place or likely to happen in the end. There is even more reason for skepticism in light of the inconsistency and lack of honorable standards of selection on the part of intervening states, in deciding where to intrude militarily and where to stay away purportedly out of respect for state sovereignty in domestic matters. This is especially so when individual nation-states instigate military invasions on their own or in collaboration with a few other states; but even the United Nations and the North Atlantic Treaty Organization, for example, can be manipulated by a few of these militarily and economically powerful nations whose interests have little to do with humanitarianism, to send or not send "peacekeeping" troops into conflict areas. Again, in any of these cases where multiple self-serving national agendas are involved the distinction between aggression and defense of the innocent easily blurs, and official proclamations that these violent means will bring about sustainable peace are very difficult to believe.

The second problem can be formulated as follows: In many regions of the world the material and social damage from previous widespread injury and injustice is extensive enough, that significant improvement in the lives of those affected appears to be still many years off, if it ever happens at all. How can people in these circumstances sustain efforts at nonviolent social transformation in the direction of positive peace, when there is little hope for things getting substantially better in their own lifetimes? For survivors of "ethnic cleansing" campaigns, or systematic terrorizing by governments or insurgent groups, or institutionalized and violently enforced apartheid, or multi-generational impoverishment and exploitation by a landowning class, or military occupation and subsequent terrorism by a foreign power, the trauma associated with what they have gone through naturally can be quite debilitating. When the psychological damage is bad enough, not only is post-traumatic stress disorder (PTSD) a common affliction (as it is also for military personnel who survive combat), but many victims just "give up" on the future in one way or another. Depending on cultural norms this can mean greater likelihood for suicide or, as shown by studies of people living for long periods in refugee camps, a basically amoral, survivalist opportunism can set in which replaces the individual's former morally organized worldview, and this reactive constriction of one's social sensitivities can last possibly for the rest of one's life.

Both in situations where people are recovering from a period of large-scale violent conflict and in conditions of ongoing political or economic oppression backed up by violence, hope plays a crucial role, and yet it does not necessarily contribute to good outcomes. Although normally we might think it strange to encourage feelings of hopelessness in someone, since hope itself is a feeling that what we desire will in fact happen, it obviously can be misplaced or based on inaccurate information and false beliefs about the future, and thus unjustified if not counterproductive. It also seems to me that hope can be inauthentic as well as authentic, the former often involving the attempt to deceive oneself into believing that, in spite of the evidence, "things will work out for the best," so that one can avoid the additional discomfort of having to reevaluate and probably change one's current understanding of a problematic situation. Inauthentic hope in this sense can amount to a strategy of self-distraction or an escapist refusal to face the facts, and can motivate a person to inaction and passive acceptance of existing states of affairs (and/or the policies of existing authorities) no matter how bad they really are. On the other hand, trying to bring about major social improvement in difficult circumstances *without* the motivation provided by an authentic hope for eventual success also seems unrealistic in its own way, and can make the task seem impossible or simply not worth it.

It is easy to cite current examples around the world where people are struggling with this problem of rebuilding their society for the benefit of all rather than just for an elite minority without giving up in despair, or, giving in either to reactionary forces aimed at reestablishing old hierarchies of power and control or to the temptations of violently removing perceived social obstacles. The continuing tensions between the working classes and the government in Guatemala years after the official end of a decades-long civil war; the problems still faced by South Africans in their creation of a functional multicultural society after so many years of atrocities against the non-white populations by the white minority government to enforce its system of apartheid; the state of inter-ethnic relations in places like Rwanda, Sierra Leone, Somalia, and Bosnia, where people are still trying to recover from earlier years of widespread brutalization, mass murder, and trauma; all these cases illustrate how the resulting psychological as well as material damage can make even an approximation of positive peace appear beyond reach.

Not surprisingly, different social theorists in recent times have been more pessimistic or more optimistic regarding the possibilities of social transformation that was both progressive and nonviolent after an era of massive suffering and destruction. In his assessment of the Algerian war of liberation against French colonialism (1954-62), and anti-colonialist struggles across Africa generally after World War II, the psychiatrist and activist Frantz Fanon (1925-61) argued in *The Wretched of the Earth* (1961) that "... decolonization is always a violent phenomenon" (p.35). This was so largely because of what he called the "Manicheanism" of good and evil created in the colonial world, originally by the colonial invaders themselves in their treatment of the "natives" as effectively subhuman in contrast to their own morally superior European civilization. The subjugated peoples over time tended to internalize this absolute duality of human worth according to Fanon, and thereafter live with the inner conflict of seeing themselves as their racist colonial masters saw them while simultaneously resenting and resisting this self-devaluation. Eventually when the "natives" were able to organize and rise up against the "settlers" and the occupation government protecting the latter, the former would reverse the duality in their self-understanding and see all colonists as absolutely evil, and colonial power as a totally demonic force to be totally destroyed with force by the "united people" in the name of their reclaimed humanity. If decoloniza- tion succeeds for a people to the point of political emancipation, construction of a new society can begin even in conditions where the precolonial traditional culture has been mostly rendered inoperative. But for Fanon it required the outgrowing of this Manicheanism in order to focus on this new task, and to allow for the "healing" necessary to progress toward better ways of living as human beings, and he saw how easy it was to fail to make that psychological transition.

Like Fanon, the Brazilian philosopher of education Paulo Freire (1921-97) advocated revolutionary uprisings against colonial occupation and against im- perialist exploitation of impoverished peoples around the world, though his primary focus was on the dynamics of class relations in the "postcolonial" so- cieties of Central and South America. In *Pedagogy of the Oppressed* (1970) he was responding to the situation of the rural and urban "dispossessed" in Latin America, who were not only desperately poor and quite often illiterate, but who also lived in what he called a "culture of silence." What he meant here was that peasants in the countryside shared with unemployed and marginally employed slum-dwellers in the cities a view of themselves as passive victims of external social forces beyond their control or comprehension, where it was simply their fate to be mere "things" for various economic and political elites to use and abuse as they wished, and where they had no right to speak out against this kind of objectifying, dehumanizing domination by others. Although this "culture of silence" had become well-entrenched as it was passed on from generation to generation, and the ruling classes did everything they could to reinforce it (often violently) in order to preserve their control of the masses of people, it was not impenetrable according to Freire. He thus got involved in literacy and edu- cation campaigns among the poor, which had as a central goal their empower- ment as persons who develop a "critical consciousness" about themselves and their social conditions, and who recognize that they are capable of "speaking up" for and affirming themselves as active, autonomous subjects rather than continuing to live as passive objects. Also, even though Freire apparently did not assume that nonviolent means always would be sufficient in organized ef- forts by the oppressed to liberate themselves from their oppressors, he was more optimistic than Fanon in this regard. This was largely because his program of "education for liberation" emphasized as most important changes in the con- sciousness of the "dispossessed," so that the social-psychological power of the ruling elites could be negated and their economic and political domination as a direct result made untenable. And, one of the beneficial consequences of a person acquiring "critical consciousness" was coming to understand and then reject the kind of "Manicheanism" Fanon warned against, whereby oppressors and oppressed treat each other as categorically and eternally Other with completely opposite value, and where the oppressed never get beyond the desire to simply trade places with their oppressors.

While we are justifiably asserting the immorality of political oppression, enforced material scarcity, organized campaigns of terror, torture, the use of rape as a weapon of war, and mass killings of civilians, along with the colonialist and imperialist practices that regularly have led to these other kinds of injury, we cannot at the same time overlook surviving victims' desperate need for some degree of healing. Of course extensive medical resources are needed for physical recuperation, but psychological healing for those victimized is just as necessary and yet often even harder to accomplish. Emigrants fleeing a civil war, persecution, or severe deprivation in their homeland may have been traumatized already, and then traumatized again by their experiences as refugees or as aliens in a new country. For people who couldn't or wouldn't flee those same circumstances, there are not only the problems of coping with the personal suffering they may have undergone or the horrors they witnessed, but also the problem of how to continue living in the same society as the perpetrators of these evils. As emphasized throughout this book, social justice is so much more than just retribution, but most of those involved in social rebuilding programs after times of massive harm inflicted by some groups on others argue that the victimized will not be able to get on with their lives in any healthy way, unless some meaningful form of accountability and/or punishment is imposed on the agents of atrocities, "crimes against humanity," or wanton slaughter. Forgiveness of perpetrators who are unrepentant, or who deny responsibility for their violent actions, or who appear to have effectively gotten away with and even benefited from their crimes, is not a realistic possibility for most victims, nor would it usually promote adequate healing according to many researchers. At the same time, giving free rein to the desire for revenge easily leads to a cycle of inter-group "payback" which tends to escalate and become increasingly difficult to stop over time (as indicated in Chapter 6, Section 3), and practically guarantees that real progress toward positive peace will not happen.

Since the establishment of the United Nations and the World Court after World War II, the recognition of the need to balance the demands of vengeance and reconciliation in organized attempts to help societies "mend" after collective experiences of widespread violence and injustice has led to the formation of numerous situation-specific investigative commissions (with or without punitive powers). Many have been UN sponsored or in some other way international, such as the United Nations Truth Commission for El Salvador and the International Criminal Tribunal on the former Yugoslavia, while others have been more the result of an internal national effort, such as the Truth and Reconciliation Commission in South Africa. In some instances the primary focus has been on finding out who the perpetrators really were, in other instances the emphasis was on providing opportunities for victims to tell their stories, while in other public investigations survivors mainly wanted information about where the bodies of their murdered loved ones were buried, and who among the perpetrators could tell them that. The success of these various commissions and tribunals is debated, partly because there isn't usually complete agreement about the criteria of success, and partly because the results of the official proceedings still leave at least some parties with feelings of dissatisfaction and lack of closure. Also of course, some people want to forget the horrible past as much as possible, while others become obsessed with it to the point where the future becomes irrelevant and lifeless for them; and personal agendas here have a lot to do with whether one was a perpetrator, a victim, or a "bystander" who may or may not have been so innocent. But as uneven as the outcomes of these investigations have tended to be, there does seem to be quite a bit of agreement in the diverse field of conflict resolution that some such efforts are required, if something as crucial and yet as difficult to calculate as the healing of whole communities is ever to occur.

Whether people are living at present in an environment of violence, insecurity, and scarcity created by hierarchical social organizations of power, privilege, and exploitation; or they are trying to recover from past times of war, persecution, or state-supported terrorism; or they are trying to cope with both present and past horrors, the motivational energy provided by a realistic hope for the future is an essential resource. Again however, at best it is a necessary but not sufficient condition for actual improvement in people's lives, and so both personal and collective action is needed within a wide range of governmental and non-governmental arenas, grounded in accurate assessments of what in fact is possible to achieve and in how much time. In different situations immediate priorities will differ, of course, so that the emphasis sometimes may be on retribution for atrocities committed and reparations for victims, at other times on the resolution of land issues and political boundaries, and in other circumstances the focus will be on economic and cultural reconstruction upon the ruins of a violent colonial past. And, in all cases it is possible that no matter how hard people try they may fail to make substantial progress, since there does not seem to be anything inevitable or inexorable about the achievement of positive peace either locally or globally. Our views on human nature will influence our optimism or pessimism here as well, regarding someone's resilience in the face of injury caused by design, indifference, or the ignorance of others, and what it will take to "hang in there" and keep working for a better future for oneself and one's descendents.

If we believe it is morally desirable and achievable that many more people on the planet live in social conditions characterized by nonviolence, peace, and justice, we are also thereby embracing the goals of cooperative rather than competitive economic improvement and sustainability for all, cultural co-existence based on a common foundation of positive and negative rights of persons, and security established through widespread mutual support and respect rather than military force. What any of us can actually do to contribute to these goals will again depend on our own circumstances, resources, and opportunities, whether we live in more affluent societies or in more impoverished societies, or whether we have materially benefited from institutional violence or have been harmed by it. Yet every conscious, competent human being with any knowledge of these goals has available to him or her at least some range of viable choice about what could be done, which can only be ignored through self-deception and moral cowardice. Choices of action may be extremely limited for some people weighed down with their own suffering or past injury, or quite expanded for others living fairly comfortable, educated lives free of disability. But whether we as moral agents focus on interpersonal, inter-group, or international relations, it seems safe (in fact platitudinous) to say that the surest way to increase the chances of more violence, more insecurity, and more injustice for more people is to choose to do nothing significant in one's life to change all this for the better.

FURTHER READING

Section 1

Ward Churchill, editor, *Marxism and Native Americans* (Boston, MA: South End Press, 1983).

Louise Diamond and Elizabeth Slade, *How to Raise a Peaceful Child in a Violent World*, second edition (Bristol, VT: The Peace Company, 2005).

Haim Gordon and Leonard Grob, editors, *Education for Peace* (Maryknoll, NY: Orbis Books, 1987).

Patrick Joyce, editor, *Class* (Oxford: Oxford UP, 1995).

David Korten, *The Post-Corporate World: Life after Capitalism* (San Francisco, CA: Berret-Koehler, 2000).

V.I. Lenin, *Imperialism: The Highest Stage of Capitalism* (New York: International Publishers, 1939).

Kathleen McGinnis and James McGinnis, *Parenting for Peace and Justice* (Maryknoll, NY: Orbis Books, 1981).

Jack Nelson-Pallmeyer, *War against the Poor: Low-Intensity Conflict and Christian Faith* (Maryknoll, NY: Orbis Books, 1989).

Baruch Nevo and Gavriel Salomon, editors, *Peace Education: The Concept, Principles, and Practices around the World* (Mahwah, NJ: Lawrence Erlbaum Associates, 2002).

Marge Piercy, *Woman on the Edge of Time* (New York: Ballantine Books, 1976).

Leslie Poynor and Paula M. Wolfe, *Marketing Fear in America's Public Schools: The Real War on Literacy* (New York: Routledge, 2005).

Tsenay Serequeberhan, editor, *African Philosophy: The Essential Readings* (New York: Paragon House, 1991).

Anne Wilson Schaef, *When Society Becomes an Addict* (San Francisco, CA: Harper and Row, 1987).

Worldwatch Institute, *State of the World, 1984-2009: An Annual Report on Progress toward a Sustainable Society* (New York, NY: W.W. Norton and Co.).

Section 2

Michael Albert, *Parecon: Life after Capitalism* (London: Verso, 2003).

Ernst Bloch, *The Principle of Hope*, 3 Volumes, translated by Neville Plaice, Stephen Plaice, and Paul Knight (Cambridge, MA: The MIT Press, 1986).

Leonardo Boff and Clodovis Boff, *Introducing Liberation Theology* (Maryknoll, NY: Orbis Books, 1987).

Barbara Deming, *Revolution and Equilibrium* (New York: Grossman Publishers, 1971).

Frantz Fanon, *The Wretched of the Earth*, translated by Constance Farrington (New York: Grove Press, 1961, 1963).

Paulo Freire, *Pedagogy of the Oppressed*, translated by Myra Bergman Ramos (New York: Continuum, 1970, 1993, 2003).

——, *Pedagogy of Hope: Reliving Pedagogy of the Oppressed*, translated by Robert R. Barr (New York: Continuum, 1992, 1994, 2004).

Peter Gelderloos, *How Nonviolence Protects the State* (Cambridge, MA: South End Press, 2007).

Nelson Mandela, *The Struggle is My Life* (New York: Pathfinder Press, 1986).

Peter Singer, *The Life You Can Save: Acting Now to End World Poverty* (New York: Random House, 2009).

James D. White and Anthony J. Marsella, *Fear of Persecution: Global Human Rights, International Law, and Human Well-Being* (Lanham, MD: Lexington Books, 2007).

John P. Wilson and Boris Drozdek, editors, *Broken Spirits: The Treatment of Traumatized Asylum Seekers, Refugees, War and Torture Victims* (New York: Routledge, 2004).